W9-BKE-829

MAY I DIVORCE AND REMARRY?

An exegetical study of
First Corinthians Chapter Seven

By
SPIROS ZODHIATES, TH.D.

AMG PUBLISHERS
CHATTANOOGA, TN 37422

© 1984 by SPIROS ZODHIATES
All Rights Reserved.

Revised edition, 1992

ISBN–0–89957–600–1

Printed in the United States of America
99 98 97 96 95   6 5 4 3 2

*To Gordon and Ruth Peters
as a token of appreciation for demonstrating what a
truly blessed Christian marriage ought to be.
Gordon and Ruth are dedicating their retirement
years to serving Christ as volunteers with AMG
International. This dedication is in gratitude of
their unselfish service to our Lord*

CONTENTS

Contents

Contents

ix

PREFACE

God instituted marriage as a lifetime commitment. The Pharisees of Jesus' day, realizing that God meant it that way and that Jesus confirmed it, tried to entrap Him.

You might expect the Pharisees to want the God of the Old Testament and the Lord Jesus to justify a man dismissing his wife for any reason. But when the disciples asked Jesus privately whether He really meant what He had said, one wonders whether they too were not confused about marriage being a lifetime commitment.

"If the case of the man be so with his wife, it is not good to marry," they said (Matt. 19:10). In other words, if by getting married one is bound for life, it is better not to get married. Why did the disciples of Christ ask such a question? Did they really believe that if they could not change partners if they were unhappy, that it would be better not to get married at all?

Practically, there are many people who are afraid of marriage. What am I going to do if it doesn't work out? If I am a true Christian or Jew, am I really stuck with the same marriage partner for life? This fear causes some today to remain single throughout their lives.

Others bypass the God–appointed ordinance of marriage that binds a husband and wife together and prefer to engage in sexual relations in complete disregard of the laws instituted by God for happiness in marriage. Such are condemned to the sad consequences of their choice. Indeed we can choose a sinful way of life, but we cannot choose the God–ordained destructive consequences of our sinful choice.

In my first volume on the general theme of marriage, divorce, and remarriage, I examine very thoroughly from the Greek text the following passages of Scripture which have perplexed the many millions of readers of the various translations of the New Testament, namely: Matthew 5:27–32; 19:3–12; Luke 16:18; and Romans 7:1–3. The study of this first volume entitled *What About Divorce?* is a must if you want to fully understand the total subject.

Because the pertinent passages examined in my first volume left many questions unanswered, I have delved into Paul's discourse in First Corinthians chapter seven on the subject. The issue of marriage confused the Christian believers of his day, especially those who lived in the pluralistic, heathen, secular, and materialistic environment of Corinth. So the apostle Paul decided to answer their questions precisely, extensively, and candidly.

What the questions were that prompted Paul to write First Corinthians chapter seven we do not know. Consequently, it is more difficult to understand the answers. Perhaps this is the reason why so many Bible commentators have not given this difficult chapter the proper and thorough attention that it deserves. I have come to the conclusion that reading this chapter in a translated rendering makes it almost impossible to understand adequately and to catch its intended purpose. This is the reason that I have thoroughly examined every Greek word in this passage. The content may become a little tedious and repetitious, but it is the only safe way. Safe behavior in as serious a matter as marriage is advisable no matter how much study it takes to understand the various issues.

I have come to the conclusion that Paul had decided to remain unmarried, and in First Corinthians chapter seven he explains why. But Paul does not expect others necessarily to follow his example. If Christians are so motivated by a higher calling and believe that celibacy is the state whereby such a goal can more efficiently be reached, then celibacy is to be preferred.

But once a person is married, there is no changing one's mind and coming to the conclusion that celibacy would have been better. Such a subconscious philosophy of life in a husband or wife will undermine the happiest of marriages.

If one does not believe that marriage is for life, bitterness and resentment can easily creep in and ferment. Any and all kinds of excuses are then a reason to break that relationship. If one believes that marriage is for life, then he or she will make the necessary adjustments in his or her personal make–up and behavior so that the marriage may not only last, but become sweeter as the years roll by.

I know that because I have thus far lived in 44 years of honeymoon with my one–time wife, Joan. It is not because I am perfect or that she is, but because we complement each other and try daily to bury self in its many insidious manifestations. Try dying to self as a furtherance to longevity of marriage and increasing happiness in it.

Paul's rules for a happy marriage are specific and worth careful study by any person, either married or single.

One of the characteristics of the marriage manual called First Corinthians chapter seven is that there are decisions that can only be made by the individual marital partner.

Because of the presence of sin, life is made so complex that frequently there are no pat, simplistic answers to complex questions.

What is to be done when only one spouse becomes saved, believing on the Lord Jesus, and seeing his or her life be completely changed? That spouse becomes sanctified in that he or she abstains from fornication from the moment of his or her spiritual rebirth (1 Thess. 4:3, 7). The believer's body then becomes the temple of the Holy Spirit (1 Cor. 6:19).

But suppose that the believer's marital partner does not come to know Christ and abstain from fornication. What is the Christian spouse then supposed to do? Is she to remain married and have her body used by an adulterer husband or is she given the choice of divorcing and remarrying? Such problems Paul deals with in First Corinthians chapter seven.

Whatever your state of being may be, unmarried, divorced, unhappily or happily married, this is a book that you cannot miss. It will help you as it has helped me, even in my own state as a happily married man, to find the real undergirding principles of a happy marriage.

Marriage, as any other circumstance of life, should never become the goal of life, but only a means to an end. And that end should always be a closer walk with our Creator. In Christ and through Christ, I can do all things because He strengthens me (Phil. 4:13).

My prayer is that in whatever state you may be, Christ will bring to you that measure of His sustaining strength.

My deep gratitude is expressed to my dear wife, Joan, who diligently labored in editing and improving the manuscripts. Both of us will be praying that every reader of this book may find the strength for life that we have experienced.

Last, but not least, I wish to stress that the words "man, woman, he and she, him and her," are used generically in this book. God does not have two standards, one for men and one for women. In His sight we are all equal. "There is neither male nor female: for ye are all one in Christ Jesus" (Gal. 3:28). There is a God–designed place for a husband and a different one for a wife, one for a father and one for a mother. But that does not mean that God chooses favorites—men or women. They are both human beings that God in His relationship with them considers equal.

Spiros Zodhiates

1

MARRIAGE OR CELIBACY
IN 1 CORINTHIANS 7:1–7

*Now concerning the things whereof ye wrote
unto me . . . —1 Corinthians 7:1*

The Corinthians had been visited by Paul, who brought the gospel to their cosmopolitan city which was given to debauchery. After he left them, following an eighteen month's ministry, they had a number of questions concerning marriage.

As we read of what Paul had to say concerning this important, divine institution that had lost its sanctity, it is necessary to remember a few basic facts about the Corinth.

Corinth was primarily a Gentile city, a colony of Rome; however, a considerable number of Jews did maintain a synagogue there (Acts 18:4). Among the Corinthian Jews were a certain number of Christian converts including prominent persons who joined St. Paul (Acts 8:4, 8; Rom. 16:21; 1 Cor. 9:20). The church at Corinth, however, consisted chiefly of non–Jews (1 Cor. 12:2).

Problems of Marriage to an Unbeliever in the Early Church

When both Jews and Gentiles accepted Christ and became Christians, problems arose in regard to their marital status. It seems that when one of the two partners became a Christian and the other remained an unbeliever, the question of "What should the believer do?" would be asked.

This problem is with us today. How should marriage between an unbeliever and a believer be regarded by the Christian Church and Christians in general? Is there only one rule pertaining to this situation in marriage, or does any action taken depend on the philosophy of life of the partners and the community in which they live?

James Hastings in his *Dictionary of the Apostolic Church* in the article on "Corinthians" under the subtitle "Marriage and the Position of Women" writes the following:

> St. Paul's teaching upon this question is conditioned by the attitude to women common in the world in which he lived, and also by his expectation of the *Parousía*. As the time is so short, it is best for people to remain in the external circumstances in which they were when they were converted (1 Cor. 7:18–20). As to the desirability of marriage, he lays stress upon the necessity of the avoidance of anything that can distract the Christian from the

service of God. In most cases he thinks marriage will constitute a distraction. Therefore, for most people celibacy is desirable. But if celibacy constitutes a greater distraction than marriage, then Christians should marry. There is no hint of any view of conjugal relations as being in themselves evil. The only consideration present to his mind is as to whether marriage will help or hinder a Christian in the service of God. His view that celibacy from this point of view is the best state is put forward on his own authority.

But for the indissolubility of Christian marriage, he claims the authority of Christ Himself (1 Cor. 7:10, 11). As to this he is quite explicit (Vol. I, p. 258).

In Answer to Questions

From the answers Paul gives in this chapter, we can deduce the questions the Corinthians asked concerning marriage. How wonderful it would have been if the exact questions had been preserved in the Scriptures for us.

The Corinthian Church was very similar to the church of today. We in a pluralistic society have similar problems to face relative to the many opinions and views on ethics and the family structure. This is the reason why a very careful examination of the answers given by Paul in First Corinthians chapter seven is necessary. "Now concerning the things whereof ye wrote unto me."

2

TOUCHING A WOMAN!

. . . It is good for a man not to touch a woman.
—1 Corinthians 7:1

The first answer Paul gives is: "It is good for a man not to touch a woman." What question did Paul answer with this statement?

Asceticism and Celibacy Is Not the God–Ordained Way of Life

First let us examine what he could not have meant. Even a cursory examination of the Scriptures show that he was not teaching that asceticism and celibacy is the God–ordained way of life. If this were true, Paul would have been setting himself against God's direct assessment and commandment concerning marriage. God's assessment was: "It is not good that the man should be alone; I will make him an help meet for him" (Gen. 2:18). And then in Genesis 2:24 God said: "Therefore shall a man leave his father and his mother, and shall cleave unto his wife: and they shall be one flesh." And in Genesis 1:27, 28 we read:

5

"So God created man in his own image, in the image of God created he him; male and female created he them. God blessed them, and God said unto them, Be fruitful and multiply and replenish the earth, and subdue it."

In Proverbs 18:22 we read: "Whoso findeth a wife findeth a good thing, and obtaineth favor of the Lord." (See also Jeremiah 29:6.) It is therefore inconceivable that Paul would attempt to change God's rule and institute celibacy as the rule instead of encouraging marriage.

Paul Esteemed Marriage

Paul would be contradicting himself if celibacy were the general principle he believed and taught since he wrote that even the officials of local churches should be married. He wrote to Timothy: "Let the deacons be the husband of one wife, ruling their children and their own houses well" (1 Tim. 3:12). And then in 1 Timothy 5:14 he writes: "I will therefore that the younger women marry, bear children, guide the house, give none occasion to the adversary to speak reproachfully."

God Presents Himself as Husband of His People

When God sought a figure to illustrate His union with His people, the church, He chose the bond of marriage. "For thy Maker is thine husband" (Is. 54:5). "For as a young man marrieth a virgin, so shall thy sons marry thee: and as the bridegroom rejoiceth over the bride, so shall thy God rejoice over thee" (Is. 62:5). "Turn, O backsliding children, saith the Lord; for I am married unto you" (Jer. 3:14). "And I will betroth thee unto me forever; yea, I will betroth thee unto me in righteousness, and in judgment, and in lovingkindness, and in mercies" (Hos. 2:19).

Marriage in Christ's Parabolic Teaching

Note how many times our Lord used the ceremony of marriage in His parabolic teaching. In Matthew 22:2 we read: "The kingdom of heaven is like unto a certain king, which made a marriage for his son." In the parable of the virgins, we have the scene of a wedding with the unexpected coming of the bridegroom referring to His second coming (Matt. 25:10).

The Church, Christ's Bride

The Church is presented as Christ's bride by Paul in his second epistle to the Corinthians: "For I am jealous over you with godly jealousy: for I have espoused you to one husband, that I may present you as a chaste virgin to Christ" (2 Cor. 11:2).

The Church as Christ's Bride in Revelation

Revelation states, "Let us be glad and rejoice, and give honor to him: for the marriage of the Lamb is come, and his wife hath made herself ready" (19:7).

"And I John saw the holy city, new Jerusalem, coming down from God out of heaven, prepared as a bride adorned for her husband" (Rev. 21:2).

"And the Spirit and the bride say, Come. And let him that heareth say, Come. And let him that is athirst come. And whosoever will, let him take the water of life freely" (Rev. 22:17).

Paul Does Not Teach Sexual Relations Are Wrong in Marriage

Secondly, Paul does not teach that sexual intercourse between husband and wife is wrong or immoral. How easy it is to arrive at this conclusion upon reading the words "It is good for man not to touch a woman" (1 Cor. 7:1). This clause when taken out of its context would surely indicate that it means just that, but it should really be taken with its preceding clause: "Now concerning the things whereof ye wrote unto me." It is related to a specific question or questions asked by the Corinthians. Since we don't have those questions, we can only attempt to reconstruct them.

Touching a Woman to Whom a Man Is Not Married

Perhaps someone asked if it were permissible for an unmarried man to touch a woman. Since the word "unmarried" was probably in the question, it was not necessary that it be repeated in Paul's answer. He simply said, "It is good not to touch a woman." If it is not good, then it is wrong.

Notwithstanding, when it comes to a man's wife, it is good, for love requires him to touch her and assure her of his love and vice versa, which Paul assures us in 1 Corinthians 7:5. But when a woman is not one's wife or when a man is not one's husband, the Christian must be so circumspect as to avoid even the touch.

Isn't this also what the Lord Jesus actually taught in the Sermon on the Mount? His teaching on divorce and remarriage does not begin with Matthew 5:31, 32 but with verse twenty–seven: "Don't commit adultery."

And how does it all start? By the constant look and the constant touch: "Everyone seeing (constantly) a woman to lust after her has already committed adultery against her in his heart . . . and if thy right hand offends thee or scandalizes thee or becomes a trap (unto adultery), cut it off" (Author's translation). "Keep your hands to yourself," is not only what Paul says, but what Christ says too. Paul is simply reiterating Christ's teaching.

What Does the Word "Touch" Mean?

In its basic meaning in the active voice, the word "touch"[1] as applied to things means "to set fire to, to kindle, to light" as in Luke 8:16; 11:33 and 15:8. It is also "to put one thing to another, to adjoin, to apply." When it is used in the middle voice or as a deponent verb (a verb in the middle voice but with an active meaning), then it means "to apply oneself to."

There is another Greek verb *thiggánō* which Paul could have chosen to use which has more of a sense of mere touch. (See Col. 2:21; Heb. 11:28 and 12:20.) *Háptomai* has a stronger meaning, that of "handling," which goes beyond the mere touch. It is handling an object or person to exert a modifying influence upon it.[2] The Lord touched the leper in order to have an influence upon him (Matt. 8:3). He touched Peter's mother–in–law's hand to heal her (Matt. 8:15). The woman with an issue of blood touched the hem of Jesus' garment in order to be healed (Matt. 9:20, 21). Christ touched the eyes of the two blind men in order to give them their sight (Matt. 9:29). It is touching for the purpose of being influenced by someone or of influencing someone. It is not just an indifferent, objective touch which would be expressed by the verb *thiggánō.*

In 1 Corinthians 7:1, the verb *háptesthai* means not a mere touch, but a touch that is like the look unto lust or the roving of the right hand of which the Lord Jesus spoke in Matthew 5:27–32. It is that touch that arouses a man to a passion for a woman who is not his wife which Paul condemns. The verb is in the present infinitive middle which means a continuous touching, even as the present participle *blépōn* of Matthew 5:28: "Everyone looking constantly upon a woman to lust after her."

Actually, this is a basic general injunction of Paul in this total marital relationship chapter. It applies to the unmarried as well as to the married if the person the married one touches is not one's own spouse.

Is Caressing Permissible in the Single State?

But you may say, "Could it not apply only to some who have the special call to remain unmarried as in the case of Paul himself?" No, it applies to all who are single, and is not an exception pertaining to a class of people to whom the special grace of God is given. This word of Paul should not be interpreted as referring to a group of Christians who belonged to a Pauline party of unmarried people. These were not those who said, "We are of Paul's celibate group, and the rest of mankind are of Peter's party" (1 Cor. 1:12).

We must remember in this connection the words of the Lord Jesus in Matthew 19:11, 12: "All men cannot receive this saying, save they to whom it is given. For there are some eunuchs who were so born from their mother's womb." In other words, they are equipped by God in their constitution to be able to remain unmarried and to not burn with sexual desire which would be more destructive than if they had a wife and children.

The Lord Jesus continues: "and there are some eunuchs, which were made eunuchs of men. . . ." This second category includes those who because of circumstances of life, emasculation, health, social or other related reasons, are unable to marry. It is the physical or social situations of life that necessitate their not touching a woman. The third category is that to which the Apostle Paul himself belonged. ". . . and there be eunuchs, which have made themselves eunuchs for the kingdom of heaven's sake." It is for the love of God and His service that they deprive themselves of the privilege of marriage.

But the most important statement is at the end of this verse: "He that is able to receive it, let him receive it." And to this we must connect the words of our Savior in verse eleven: "All men cannot receive this saying, save they to whom it is given" which is by God, of course, as a special enablement of His grace.

---

[1]In Greek, it is the verb *háptesthai*, the present infinitive middle of *háptō*, "to touch."

[2]Trench, Richard C. *Synonyms of the New Testament* (Grand Rapids: William B. Eerdmans Publishing Company, 1953), pp. 58–60.

3

IS THE CELIBATE LIFE HOLIER THAN MARRIED LIFE?

Now concerning the things whereof ye wrote unto me: It is good for a man not to touch a woman.—1 Corinthians 7:1

What are the feelings that stir within when we see a celibate servant of Christ? We may immediately judge such a person as missing the joys and comfort of marriage which in our estimation is the best state for man. Is it good to be married and bad not to be? We are so apt to recognize only two colors, black and white. In morals we only see what is bad and good, sinful and holy, joyful and sorrowful. Can't there be degrees within these moral states? Of course there can be, and we will do well to recognize them.

See God in Your Circumstances

Without doubt, what God wants us to be or what God permits us to be is the best for us. To attain the closest possible relationship with Him is His goal for our lives. This may be accomplished either through marriage or through celibacy. Neither should be sought as an end in itself.

How foolish some modern authors have been to entitle their books on marriage, "You Can Be Happy Though Married." Neither the single nor the married state is necessary to happiness, rather, a commitment to be what God wants us to be in either state. And He will equip us to be happy in that which He has ordained us to be. The same apostle who wrote, "It is good for a man not to touch a woman," also said in Philippians 4:11, "I have learned in whatsoever state I am, therewith to be content." If the Lord wanted Paul to be married, Paul would have said, "It is good for a man to be married."

Paul's primary purpose in life was to please his Lord and to accomplish the most for Him. And since in his own case he could best serve the Lord by not being married, that state of celibacy was best for him. This does not mean that the state of marriage is bad.

Expecting Others to Be What We Are

For Paul to have imposed his state on others would have been wrong. There is no indication that Christ ever asked any of His servants to stay single, and no religious leader has the right to command that which Christ never commanded. However, we can make choices that are personal and strictly individual. One's choice does not have to be branded as bad and another's as good. It all depends on the measure of God's grace to each individual.

When Paul says, "It is good for a man not to touch a woman," he means that celibacy is a satisfactory state as long as it enables a person to be and do his best for the Lord.

Celibacy Uncommon in Paul's Day

Celibacy was extremely uncommon both among the Jews and among the heathen in the first ages of the Church. It was not part of the Nazarite vow (Num. 6:3–5), though no doubt many Nazarites, like John the Baptist (if indeed he was one of them), were celibates. And there were some, but not all, of the Essenes who preached the requirement of abstinence from marriage and admitted members to their group only after a probation of three years to test their continency (Josephus BJ II VIII 2, 7). In them we see the germ of gnostic dualism which taught the inherent evil of matter (Lightfoot, *Colossians,* ed. 1900, p. 85). In this respect, the Essenes were in direct antagonism with the Pharisees who strongly supported marriage. However, the Essene practice did have some influence in promoting Christian celibacy in the post–apostolic age. Among the heathen, celibacy can hardly be said to have existed.

As we have seen, the Lord Jesus, while teaching the holiness of marriage, nevertheless commended celibacy for those "to whom it is given" and who are "able to receive it" (Matt. 19:11ff).

Paul is in full agreement with his Master when he says in 1 Corinthians 7:7, "every man hath his proper gift of God, one after this manner, and another after that." Nowhere in the New Testament is marriage referred to as a state inferior to that of celibacy however much the latter may be commended under certain circumstances to specific persons. Neither should those who marry be considered as carnal Christians and be depreciated by those who choose to stay single because they are so divinely enabled.

Paul's Changing View in Regard to Marriage and Celibacy

In the teaching of the Apostle Paul there appears to be a certain change of view between the earlier and later Epistles.

In the earlier Epistles, the Apostle plainly expected that the coming of the Lord was imminent as expressed in 1 Thessalonians 4:17: "We that are alive, that are left." If the coming of the Lord was held to be so imminent, a belief that arose out of prevailing persecution from which the *Parousía* would liberate the believers, it followed that the increase of the human race and Christian community through childbirth would not be of primary importance.

Therefore, while marriage was entirely lawful (1 Cor. 7:28), and indeed imperative for those who had not the gift of continency (1 Cor. 7:2, 9), celibacy was encouraged. In this chapter, we find Paul saying: "It is good for a man not to touch a woman"; "I would that all men were even as I myself"; "It is good for them if they abide even as I" (vv. 1–8ff); "It is good for a man to be as he is [whether he was a widower or single]" (v. 26). Yet Paul does not say that celibacy is a higher state, but only that it was expedient by reason of the present distress (v. 26), because the time was shortened (v. 29), and he would have Christians liberated from marital and family cares (v. 32).

The lawfulness of marriage is further emphasized by the assertion of the right to marry by Paul himself "even as the rest of the apostles, and the brethren of the Lord, and Cephas" (1 Cor. 9:5). Since the apostles were traveling missionaries even as Paul, the conclusion must be drawn that the married state was not inconsistent with the work of a traveling missionary. Aquila, who was a great Christian worker, traveled about with his wife, Priscilla (Acts 18:2, 26; Rom. 16:3; 1 Cor. 16:19; 2 Tim. 4:19).

In the Epistles that Paul wrote from prison, marriage is mentioned as the normal state and nothing is said in favor of celibacy (Eph. 5:31ff; Col. 3:18ff). We also notice that in these Epistles little is said of the nearness of Christ's coming with the exception of Philippians 4:5.

In the Pastoral Epistles marriage is accepted or required for the local church leadership (1 Tim. 3:2, 4ff; Titus 1:6) and is also advised for young widows. Paul desired his local church officials, the elders (bishops or overseers) and deacons to be, at least as a rule, married men. The Greek Orthodox Church demands her parish priests be married and their wives must be alive.

Is It Good to Be Single and Bad to Be Married?

The term *kalón*, "good," Paul uses four times in this chapter. Also in 1 Corinthians 7:8 he says, "I say therefore to the unmarried and widows, It is good (*kalón*) for them if they abide even as I." Here he refers to his state of not being married. Not only is it good not to touch a woman, not to take liberties with women that would lead to illicit relations, but according to Paul, an unmarried person could be what he chose to be and not miss what is considered fulfilling in the state of marriage.

In 1 Corinthians 7:26 we read: "I suppose therefore that this is good (*kalón*) for the present distress, I say, that it is good (*kalón*) for a man so to be." Paul here is referring to difficult times which were about to break out in Corinth. If one were married, the concern would be greater than if one were single. So there are times that being single is beneficial.

Whatever helps us to accomplish God's purpose in our lives is good. Some of us accomplish it while married, and some of us while unmarried. Each state is equally as good. We must not consider the unmarried as lacking in anything, and if unmarried, consider the married as subject to sinful desires. Marriage is moral, but whether one is married or unmarried, he must be careful to be moral. This is what Paul means by the word "good" in this chapter and this particular verse.

That this verse is not a blank endorsement of celibacy as a better state than married life is made clear by reference to the evil of the last times when people will be "forbidding to marry" (1 Tim. 4:3).

4

WHAT WOULD BE THE RESULT IF MARRIAGE WERE PROHIBITED?

Nevertheless, to avoid fornication, let every man have his own wife, and let every woman have her own husband.—1 Corinthians 7:2.

What Paul said in 1 Corinthians 7:1 is that touching a woman who is not one's wife is immoral since it may lead to illicit sex. Therefore stay at a distance.

But what does a person do when he has sexual passions and finds it difficult to restrain himself? Paul recognizes that there are some people who have difficulty in containing themselves in the expression of their sexual desires whether married or unmarried.

Fornication Absolutely Prohibited

There is one general moral rule that is all–binding; fornication is contrary to God's provision for the

21

satisfaction of anyone's sexual drive. The Greek word used for all illicit sex is *porneía*. It must be absolutely avoided. It is sin. It will affect your relationship with God and it will destroy family, society, and humanity itself. It will reduce man to the level of a mere animal.

One must remember that Corinth was a pagan city in which, while adultery (*moicheía*) was regarded as wrong on a woman's part mainly on the ground that it infringed upon the husband's rights, fornication (*porneía*) or sexual intercourse outside the marriage bond, especially by husbands, was allowable.

The Apostle Paul demanded chastity from married men in particular as in 1 Thessalonians 4:3–5:

> For this is the will of God, even your sanctification, that ye should abstain from fornication: That *every one of you* (note that there are no exceptions admitted) should know how to possess his vessel in sanctification and honor; Not in the lust of concupiscence (desire in a bad sense), even as the Gentiles which know not God.

Paul recognizes that the flesh has strong desires. But no lustful desire, no matter how strong on the part of either a man or a woman, needs to be satisfied in defilement of one's body. Chastity is not only possible; it is mandatory. The heathen world considered fornication and adultery not only as normal, but as a necessity of nature. This is what Paul combats in 1 Corinthians 6:12–20:

> All things are lawful unto me, but all things are not expedient (will not contribute to pulling me together, *sumphérei*): all things are lawful (*éxestin*, really meaning 'are taken by me as permissible') for me, but I will not be brought under the power of any . . . Now the body is not for fornication, but for the Lord; and the Lord for the body . . . Know ye not that your bodies are the members of Christ? shall I then take the members of Christ, and make them the members of an harlot? God forbid. What? know ye not that he which is joined to an harlot is one body? for two, saith he, shall be one flesh . . . Flee fornication. Every sin that a man doeth is without the body; but he that committeth fornication sinneth against his own body. What? know ye not that your body is the temple of the Holy Ghost which is in you, which ye have of God, and ye are not your own? For ye are bought with a price: therefore glorify God in your body, and in your spirit, which are God's.

You Can Live a Life of Continence

What Paul asserts here is that lustful desire and sex is not a natural necessity like food. A man cannot live without food, but he can live without sex. While the digestive system of man belongs to the perishing form of man and this world, the body as such is the organ of the spirit and the temple of the Holy Spirit, bought by Christ for His own service. Therefore, to unite one's body with the body of a harlot is an act of sacrilege, of self–violation, and it breaks the union between Christ and the believer.

In Revelation 22:15, the Lord Jesus appeared to John and revealed to him those who are going to be kept outside the Kingdom of God, Heaven: "For without are dogs, sorcerers, and whoremongers (*pórnoi*), and murderers, and idolaters, and whosoever loveth and maketh a lie."

Whoremongers (*pórnoi*) here are equated with dogs. And truly they are for they act very much like dogs. Instead of subjugating lustful desires to the limitations of marriage or to sublimation through the control of his God–influenced spirit, man has sexual relations on a level no higher than that of a dog.

5

MARRIAGE'S PRIMARY PURPOSE IS NOT TO AVOID FORNICATION

Nevertheless, to avoid fornication, let every man have his own wife, and let every woman have her own husband.—1 Corinthians 7:2.

In 1 Corinthians 7:2 the words "to avoid" are in italics which indicates that these words are not found in the Greek text, but rather they are necessary to the English translation of the Greek.

Intercourse Within Marriage Is Not Evil

The Greek reads: *"Diá tás porneías"*—which literally means, "for the fornications." This rendering may be misunderstood as classifying intercourse within the bond of marriage as "acts of fornications." Hence, intercourse between spouses may take an evil connotation instead of the beautiful, conjugal relationship it is meant to be. Indeed, marriages can be destroyed when one partner considers the sex act as evil and the other desires it as an expression of the love that joins the two together. In marriages that have not been harmonious, mothers have sometimes instilled in their daughters a sanctimonious feeling toward sex even within marriage. The exercise of this intimate relationship within marriage ought not to be considered as an act that damages one's spirituality. There are no "fornications" within marriage when the relationship is between the two conjugal partners. Sexual intercourse is a God–given act of union within marriage and an abomination to the Lord outside of marriage.

Why "Fornications" and Not "Fornication"?

Porneías, "fornications," in the Greek text is in the accusative plural. It is not "fornication" as the translations have it, but *porneías*, "fornications."

    The New International Version and *The New King James Bible*, in an attempt to correct the inadequacy of former translations, have instead worsened it: "But since there is so much immorality, each man should have his own wife, and each woman her own husband" (NIV); and, "Nevertheless because of sexual immorality, let each man have his own wife, and let each woman have her own husband" (NKJB). These translations give the impression that Paul is teaching that the purpose of marriage is simply to avoid sexual immorality outside of marriage, which view is totally outside of the proper concept of marriage within Christianity.

Fornication Causes Separation

Greek grammar specifies that the preposition *día* in its root meaning is related to *dúo* or *dís*, "two" or "twice." It involves separation, meaning "passing between or through." But when it is used with an accusative noun as here, *porneías*, it means "because of, for the sake of, or on account of." The notion of between is still present as in Matthew 27:18 for instance: "for envy they had delivered him." In Greek this is *diá phthónon*. Envy was the reason that prompted the betrayal of Jesus, and so it came in between and caused the act.

The King James Version is correct in exegetically translating *diá tás porneías* with the periphrastic expression "to avoid," but in so doing, unless it is qualified, it can lead to serious difficulties in the correct concept of marriage.

Intercourse Within Marriage Is Not Fornication

Unless this prepositional phrase is qualified, it may give the idea that the act of intercourse within marriage, as already stated, should be equated with fornication, which it is not. That act has God's blessing upon it. Immediately after God created male and female He said to them: "Be fruitful, and multiply, and replenish the earth" (Gen. 1:27, 28). The only way this could be done is through conjugal intercourse. This is not *porneía*, "fornication."

27

The Christian Concept of Marriage

This whole passage of First Corinthians chapter seven leads us into the consideration of the Christian concept of marriage.

During the apostolic age, the Church was both Jewish and Gentile, and its ideas on marriage had a double background which came from both the Old Testament and the heathen, which is still true today. The Christian Church faces some real problems, as among its ranks are those from Jewish and heathen backgrounds. Ask any missionary working among polygamous peoples and he will tell you what a problem it is when a heathen who has multiple wives is made a new creature in Christ. Whom does he choose to be his wife from the moment of his salvation? Does he keep one in the Christian concept of marriage and abstain from the others? To keep all of them as wives is definitely prohibited by the Bible, but to desert them and their children could result in extreme hardship. Such were the problems faced by Paul as a missionary among Jews and Gentiles (heathen) in Corinth particularly. It is these specific problems he is trying to solve. The Jewish and heathen background must be taken into account as we study Paul's epistles to these Corinthians concerning Christian marriage.

The gravest danger was that the laxity of heathenism with regard to marriage should continue among Christian converts from such a background. This is the greatest danger in the Christian Church today; adopting the laxity of secularism and humanism in this all–important matter of marriage. It spells the danger of incipient destruction of the Christian Church. Such laxity occupied Paul and it ought to occupy us. We must not seek the least painful way of conforming to secularism and humanism, but the firmest, most loving way of applying Christ's teaching even as Paul did. The Corinthian Church was but a replica of the Church of the twentieth century.

In the heathen world, though the marriage ceremony was in some cases a type of a sacred act, the marriage itself was looked on as an easily–broken contract which either party might dissolve at will. It is not surprising, therefore, that one of the earliest questions which the Corinthians put to Paul should be on the subject of marriage, which is apparent in reading 1 Corinthians 7:1: "Now concerning the things whereof ye wrote unto me."

In the second verse, the first thing he points out is that marriage is partly a remedy against *porneías*, "fornications," which is sin. But if it is sin, it cannot be part of marriage.[1]

The Higher Jewish Concept of Marriage

The Jews had a much higher concept of marriage than the heathen. Almost all of them were married, as is the case in the present day with practically the whole of the Christian, Jewish, and Muslim populations of the Near East. The exceptions are very few. Marriage was considered a sacred and holy duty.

Yet the Jews had not wholly escaped from heathen contamination.

Our Lord greatly raised the concept of marriage, even as compared with that of the Jews of His time. Marriage was intended only for this life, for there are no marriages in heaven (Matt. 22:30; Mark 12:25; Luke 20:35). These passages, however, do not teach that loved ones will be parted hereafter.

Paul Taught the Sanctity of Marriage

Paul, following his Lord, insists on the holiness of marriage in Ephesians 5:22–33. It is obvious everywhere that Christianity stresses that marriage can only be the union of one man to one woman. On the conclusion of his injunctions as to how the spouses should behave toward each other, he says in verses thirty–one through thirty–three: "For this cause shall a man leave his father and mother, and shall be joined unto his wife, and they two shall be one flesh. This is a great mystery: but I speak concerning Christ and the church. Nevertheless let every one of you in particular so love his wife even as himself; and the wife see that she reverence her husband." One to one, no matter what the previous cultural background. Can these be the words of a man who did not believe in marriage and its sanctity?

Paul was single, and yet he denounced as a heresy the prohibition of marriage. In 1 Timothy 4:1, 3 he writes: ". . . in the latter times some shall depart from the faith, giving heed to seducing spirits,

and doctrines of devils; . . . forbidding to marry . . ."
How could he himself be advocating what he calls a
doctrine of devils in First Corinthians chapter seven?
Such an interpretation of the chapter must be considered erroneous. It must be remembered, however,
that when Paul wrote 1 Timothy, almost ten years
had gone by since he wrote First Corinthians chapter
seven.

Which of the officials of the early church remained single besides the apostle Paul and which
were married? Philip the Evangelist had four daughters "who prophesied" (Acts 21:9), while the apostle
John, who Tertullian called a "celibate of Christ,"
was frequently known as a *parthénos*, "virgin." It
must be remembered that the New Testament does
not teach any special blessing for celibates as officials of the Apostolic Church. On the other hand, it
does not exclude one who is not married from being
either an elder or a deacon. It does, however, instruct
that elders and deacons who marry should be the
husbands of one wife (1 Tim. 3:2, 4; Titus 1:6).

---

[1]The same truth he stresses in 1 Thessalonians 4:3; Romans
1:24, 28; 6:12ff; 13:14; 1 Corinthians 5:1, 9–11; 6:13–20;
2 Corinthians 12:21; Galatians 5:16–24; Ephesians 2:2ff;
4:17–19; 5:3; Colossians 3:5–8; 2 Timothy 2:22. Other New
Testament writers give similar warnings such as we find in
1 Peter 1:14; 2:11; 4:2ff, 2 Peter 2:18, and Jude 1:16, 18.

6

SEXUAL INTERCOURSE IS THE NATURAL AND LEGITIMATE PRIVILEGE OF MARRIAGE

. . . Let every man have his own wife, and let every woman have her own husband.—1 Corinthians 7:2

God forbids sex outside of marriage but within marriage it is not forbidden. It is acceptable and should be exercised as part of our humanity. Marital relationships should not be considered as merely a substitute for something inherently immoral.

Another thing Paul wants to stress is that a marital sexual relationship is part of our humanity. Recall the words of the Lord Jesus in Luke 20:34, 35: "The children of this world marry, and are given in marriage." This is part of our earthly life. "But they which shall be accounted worthy to obtain that world, and the resurrection from the dead, neither marry, nor are given in marriage" (see also Matt. 22:30; Mark 12:25). The word "marry" or "to give in marriage" here is the Greek verb *gaméō* from which *gámos*, "wedding feast" or "wedding," is derived (Matt. 5:32; 19:9; 22:2, etc.). But the verb also means "to have sexual intercourse."[1]

I believe that is the meaning of the verb *gamoúsin*, "have marital relations," referring to the men in the present indicative active, and *gamízontai*, third person plural present indicative passive, and referring to the women in Luke 20:34, 35.[2] The form *gamízō* is a late form of *gaméō* and is used only in the present active and passive and imperfect passive in the New Testament.[3]

The Lord in His discussions with the Sadducees was pointing out that the resurrection is going to mean a new body for His followers. Paul calls it "a spiritual body."[4] It is going to be a body governed primarily by our spirit and will not have sexual appetites as our present body. This also infers that the multiplication of the race will not be part of our metaphysical existence. The Lord did not teach in these passages of the three synoptic gospels that in the resurrection there will be no earthly family relations maintained, but that our bodies will be so constituted that there will not be sexual relations between husbands and wives for they will be like angels in that respect. Angels are said to be neither male nor female. The same institution of marriage will not be maintained in heaven as it was here.

While we are down here on earth, however, we must realize that basically the institution of marriage is for the multiplication of the race and our mutual marital enjoyment. To disregard that function of marriage is to deprive it of its God–intended function.

The word *porneías*, translated "fornications" in 1 Corinthians 7:2, is used in the plural. The reason for this is that reference is made not to the "much immorality" that existed in Corinth as the NIV interprets 1 Corinthians 7:2 to mean, but "to the acts of fornication" to which these believers to whom Paul was writing would be tempted in view of their present bodily constitution. Outside of marriage, the fulfillment of one's sexual desires, Paul was intimating, is fornication. But when married, one's full sexual satisfaction is to be found in the acts of intercourse with one's spouse. What is an act of true love within marriage is an act of lust outside of marriage. (See A.T. Robertson, p. 408.)

A Marriage Just for Sex Cannot Last Long

Nor did the Apostle Paul want to give the idea by the admonition "to avoid acts of fornication, let every man have his own wife, and let every woman have her own husband" that the only purpose of marriage is the avoidance of "acts of fornication." That would be the poorest excuse for marriage, and if the main reason that anyone marries is to have intercourse legitimately within marriage to substitute for acts of sin outside of marriage, I can assure you that such a marriage could not last long. As Paul taught throughout his epistles, Christian marriage should be based on mutual respect and love. The word for "love" is *agápē* (Eph. 5:25, 28, 33) which means not meeting one's own need of the flesh, but meeting the total need, physical, spiritual and emotional, of one's spouse. Marriage based on lust instead of love, on sexual self–satisfaction instead of mutuality of respect of the need of the other, is not in accordance with God's plan.

May Those Who Find It Impossible to Marry Engage in Acts of Fornication?

We find in the expression "let every man have his own wife, and let every woman have her own husband" (1 Cor. 7:2) that the Greek word for "every man" and "every woman" is the pronoun *hékastos*. The fact that it is in the masculine presupposes the word "man" or "male." In this instance it is used as an adjectival noun. It has the meaning "each one" with some individual distinctiveness to the person referred to. It does not refer to the totality of people, but rather to each individual within the totality. The Apostle Paul fully realized that it was and is impossible for every man and every woman to get married and, by virtue of that marriage, to avoid sexual relationships outside of marriage which would constitute acts of fornication.

But what about those who cannot marry because of health, social, economic or any other circumstances? Can they then, because of such inability to marry, engage in acts of fornication? Nowhere in

Scripture is this permitted. All cannot marry, but each one who can and feels the necessity, let him marry. No one can just cohabit with another person of the opposite sex and call that cohabitation marriage.

One Spouse Belongs to Another Exclusively

Let each man have "his own wife." He is not to have any woman, but only the one he gives his vow to. And let each woman have her own husband. There are two Greek words used here translated as "own."[5] The reference is to a woman who becomes part of himself, one flesh forever as our Lord taught. And to the woman it is said, "let each one have her own husband." The word for "her own" is *ídion*, "one's own." It denotes property or a peculiar relation. This man cannot belong to anyone else. He is exclusively hers. That this refers to the legitimate marriage recognized by God and society there is no doubt whatsoever.

It is interesting to note that it is the woman who is said to possess the husband. This is in contradistinction to the Old Testament concept of a husband always possessing the wife.

What Paul says in 1 Corinthians 7:2 cannot be taken as a command for everyone to marry since later on in verse seven he expresses the desire, "For I would that all men were even as I myself. But every man hath his proper gift of God, one after this manner, and another after that." And in verses twenty–five through thirty–eight, he deals with the virgins expressing the opinion that there are exigencies in life that would make celibacy preferable.

---

[1]Brown, Colin. *New International Dictionary of New Testament Theology (Theologlsches Begriffslexikon Zum Neuen Testament)* (Grand Rapids: Zondervan Publishing House, 1975), vol. 2, p. 575.

[2]Robertson, A.T. *A Grammar of the Greek New Testament in the Light of Historical Research* (New York: George H. Doran Company, 1923), p. 392.

[3]Op. Cit. p. 1213.

[4]1 Cor. 15:44—See Author's volume on 1 Cor. 15, *Conquering the Fear of Death*, pp. 663–670.

[5]*Heautoú* is a pronoun compounded of the Ionic *héo*, "for," *hoú*, "of his own," and *autoú*, "him."

7

MUTUAL CONSIDERATION OF HUSBAND AND WIFE

Let the husband render unto the wife due benevolence: and likewise also the wife unto the husband. The wife hath not power of her own body, but the husband: and likewise also the husband hath not power of his own body, but the wife.—1 Corinthians 7:3, 4

Paul ascribes the initiative of marriage to the man. In verse two he said: "Let each man have his own wife" and then, "let each woman have her own husband."

Again in verse three it is the man who is asked to render unto the wife due benevolence.

What is this "benevolence"? The Greek word is *eúnoian*. It is a compound noun from *eú* meaning "well" and *noús*, "mind." It occurs only here and in Ephesians 6:7 and is found only in the Textus Receptus. The UBS text simply has *opheilén* (accusative of *opheilé*). An *opheilén* is "a debt" which must be paid as in Matthew 18:32, or an "obligation," a service which one owes someone as here and in Romans 13:7. The Textus Receptus has the words *tén opheiloménēn eúnoian*, "the goodwill that is due to the wife." It is as if Paul is saying to the husband: "Recognize that you owe your wife something, and that something is to think well of her. Give her that which will please her and set her mind at ease." The woman is to do likewise to her husband.

There Are Needs Only a Husband or a Wife Can Meet

Each spouse must recognize that the other has a need which only he or she can fulfill. That need which Paul has in mind here is the marital, sexual need of each other in marriage.

Paul places both husband and wife on an equal level in regard to this need. In the sexual relationship, one's priority must never be to satisfy his or her own needs, but rather the needs of his or her God–given companion. Without a doubt, one really receives more when giving to satisfy his partner. How amiss some husbands are in their marital relationships. They want primarily to receive instead of to give. Even in this regard, remember the words of our Savior: "It is more blessed to give than to receive" (Acts 20:35).

1 Corinthians 7:3, 4 annuls any thought that the first verse saying, "It is good for a man not to touch a woman," means that it is good not to have sexual relations within marriage. The husband should take

the initiative for the purpose of first satisfying his wife's need of him as her husband. If this is done consistently, there need be no fear of any deterioration in the marital relationship.

And the wife is to accept that initiative and reciprocate. She is not to seek only to have her own need satisfied but seek aggressively to satisfy her husband's need. The wife should recognize that she is the only one and the God—ordained one to meet that need in her husband's life. This will certainly do much in lessening the "acts of fornication" spoken of in verse one which are so prevalent today. Let marriage be what it ought to be, a beautiful partnership of two personalities and a life of marital sexual satisfaction among other things.

Sex Within Marriage Is Not Just for Childbearing

Observe that Paul does not speak here about childbearing as the purpose of this marital relationship. If sexual relations between spouses were meant only for childbearing, Paul would not have spoken of mutual need and satisfaction, but would rather have specifically spoken about childbearing being the basic purpose of marital sexual relations. As Hebrews 13:4 says: "Marriage is honorable in all, and the bed undefiled: but whoremongers and adulterers God will judge." Since the evil practices of sin spoken about in the latter part of this verse were done only for the purposes of pleasure and not procreation, why were they contrasted with the marital act if it was only to be employed for child-bearing?

Furthermore, verse four certainly makes clear what the Apostle Paul meant by that which the spouses owe each other. "The wife hath not power of her own body, but the husband: and likewise also the husband hath not power of his own body, but the wife."

Whereas Paul in verses two and three places the initiative with the husband in that it is the man who chooses a wife and the man who takes the first step in meeting the needs of his wife, now in verse four we have first the woman spoken of as not in control of her own body when it comes to the marital relationship. "The wife hath not power of her own body, but the husband."

Paul indirectly here, as in other writings, upholds the leadership role of a husband in the marital relationship. In 1 Corinthians 11:3 he writes: "The head of every man is Christ; and the head of the woman is the man." And in verses eight and nine he writes: "For the man is not of the woman; but the woman of the man. Neither was the man created for the woman; but the woman for the man." But he stresses the mutuality of dependence by writing in verse eleven: "Nevertheless, neither is the man without the woman, neither the woman without the man." And in Ephesians 5:23 he writes: "The husband is the head of the wife," but he also stresses the husband's duty by saying in verse twenty–five: "Husbands, love your wives. . . ."

In 1 Corinthians 7:2, 3 we have indirect imperatives: "*Let* every man *have* (*echétō*) his own wife, and *let* every woman *have* (*echétō*) her own husband. *Let* the husband *render* (*apodidótō*) unto the wife due benevolence: and *likewise also* the wife unto the husband."

The Sex Act in Marriage Should Be Exercised Gently and Considerately

But in verse four there is a shift in the verbal form to the present indicative: "The wife *hath not power* of her own body." That verb in Greek is *ouk exousiázei.* There is no imperative here. It is a statement of fact. And so is the next statement concerning the husband: "and likewise also the husband hath not power (*ouk exousiázei*) of his own body, but the wife."[1] The verb comes from the noun *exousía,* which does not really refer to physical power, but to liberty, the moral right and privilege by virture of one's relationship. When we become a wedded wife or a wedded husband, we abdicate the sole right to our own body. We two become one flesh. Each owns the other's body. Since our spouse's body is actually our body, how could we ever think of forcing or harming our own body?

In considering the meaning and implications of verse four, we can then conclude that verse three must give preference to the Textus Receptus reading, allowing the noun *eúnoia,* "benevolence or goodwill," to be the exegetically correct reading instead of *opheilén*, "debt, obligation," of the UBS text. The Textus Receptus of verse three has, "Let the husband render unto the wife *due benevolence* (*tén opheiloménēn eúnoian*)," instead of merely *tén opheilén*, "that which is due." The Textus Receptus stresses the *eúnoian*, "goodwill or benevolence" as due to the wife instead of the indefinite "that which is due" without specifying what this is. Of course, from the context we know that Paul is speaking about sexual love, but in the Textus Receptus that "goodwill" or "benevolence" must be exercised in giving such to the marital partner. The sex act must not be a torture imposed on the marital partner but a "well–minded" (literal translation) act which the Greek *eúnoia* explicitly stresses.

How many marriages are greatly damaged, if not totally destroyed, because of the roughness of the exercise of power over a marital partner? Affection, love, tenderness and consideration ought to be the guiding principle of the sexual act on the part of each spouse. Set your spouse at ease, make her or his mind peaceful when you exercise your authority and liberty over your spouse's body. Remember your spouse's body is your very own.

How Should a Spouse React to a Partner's Rough Behavior?

If a marital partner does not exercise "benevolence," and in many cases, a partner can be very cruel, what are the rights of the injured member?

In such a case, a more general rule transcends the marital relationship. It is the commandment, "Do not kill." God does not only want you not to kill, but not to allow someone else to kill you. In some instances, that may mean your very own husband or wife. How many homicides occur between marital partners right in their own homes! The kitchen or the bedroom is not supposed to be a battlefield with submission to one who tries to hurt you, but a little bit of paradise on earth when the two partners submit one to the other in goodwill and love.

Besides the law of submission to one another in the marital partnership, there is also the scriptural injunction to "Let every soul be subject unto the higher powers. For there is no power but of God: the powers that be are ordained of God" (Romans 13:1). Most countries have laws protecting individuals from physical attacks by other human beings no matter who they may be, even though a husband or a wife. Such ruthless partners who consistently abuse their spouses ought to be reported to the authorities ordained by God to protect life itself. Such a spouse certainly must not be permitted to exercise power without benevolence towards his partner. No person in his right mind would demand that another person be closed in a house for all her life with a vicious animal or criminal, and yet how many well–meaning Christians insist that a fellow–Christian must, without restraint, continue to accept her mate's abuse.

[1]The verb is used only four times in the entire New Testament. In 1 Cor. 6:12 we read: "All things are lawful (actually 'are permissible', a related verb in Greek, *éxestin*) unto me, but all things are not expedient; all things are lawful (*éxestin*, 'permissible') for me, but I will not be brought under the power of any." That expression "will not be brought under the power" in Greek is *exousiasthésomai*, the future indicative passive of *exousiázo*. Paul here is speaking about purity among believers, primarily from the sins of the flesh. The other two times *exousiázo* is used are in 1 Cor. 7:4 and Luke 22:25.

8

DON'T DEPRIVE YOUR SPOUSE

Defraud ye not one the other.... —1 Corinthians 7:5

Here we have a direct imperative addressed to both husband and wife. It is "Defraud ye not." In Greek the phrase is *mē apostereíte allēlous*, "don't deprive each other." *Apostereō* is a compound verb made up from *apó* meaning "from" and *stereō*, "to deprive another of what belongs to him or her." Of course the object is the body which belongs to the spouse in the marital union.

In Mark 10:19 this imperative is used as one of the Commandments. Jesus met a young man who knelt down and asked, "Good Master, what shall I do that I may inherit eternal life? And Jesus said unto him, Why callest thou me good? There is none good but one, that is, God. Thou knowest the commandments, Do not commit adultery, Do not kill, Do not steal, Do not bear false witness, *Defraud not*, Honor thy father and mother." In this Scripture "defraud not" is *mē apostereses*, the same as in 1 Corinthians 7:5 except in the second person singular.

47

Not Depriving Your Spouse Prevents
Coveting Another Woman

In Exodus 20:17, we will find that this concerns the Tenth Commandment: "Thou shalt not covet thy neighbour's wife . . ." etc. Coveting or wanting what does not belong to a person can destroy his life, even if he never comes to possess that which he is coveting.

But what is the preventive step that husband and wife can both take in order that there may be the least possible chance of such coveting? It is the advice Paul gives: Don't deprive your partner of what belongs to him or her, your body in marriage. Such deprivation is partly responsible for such coveting. Obedience to this direct command of Paul's in 1 Corinthians 7:5 is one of the best safeguards against the possibility of divorce.

Getting Even With a Spouse by
Depriving Him or Her

Isn't it true so many times that when couples get irritated with each other, the first thing they want to do is to deprive the other of their physical availability? "I know how to get even with him or with her," says a wife or a husband! If this continues for any length of time, the results may well be catastrophic. Depriving one's wife or husband of his or her body is no way to punish or correct. It is precisely this that the Apostle Paul warns against.

Don't Be the Devil's Advocate Through Depriving

In the case of such deprivation of oneself in marriage, one is equating himself with Satan by bringing temptation to his partner. This is manifest by the conclusion: "that Satan tempt you not for your incontinency."

How careful each one of us must be as husband and wife. There are times that we do well to be continent or self–restrained as in a case of mutual agreement. But this must not be when our spouse desires us. Restraint then is inadvisable. If a partner is not well, we must show the proper respect for his or her particular circumstance. Privation, however, because of obstinate self–will is forbidden.

Many times such refusal is the hidden first step toward the calamity of divorce. The moment we resort to it as part of our self–defense and preservation of individual rights, we become devilish. The other name for Satan is "devil" which in Greek is *diábolos*, from the verb *diabállō* which means "to go in between," or to put it in more colloquial terminology, "to throw a monkey wrench in the works." By refusing a partner his conjugal rights, the devil is causing him to build a gap which will grow bigger and bigger and may become a split.

Be Benevolent (1 Cor. 7:3) Means Don't Deprive (1 Cor. 7:5)

What Paul expressed positively in 1 Corinthians 7:3 by saying: "Let the husband render unto the wife due benevolence: and likewise also the wife unto the husband," he states negatively in verse five: "Deprive ye not one the other, except it be with consent for a time." In the first positive instance, the imperative is indirect in the third person singular, *apodidótō*, "let him/her render due benevolence," what he owes her and what she owes him in kindness. But in verse five Paul becomes more stern and issues it as a direct command in the plural: "Don't you deprive each other." He wants us to realize how serious a matter this is. He speaks to both husband and wife together because he knows that either can fall into such a trap.

Equality Between the Sexes in Marriage and Mutual Satisfaction

The word translated "each other" in Greek is *allélous* (*állos, állon*, "one another"), which denotes mutuality and reciprocity without distinction of the gender. The word makes husband and wife to stand on an equality in the marital relationship. The husband is not superior to his wife and the wife is not to be passive or merely submissive to the husband when it comes to the marital relationship. The husband has no more right to want his wife than the wife her husband. The right to each other is equal. The wife is not merely a vessel for the husband to have whenever he wants, and the same is true of the wife toward her husband.

It is easy for a husband or wife to find an excuse for such deprivation of their partner. As John Calvin writes: "Paul was under the necessity of speaking of these things. . . . He knew how much influence a false appearance of sanctity has in beguiling devout minds, as we ourselves know by experience. For Satan dazzles us with an appearance of what is right, that we may be led to imagine that we are polluted by intercourse with our wives, and leaving off our calling may think of pursuing another kind of life" (Calvin on 1 Cor. 7:5).

Satisfying Oneself While the Mate Remains Unsatisfed

There is another danger in married life. One, usually the husband, may satisfy his sexual need before his mate and does not care in what state of unsatisfied emotional upheaval he may leave his partner. In the marital relationship, it should not be of primary concern to reach one's own selfish satisfaction, but to bring to the spouse equal fulfillment. A man must not defraud his wife of her due benevolence either by neglect or by design. The obligation is mutual and the rights are equal in married life.

Watch the Compulsive Desire to Abstain From Marital Relations

Sometimes in the married life, one of the partners may develop a false attitude that the sexual act is evil in itself which creates a compulsive desire to abstain. "Since I am spiritual," he reasons, "I should not touch my spouse lest I defile my body in which the Holy Spirit dwells." Such a false sanctimonious attitude may even create the unconscious desire of reverting to celibacy. To even entertain such a mental desire is extremely dangerous for the health of one's marriage and one's true spirituality.

After all, true spirituality is preservation of and perseverance in the vows that we take before God and men when we are married. Denial of those vows consciously or unconsciously is not spirituality, but lack of it.

We must remember that as a spouse we are only one half of our body. If we decide to disregard the rights and needs of the other half, we are actually guilty of physically and spiritually harming our own body. A married partner must never wish that he had remained single or that by some act of God he would again become single. "In whatever state I am, therewith to be content," is Paul's teaching in Philippians 4:11.

9

MUTUAL AGREEMENT IN ABSTAINING FROM MARITAL RELATIONS

... except it be with consent for a time, that ye may give yourselves to fasting and prayer; ...
—1 Corinthians 7:5

There is, however, one exception to this command which Paul mentions: "Except it be with consent." That phrase translated "with consent" in Greek is *ek sumphónou*. This expression occurs only here in the New Testament. It is a common expression even in modern Greek. It is a compound expression, *to sumphónon*, which means "agreement." It is derived from the conjunction *sún*, "together" or "together with," and *phōnéō*, "to speak." It is a mutually expressed agreement one with the other. It excludes unilateral action. It excludes a hidden, unspoken desire of the one which is subtly imposed on the other.

This word even denotes equality in the desire. It is not a desire which springs in the heart of the one and is imposed on the other, but it is a desire that is born simultaneously in the heart of the husband and wife who, in reality, are "one flesh." That is the one exception when the two partners in marriage can mutually abstain from intercourse.

The important phrase is *ek sumphōnou*, by mutual agreement. Are there no other circumstances besides prayer which would induce the marital partners to abstain one from the other? Of course there are, such as the avoidance of pregnancy or disease or other valid circumstances. Prayer is merely given as an example of such mutual agreement.

Abstaining Should Be for a Short Time Only

The second condition for such deprivation is "for a time." The Greek expression is *prós kairón*. The Greek word *kairós* is a little different from *chrónos.* The latter word from which comes the English "chronometer" refers to time in general. But *kairós* signifies *eukairía*, "proper time or opportunity." What Paul meant when he said "Don't deprive each other unless mutually agreed for a time" was not simply for the length of time but also for the granting of an opportunity for something else.

In other words, don't give up your marital relations just for the sake of giving them up for a time. There should be a purposeful goal, and that goal should be mutual. Of course, the word *kairós* also refers to a brief season of time when used with the preposition *prós*, "for." It actually infers that the meaning is until the goal that has been mutually set is accomplished. There must be a real purpose and that purpose must be of short duration.

The Purpose of Abstaining

This purpose is explicitly expressed with the telic *hína*, "so that you may give yourselves to fasting and prayer." The word *scholázēte* is translated "give yourselves." The Greek verb *scholázō* means much more than just "to give oneself." The verb means "to be unemployed or at leisure." With a dative as, *tē nēsteía kaí proseuchē*, "for fasting and prayer," it means to be at leisure for fasting and prayer.

It is interesting that the word for "school" in Greek is *scholē*. Actually the English is a transliteration of the Greek. Why did the Greeks call school *scholē*, "a place of leisure"? Because it was a place where persons being at leisure from bodily labor and business could attend to the improvement of their minds.

Why then this mutual agreement to abstain from sexual relations in marriage? For the sake of a short time of leisure in order to fast and pray.

Abstaining Is Not a Necessary Concomitant to Spirituality

This should not be taken to imply that if spouses have relations, they cannot pray and fast. The one exercise is not exclusive of the other. But there are seasons of special needs and crises in a couple's life when by mutual consent and concern, marital relations ought to be set aside to provide a little more leisure to devote to fasting and prayer. Paul does not speak here about all kinds of fasting and prayer but special occasions. Prayer as per Ephesians 6:18 is an attitude and practice that is continuous. Fasting is voluntary privation of necessary food. Doing without a necessity centers our attention upon a purposeful goal which we set as a target for prayer. Our Lord said in Matthew 17:21: "Howbeit this kind goeth not out but by prayer and fasting." This concerned the healing of the lunatic boy whom the disciples failed to help.

Thus Paul teaches that the only time that a couple may deprive each other of their marital obligations is when mutually agreed for a time and a purpose which is to fast and pray, and by extension, other valid purposes.

Paul did not say that husband and wife should deprive each other except in the case that children are desired. The conjugal intercourse should be frequent and mutually satisfying.

Observe that the verb *scholázēte*, "that ye may have leisure for fasting and prayer," is in the plural. It includes both husband and wife. Neither can say to the other, "I have no time for it." It must be both together agreeing to make time for fasting and prayer, but not one alone.

56

In the Greek there is the definite article before both *nēsteía* and *proseuchē*. It is "the" fasting and "the" prayer. This lends authority to the previous observation that this fasting and prayer is not the ordinary, common exercise in the believer's life, but must be something of extraordinary importance. When that fasting and prayer has been accomplished, then the physical aspect of the marital relationship is to be resumed.

10

SATAN'S TEMPTATION DURING ABSTINENCE

. . . and come together again, that Satan tempt you not for your incontinency.—1 Corinthians 7:5

Paul does not say how long an abstinence should be. No time limit is imposed. The couple together agrees on it. "And come together again"; the implication is that these mutual abstentions may be repeated from time to time as the need for such a procedure becomes apparent.[1] The reason why the couple should come together again is introduced by the second telic *hína*, "so that Satan tempt you not for your incontinency."

Human Weakness and Satan's Temptation

There are certain explicit conclusions at which we must arrive by reading these words:

1. *That we are weak in the flesh.*

In what Paul calls "incontinency," which he denotes by the Greek word *akrasía*. The only other occurrence of this word is in Matthew 23:25. Here the

Lord was speaking to the scribes and Pharisees and calling them "hypocrites!" And He told them why: "For ye make clean the outside of the cup and of the platter, but within they are full of extortion and excess."

The word translated "excess" is *akrasía*.[2] It refers to a lack of power to regulate one's appetites. And this is the same meaning we find in 1 Corinthians 7:5. We do not have sufficient strength of our own to regulate our appetites, among which is the sex desire. It is a weak spot in every one of us. There is victory within marriage by meeting each other's need. There is victory outside of marriage by the power of God enabling us to be continent. It takes His power, for we don't have it innately in our sinful nature. Paul was victorious, and through his victory he sets an example which everyone else can follow by God's enablement. If you and I, however, do not recognize or refuse to recognize our weakness in the flesh, we shall surely expose ourselves to dangerous temptation. We are warned in the Scriptures to beware when we think we stand, lest we fall.

God's strength can be manifested in our weakness. But we cannot pretend we are strong while we are weak and expect to overcome with His strength. God can only fill a vacuum. If we empty ourselves of self, He will enter and live within us and thus manifest His strength through us.

2. *There is a devil whose job is to tempt us.*

He will not spare any of us. He is real. Paul believed in his existence. Christ did too, and often battled with him. He is most active in pinpointing our weaknesses and making us succumb to them.

If your weakness is sex, recognize it and take appropriate measures to combat it. If you are married, come together with your spouse. That is your best weapon against the temptation to satisfy your sexual desire outside of marriage. If you are not married, seek God in complete yieldedness to Him. Don't expose yourself to any scene or reading material or activity which may arouse your sexual desire. What starts out as light petting is a direct road into deeper involvement. It is possible to sublimate your desire for sex and be victorious. You can rest assured of one basic principle: God will enable you to be victorious in any circumstance He directs or permits you to be in. But He will not prove His sufficiency to you in disregard of His commandments and endowments.

When God permits you to be married, He will direct you to act properly in your conjugal relationships so that Satan will not take advantage of your natural inability to control yourself sexually.

The Divine Strength of Continence When Needed

If God were to take someone's spouse, He would give the strength of continence. He will not give it before it is needed, since He permits the availability of the spouse. He will do the same in case of sickness or whatever circumstance makes it impossible or essentially inappropriate for a couple to have marital relations.

If God does not provide a marriage partner in spite of the believer's desire for one, He will provide His strength in one's weakness. But it is not wise to voluntarily choose such a state without having His special gift and then expect His sufficiency. We are to discern God's gifts and apply them in our lives. If we are His and are looking to Him for strength for each passing day, He will never allow us to be tempted beyond our ability to bear it.

Truly, Satan is alert in tempting us, but we must also recognize his limitations. At the same time, we are to do what is in our power to resist him by coming together with our spouse if married, and if not married, by avoiding situations and temptations that would lead to sin. First Corinthians 7:1 then applies here: "It is good for a man not to touch a woman." God gives us the victory through taking the first step of safeguard and precaution ourselves and not igniting those fires which are almost impossible to quench or contain. When tempted by Satan, let us inscribe upon our hearts and memories what Paul said in 1 Corinthians 10:13: "There hath no temptation taken you but such as is common to man: but God is faithful (dependable), who will not suffer you to be tempted above that ye are able; but will with the temptation also make a way to escape, that ye may be able to bear it."

God does not grant to everybody the same opportunity of marriage. A young girl or woman may want to get married and find in marriage the answer to Satan's temptation for the fulfillment not only of her sexual instinct, but her lonely existence. But it is true that such an opportunity may not be provided. It is better to depend upon God to provide either an acceptable mate or the strength to resist temptation than to push oneself into a situation which seems to be the answer for incontinence, but may become the greatest problem of life.

How careful we must be lest in our impulsiveness we create circumstances which are difficult to deal with. Let us never complain about God's insufficiency for situations we have created for ourselves. To choose to be outside of God's will is to choose to shut God's strength and victory out of our life. In such circumstances the Lord's mercy, which is His sufficiency not for the circumstances but for the consequences of our own self–chosen circumstances, will be found of great comfort. None of us can escape the circumstances of the consequences of our own choices. It is God's grace which gives us the ability to choose His will, and His mercy which provides comfort when we have failed to choose His way in our lives. This is the basic distinction between the two Greek words: *cháris*, "grace," and *éleos*, "mercy."

God Is Sufficient in Every Circumstance

Note how sufficient God was in the life of Paul as he faced a variety of circumstances:

"Not that I speak in respect of want: for I have learned, in *whatsoever* state I am (he means here whatever state God chose for him and not that which he wilfully chose for himself), therewith to be content. I know both how to be abased, and I know how to abound: everywhere and in all things I am instructed both to be full and to be hungry, both to abound and to suffer need. I can do all things through Christ which strengtheneth me" (Phil. 4:11–13).

Let us consider one more observation about the verb translated "tempt" in 1 Corinthians 7:5: "that Satan tempt you not for your incontinency." The verb *peirázē* is in the present subjunctive tense which means that Satan's activity is continuous. It is not a once–and–for–all temptation. If, in an obstinate refusal to yield yourself to your marital partner, you set Satan to work, be assured he will never quit working. Satan is active enough without our providing him with material with which to work. The resistance of the injured spouse will rise up and may build up to the proportion of explosion which is the tragedy of the breaking of the marriage. I don't know whether any studies have been made as to the unwarranted and obstinate one–sided refusal of a partner in marriage being the basis of divorce. But if the science of statistics were able to penetrate the bedrooms of couples, I would dare state that a great many divorces begin with that stubborn, self–willed "No" by one marriage partner to another. It is then that Satanic work begins in the heart and total disposition of the other. This attitude also affects other areas of conjugal living. The partners move farther and farther apart, and it becomes increasingly difficult to bring them together. One of the greatest safeguards, therefore, against divorce is a deep–seated, good–willed respect for the sexual needs of each other by the marriage partners. Don't ever take it for granted that your partner is strong and always understanding.

Paul says that a couple living together are, by nature of the bond of marriage, *ákratos*, "incontinent." To try to be otherwise is to try to set aside the laws of nature which God has ordained for married people. The continency which a marriage partner is able to demonstrate when a spouse is set aside in sickness or is taken in death is a God–given gift which God does not necessarily impart when the marriage partner is present and available. It all comes down to the very general principle that God does not do for us what we can do for ourselves and for others. He steps in with His gifts exactly when we need Him, not ahead of time. Whenever we can help ourselves, He expects us to do all we can to solve our own problems and His grace and wisdom will be our portion if we seek it.

Recall the Israelites. In the desert after having fled from Egypt, they could not grow crops to feed themselves. God intervened for the time that it was absolutely necessary by miraculously sending manna from heaven. But He stopped it the very moment the Israelites entered their land of promise. One of the greatest Scriptures concerning God's providence is Joshua 5:12: "And the manna ceased on the morrow after they had eaten of the old corn of the land; neither had the children of Israel manna any more; but they did eat of the fruit of the land of Canaan that year."

---

[1]The tenses *scholázēte*, "that ye may have leisure for fasting and prayer," and *sunérchēsthe* are the present subjunctive which are iterative.

[2]Derived from the privative *a*, "not," and *krátos*, "strength."

11

SHOULD MATTERS PERTAINING TO SEXUAL RELATIONSHIPS OF MARRIED COUPLES BE DISCUSSED?

But I speak this by permission, and not of commandment.—1 Corinthians 7:6

The first verse of 1 Corinthians shows that Paul was answering specific questions about marriage put forth to him by the Corinthians: "Now concerning the things whereof ye wrote me." As a short review, let us reiterate these principles Paul has set forth.

He starts with the principle that outside of marriage one should not sexually involve himself with women.

"It is good for a man not to touch a woman."

If God has given you the gift and special calling to remain single as Paul was then stay that way.

It is apparent and only proper that Paul is writing primarily to men, for he himself was a man, and later, in verse seven, he presents himself as an example of a chaste, single man. But by implication, the same counsel would follow for women. He could have also said, "It is good for a woman not to touch a man." Since men are generally in a position of authority over women and can so much more easily get away with the sin of fornication since they cannot become pregnant, he directs his command to men in their practice of unchastity. And in Corinth, fornication by men especially was very common. It is really ungracious to consider Paul as prejudiced against women; rather, he is protective of them.

In verse two, he proceeds to state he really has no objection to marriage. He says that marriage is basically the God–ordained method for avoiding the sin of fornication which can be such a great temptation if one is not married.

"Nevertheless to avoid fornication, let every (or each) man have his own wife, and let every woman have her own husband."

Observe how he immediately mentions the right of a woman to have her own husband. He enunciates the principle of monogamy as God ordained from the beginning, and stresses the principle of equality in the right of a man and a woman to have a partner of the opposite sex.

But then in verses three through five, Paul enunciates principles of sexual behavior within marriage that are very basic. If we were to break down these principles with a full understanding from our discussion of these verses, we would state them thus:

1. We owe to our marital partner the fulfillment of his or her physical desires.

2. The principle of the marital act should be to fill the need of our partner first and not merely to selfishly gratify our own desire.

4. Your body, whether that of the wife or the husband, is not your own property in marriage. There are no individual rights in a truly God–ordained marriage.

5. With regularity meet the need of each other with common agreement by the initiation of either husband or wife and the willing response of the other.

6. If we consistently deprive our spouse of the physical privileges of marriage, we set Satan at work in our marriage, and he will never quit until he brings separation.

7. God does not give the gift of continence within marriage unless it is necessary due to circumstances He directs or permits, such as sickness or necessary separation. God expects the marriage partner to meet the sexual need of the spouse when both are available but will give His strength of abstinence when, through such circumstances as He permits, abstinence is necessary.

8. Prayer ordinarily is not hindered by the regularity of sexual performance within a Christian marriage. They are not mutually exclusive. Intercourse is not "unholy" for a married couple.

9. There are special times when a couple may agree to abstain for awhile to deal with specific crises situations through fasting and prayer.

10. Abstinence from each other must be only with mutual agreement and not for the sake of abstinence alone, but for meeting a special situation that demands concentration and meditation.

11. Such abstinence is purely voluntary. It should not be imposed by one partner on the other or by any outside human influence. It should be by the leading of the Holy Spirit in both husband and wife, and not by one who tries to impose it on the other.

12. Such abstinence must be of short duration and purposeful.

13. Partners should come back together when both or one of the partners feels it is time to. Let the other not say, "Not yet!"

14. Abstinence from intercourse is a form of fasting even as voluntary privation from food. But it is always not just for the sake of fasting but for the sake of seeking something special from God which burdens the heart.

All of the above principles Paul summarily refers to in verse six by the pronoun "this": "But I speak *this* by permission, and not of commandment," which we shall examine in the next chapter.

12

OPINIONS, NOT
COMMANDMENTS

But I speak this by permission, and not of commandment.—1 Corinthians 7:6

The first thing we must determine is what Paul means by the expression, "I speak . . . by permission and not of commandment."

The word "permission" in Greek is *suggnómēn* (*suggnómē*—nominative case), and occurs only here in the New Testament. It is a compound word made up of the conjunction *sún* meaning "with" and *gnómē* meaning "opinion, sentiment, will." The word in ancient Greek meant "sympathetic" or "an attitude of good will toward someone, lenience, indulgence." It also means, when it is used as "I have *suggnómēn*," that I have forgiveness for some wrong. Actually it is used in modern Greek with this meaning. One can say, "*Suggnómēn*," meaning, "Excuse me, please forgive me."[1]

Actually, Paul is asking the indulgence of the Corinthian Christians for bringing such intimacies

73

of the marital relationships to their attention. It is as if he is saying: "Please forgive me for doing so." And really, I would feel likewise if I were to speak to a congregation of believers on such personal matters, or if I were writing to them, I would offer an apology or ask for their indulgence for doing so, not really their permission. Probably Paul went into greater details about marital behavior than he wanted to, but he felt it necessary for their sakes. These private matters of conduct do greatly and seriously affect the general conduct and testimony of Christ's Church in the world.

The Freedom and Necessity of Regulating Our Own Private Lives

The counsel which Paul gave from verses three through five was not to be taken by the Corinthians as a direct revelation from God in relation to doctrine and one's relationship toward God. There is a great deal of freedom in determining our interpersonal relations as believers. God has not revealed to us in the New Testament such explicit directives as He did in the Old Testament. Our relationship to God is made possible through Jesus Christ coming to indwell us in and through the energy of the Holy Spirit. He then becomes God's fulfillment in us, our teacher and our guide.

But when it comes to our relations with our spouses and with our children or with our fellow humans, it is His general principles of kindness, selflessness and love that should direct our day by day and moment by moment choices. There is a great deal of freedom in Christian behavior. And if Paul felt that he needed the indulgence of these Corinthian believers as he, with concern, entered their private lives, how much more must each one of us who dares enter the private lives of our fellow believers and humans need their indulgence. Much humility without arrogance or a know–it–all attitude is necessary. We must not be presumptuous and attempt to regulate someone else's private life. Shun any Bible teacher or counselor who tries to prescribe remedies of fixed laws and detailed procedures instead of basic principles on which to base your individual choices.

Spiritual Leaders Should Not Attempt to Regulate Individual Choice

Paul concludes verse six with "and not of commandment." Actually the conjunction "and" is not in the Greek text. In contrast to a command that he could give as an apostle and a spiritual father, he merely seeks the same indulgence he is asking them to show.

Paul's attitude in 1 Corinthians 7:8 is different than that in 1 Corinthians 5:1–5. In these latter verses, he is direct and commanding because he is dealing with a definitive sin: a young man having relations with his mother or stepmother. So Paul is resolute and unyielding, saying: "For I verily, as absent in body, but present in spirit, have judged already, as though I were present, concerning him that hath so done this deed. In the name of our Lord Jesus Christ, when ye are gathered together, and my spirit, with the power of our Lord Jesus Christ, to deliver such an one unto Satan for the destruction of the flesh, that the spirit may be saved in the day of the Lord Jesus."

Paul Recognized the Areas in Which His Apostolic Authority Was or Was Not Applicable

The Apostle admits that the Lord, whose special apostle he was and equal to those Christ had selected during His earthly ministry (1 Cor. 9:1, 2), did not specifically give any commandment pertaining to the subject under discussion. He, therefore, being an honest man, had to present the principles he spoke about exactly for what they were.

He chose to state some principles on marriage, but he wanted it clearly understood that such were expressions of his opinion and not commandments of the Lord or precepts of his own apostleship.

---

[1]D. Demetrakou, *Great Dictionary of the Greek Language* (Athens: Demetrakos, 1952), Vol. 8, p. 6747.

13

APOSTOLIC COMMANDS AND APOSTOLIC ADVICE

But I speak this by permission, and not of commandment.—1 Corinthians 7:6

If you read Paul's epistles, you will find that whenever he speaks only of himself, he introduces himself as "an apostle of Jesus Christ." Whenever he introduces other names with his, he never refers to them as apostles but usually as brothers or servants. He never concedes apostleship to any of them unless they were apostles in the restricted sense that he was. Let us look at the introductory verses.

Romans 1:1: "Paul, a servant of Jesus Christ, called to be an apostle."

1 Corinthians 1:1: "Paul, called to be an apostle of Jesus Christ through the will of God, and *Sosthenes our brother.*" He does not include Sosthenes as an apostle. He is "the brother," *ho adelphós*, as the Greek text has it.

2 Corinthians 1:1: "Paul, an apostle of Jesus Christ by the will of God, *and Timothy, our brother.*"

Galatians 1:1, 2: "Paul, an apostle, not of men, neither by man, but by Jesus Christ . . . and *all the brethren* which are with me. . . ."

Ephesians 1:1: "Paul, an apostle of Jesus Christ by the will of God."

Philippians 1:1: "Paul and *Timothy, the servants* of Jesus Christ, to all the saints. . . ." Here, because Timothy is included, Paul does not refer to himself as an apostle nor include Timothy as one, but he calls both of them "servants of Jesus Christ."

Colossians 1:1: "Paul, an apostle of Jesus Christ by the will of God, and *Timothy our brother.*" Here he calls only himself an apostle, but not Timothy.

1 Thessalonians 1:1: "Paul, and Silvanus, and Timothy. . . ." Here he avoids calling these three anything. The same is true in 2 Thessalonians 1:1.

1 Timothy 1:1: "Paul, an apostle of Jesus Christ by the commandment of God our Savior. . . ." Here the word for "commandment" is exactly the same as in 1 Corinthians 7:6, *epitagē.*

2 Timothy 1:1: "Paul, an apostle of Jesus Christ by the will of God. . . ."

Titus 1:1: "Paul, a servant of God, and an apostle of Jesus Christ. . . ."

Philemon 1:1: "Paul, a prisoner of Jesus Christ, and *Timothy our brother. . . .*" Because of the special character of this epistle to an individual, Philemon, about his slave Onesimus, Paul decided to call himself a prisoner instead of an apostle.

Paul, in writing to the Corinthians about regulatory principles of marriage, decided to let them know that he was writing "not of commandment" (*kat' epitagén*),[1] an expression in Greek which means an order brought upon something or someone. In its verbal form, it is *epitássō*, from which *epitagé,*[2] "commandment," is derived.

From the study of the verb *epitássō* in its use in the New Testament we conclude that the meaning is that of ordering or commanding with the expectation that it will take place. The person or persons ordered to do something do not have any choice in the matter. They must do what is ordered. There is no freedom to exercise personal judgment on the part of the one who is thus ordered.[3]

Paul's Personal Opinions

Paul's aim was to make it clearly understood by the Corinthians that what he was saying to them in this immediate context was not intended to be taken by them as a command that had to be obeyed, but rather as a piece of advice which he hoped would be seriously considered. When he said, "I speak this by permission and not of commandment," he did not relate it to the Lord, i.e., by permission of the Lord and not as a commandment of the Lord, but "by your permission, Corinthian believers." It was as if he were saying, "Excuse me for saying these things. What I am saying is not really to be taken as commandments from God. It is counseling to be considered by you. It is not to be obeyed without consideration on your part of your particular personal makeup and circumstances. What may apply and be good for one may be bad or of none effect for another. It is not a commandment such as 'thou shalt not commit adultery' or 'thou shalt not steal,' etc. It is my advice. Stay single if you are able and you believe that through your singleness you can glorify God more than through marriage. I am not *commanding* any of you to stay single as I am, although I believe, judging from my own circumstances, that it is better. I have also expressed an opinion about your conjugal happiness: Don't deprive each other except when there is mutual agreement to abstain when you face a crisis situation for which you need to fast and pray. Actually, abstaining from sexual relations within marriage is a form of fasting. But such prayer and fasting in general are not a command. Conjugal relations and prayer are not exclusive of each other.

"All that I have said about staying single and the behavior of spouses within marriage is counsel I give with your permission. Don't take it as a command from me."

This *ou kat' epitagén*, "not of commandment," actually does not involve the Lord at all, but Paul himself as an apostle of Jesus Christ, affirmed at the beginning of his epistle to the Corinthians. As an apostle, he had the authority to give commands and simply to give counsel. Whether he gave the one or the other depended on the Lord's direct commandments to humanity and on the authority vested in him as an apostle. Paul knew the difference between the two, that which constituted a command which had to be obeyed, and that which was advice which could be weighed by the individual and rejected or accepted either partially or totally. Blessed is the preacher who has the same discernment as Paul in knowing what has to be a command and what is only advice. And blessed is the believer who can distinguish between the two and exercise proper judgment and discernment, taking into account his strengths and weaknesses as well as his or her particular circumstances.

General Principles to Be Studied by the Individual

It is interesting, of course, that Paul chose to make such a clear distinction between his counseling and his apostolic command in the chapter dealing with marriage and divorce. Paul knew how complex and private these matters were and how varied the circumstances. It was absolutely impossible for him to cover every eventuality. Therefore, he was satisfied in giving general principles which should be thoroughly studied and applied by individuals. There are decisions in regard to marriage that no one else can make but the person or persons involved. For this reason it behooves us to accept our responsibility to make those decisions so that we need not be ashamed when we face the Lord one day in judgment. He certainly knows the true circumstances and the true motives. And we who are entrusted with the awesome responsibility of counseling others in their marital problems should beware lest we assume more authority to command than even the Apostle Paul felt was his prerogative to assume.

Distinguishing Between the Lord's Commands and Apostolic Preferences

Paul was a man big enough to make the distinction between his own personal opinion and a direct or indirect command of the Lord.

In 1 Corinthians 7:12 he wrote: "But to the rest speak I, not the Lord: If any brother hath a wife that believeth not, and she be pleased to dwell with him, let him not put her away," etc. He did not hesitate to make clear that this was his own opinion. Going contrary to it, therefore, is not rejecting any of God's commandments but just not accepting apostolic counsel. Nor did Paul want it considered as an apostolic command which must be adhered to by believers. Paul as an apostle not only transmitted the Lord's commands but issued personal opinions in amplification of some basic principles and commands. This is due to his unique insight as a result of his special apostolic relationship to Jesus Christ.

Another important declaration in respect to this is verse seventeen: "But as God hath distributed to every man, as the Lord hath called every one, so let him walk. And so ordain I in all churches." Of course we shall fully examine this verse and all that it teaches later on. But at the moment, as we consider the Christian's duty in relation to apostolic counsel or a command representing Christ's command, we glean the following thoughts:

God distributes His grace unevenly and variously to each individual.
Consequently, not all can live for God and produce for God equally. "To each one (*hekástō*) individually God distributed" (v. 17). He made us individuals with basic simi-

larities but with distinctive abilities and idiosyncrasies not totally of our own making. Therefore, we must not, as square pegs, try to fit into round holes.

All people do not have the same calling.
To each one God gives a unique calling: "As the Lord hath called every one (*hékaston*, 'each one as an individual')." It is His calling each one has to follow, not a self–chosen path. But His calling is different for each individual, and no one can accomplish what God has called another to accomplish. There is a particular assignment by God for each individual, and if neglected, it will remain undone. In most cases, it is the task immediately at hand, and if that task is done faithfully, God will entrust more and greater duties.

Church Rules but Individuals Choose.
But now observe the third thing Paul says: "And so ordain I in all churches." The word for "ordain" in Greek is *diatássomai*.[4]

In the New Testament *diatássō* means "to issue an edict" (Acts 18:2; 23:31; 24:23).[5]

Here in 1 Corinthians 7:17, when the matter is not individual believers weighing the applicability of apostolic counseling in their lives, but the God–ordained order in the church, Paul says *diatássomai*, "I give orders or commands," or as the King James Version has it: "And so ordain I in all churches." The NIV translates it: "This is the rule I lay down in all the churches." Here there is uniformity of rule and a general order that applies to all the churches. God does not give to individual churches specific abilities, but He does to individuals. The churches do not have the liberty that individuals have. There is a church discipline that is universal in its application.

---

[1]This is not the common word for "commandment" which is *entolé*. *Epitagé* is a compound word made up of *epí* meaning "upon" and *tagé* from the verb *tássō*, meaning "to order."

[2]From the verb *tássō*, we have the substantive *táxis* which means "order, category." *Epitagé*, the substantive of *epitássō*, has the meaning of irresistability. It is used principally in Mark and Luke of the Lord Jesus commanding or ordering the unclean spirits to come out as in Mark 1:27; 9:25, and Luke 4:36. These evil spirits had no choice when they were commanded to come out. The will of the Master had to be obeyed. In the other instances also there is implied the irresistible compliance to the command. The head of John the Baptist was commanded to be brought to the king (Mark 6:27). The multitudes showed no resistance when they were commanded to sit down and be miraculously fed by Jesus (Mark 6:39). The winds could not exercise a choice when they were commanded to be stilled in their tempestuous fury (Luke 8:25). The demon in the Gadarene demoniac requested Jesus not to command him to enter into the abyss of the lake, because he knew that once Jesus so commanded, he could not escape (Luke 8:31). The servant told the master of the supper that it was done as he had commanded, i.e., the ones invited

from the squares, streets and towns were seated (Luke 14:22). His obedience to seat them was unchallenged.

³The Apostle Paul uses the preposition *katá* with the accusative *suggnómēn*, "permission or indulgence with the opinion of another," and the accusative *epitagén*, "order, command." In the English translation this one Greek preposition *katá* is translated once as "by permission" and as "of commandment." This use of a preposition with an accusative is very common with *katá*, "the notion of tendency or aim appears" (A.T. Robertson, *Grammar*, p. 609).

⁴Another derivative of the principle verb *tássomai*, or *tássō*. The only difference between *epitássō* and *diatássō* is the prepositional prefix. In the one it is *diá*, meaning "through," or used simply for emphasizing the basic meaning of the verb. The other preposition is *epí*, "upon."

We saw that in the New Testament *epitássō* (1 Cor. 7:6 used the substantive *epitagé*, "commandment") means giving a command which does not allow the freedom of choice in its being followed or not. *Epitássō* also has the implied meaning of seizing and taking something or someone under one's possession. The substantive *epitáxis* was used as an injunction or as an assessed taxation. Even in modern Greek it means exactly the same thing, seizure or confiscation or conscription. And another substantive, *epitagé*, meant the enforcement of the laws or imposed tribute or taxation. In modern Greek *epitagé* has come to mean a check which is actually an order to a bank with which a person has a deposit to pay to the bearer the stated amount on it providing there is a sufficient deposit. It is not the bank's prerogative to pay or not to pay. It is an order that cannot be refused.

Diatássō, or the middle form *diatássomai*, has the prepositional prefix *diá* meaning "through." It implies not an imposition, but a distinction. And the basic meaning of *tássō* or *tássomai* is to place in one's proper category or order. In the middle form, *diatássomai* means "to arrange for oneself, get things arranged" (Liddell and Scott. *A Greek–English Lexicon* [Oxford: Clarendon Press, 1958]). It is penetrating a situation, implied through the preposition *diá*, "through," and *tássomai*, "putting things and people in their proper categories" as, for instance, to set an army in battle order, to place each unit in its proper post.

[5]In Luke 17:10, it is applied to God's concrete directions which fill life with works of obedience. In Matthew 11:1, it means the imparting of detailed instructions for the disciples' missionary work. In 1 Corinthians 9:14, Paul refers to one of the special orders of Jesus in His address on sending out the disciples. The detailed instructions of the Apostle Paul with reference to the collection in 1 Corinthians 16:1, the regulation of questions of worship in 1 Corinthians 11:34 and in 1 Corinthians 7:17, are all obviously responsibilities he discharges with reference to his apostolic office.

14

I WANT OTHERS TO BE LIKE ME, BUT!

For I would that all men were even as I myself: But every man hath his proper gift of God, one after this manner, and another after that.—1 Corinthians 7:7

There is little doubt that the Apostle Paul was unmarried. He makes this clear in verse eight: "I say therefore to the unmarried and widows, It is good for them if they abide (remain) even as I." Later in the epistle (9:5), speaking of his freedom in Christ, he says, "Have we not power to lead about a sister, a wife, as well as other apostles, as the brethren of the Lord, and Cephas?" implying that he was free to be married, as were other apostles, Jesus' brothers, and Cephas (Peter). Paul, however, having received grace from God to remain single, chose to do so in order to better serve God's purpose for his life.

Marriage Is Not an End in Itself

For Paul, being single or being married was not the important thing. Marriage, as so many other states in this life, is not and should not be an end in itself but a means to an end. The end for Paul, as it ought to be for every believer, was the glory of the Lord Jesus Christ and the closest possible relationship with Him. Man's happiness consists in knowing whom and what to make the goal of his life and what to use as the means to achieving that goal.

Paul Desired Imitators of Himself; Not in Celibacy but in the Utmost Accomplishments for Christ

In view of the fact that Paul did not make single-ness the goal of his life, but only the most convenient way to reach his goal of doing his utmost for his Lord, what did he mean when he said: "For I would that all men were as I myself"? Did he mean single? I don't believe so. I think he meant: I wish that every man would endeavor to accomplish his utmost for the Lord in whatever state God's grace permits him to be, whether single or married.

Had he meant that he wanted all men to be single, he would have declared himself to be against the divine institution of marriage. Such a thing Paul would not do.

Paul treats marriage as a gift of God in the lives of people. Staying single as he did had a sublime purpose, but he acknowledges that he was especially endowed by God's grace to accomplish this.

He realizes, however, that most people are not so endowed. Therefore, to encourage them to be what God may not have equipped them to be—that is, single—would have been contrary to all his principles.

Paul's Desire Was for Others to Follow His Commitment to Christ

Paul should not be thought of as thinking too highly of himself when he said, "I would that all men were even as I myself." Likewise in 1 Corinthians 4:16 where he said, "I beseech you, be ye followers of me." But in 1 Corinthians 11:1 he said, "Be ye followers of me, even as I also am of Christ." Paul was absolutely committed to being a faithful follower of Christ. Thus he felt that only in respect to this fidelity to Christ should others be followers of him.

Observe that the second part of 1 Corinthians 7:7 begins with a "but." ". . . But every man hath his proper gift of God, one after this manner, and another after that." In my case, Paul reasons, I was the best follower of Christ by remaining single. But in your case, you are the best follower of Christ by being what God desires you to be. We don't all arrive at the desired goal via the same road. There is the road of celibacy and the road of marriage.

God Will Never Lead Us Where His Grace Cannot Sustain Us

There are two words in the Greek text that need to be explained in this case. The first is "all" in the clause "I would that all men were even as I my-self." The Greek word is *pántas*, the plural of *pás*. On first glance, one would think that it refers to the totality of humanity. But it doesn't. It refers rather to the individuals within the totality, and there is not any within that totality that God cannot enable to be as Paul, if it is His will. If God's grace was sufficient for enabling Paul to be single and accomplishing what He wanted him to accomplish, it would be sufficient for any one individual within the totality of humanity. Thus, if God allows His child to be in a state or situation which he or she has no power to alter, He will also give the necessary grace. God will never lead us where the grace of God is inadequate to keep us. Paul, therefore, is not saying that he wants all people to accomplish what he did by being single as he was. What he is saying is: Anyone can abide holy within the single life, and if God leads him thus, He will also enable him to be victorious over his sexual desires.

God Does Not Give Each One the Same Gift

The other word is *hékastos*, "every man," in the clause: "But every man hath his proper gift of God." The word *hékastos* would have been better translated "each man," as the NIV translates it. God does not give all men one–and–the–same gift. This is the fundamental teaching of 1 Corinthians chapter twelve. Verse four of that chapter says: "Now there are diversities of gifts, but the same Spirit." And in verse eleven we read: ". . . the selfsame Spirit, dividing to every man [here again, the Greek text has *hekástō*, 'to each man' as an individual] severally as he will." The idea promulgated in 1 Corinthians 7:7ff is that "each one" has a particular gift from God.

God's Gifts Are Tailor–Made

The word translated "his proper" in Greek is *ídion* which means "his own." Each man has his own gift from God. It refers to what is peculiar to one and possibly absent in others.

What Paul really declares in this verse is that none of us can expect another to be what he is. If the Lord has given me the grace to be a bachelor and abstain from sexual activity, it gives me no right to demand and expect others to be as I am. I am what I am because God gave me the grace to be what I am. He may have so constituted me that I can be a bachelor. It is then my own particular gift that has come from God. Virginity, therefore, is a special gift not common to all.

The word *ídion* translated in the King James Version as "his proper," referring to the gift, is something that pertains to a private person and not to the public. It should have been translated "private, particular, individual" as opposed to *démios* or *démosios*. It is the same word that is used adverbially in 1 Corinthians 12:11, *idía*, translated "severally," which would have been far better translated "individually, particularly." God made each person with a different individuality capable of following a certain way of life and capable of a certain particular learning. To discover one's own gift is really to discover one's own potential. Not all people can become musicians or scientists, and to attempt to fit into a mold for which one is not gifted only brings frustration.

Paul says over and over in 1 Corinthians 12, in which he discusses God's gifts (*charísmata*), that it is the same God who distributes His gifts, but He gives to each one particular gifts. The recipient must not try to impose his gifts upon others or to criticize others for not having them; rather he should carefully discover and develop that gift which God has given him. If, therefore, as the Apostle says, you have God's gift of being able to remain single, by all means do so. Consider your state of being as the best state whereby you can accomplish what God has ordained for you to accomplish in life. Don't impose impossible situations upon yourself.

All That We Are and Have Comes From God

There are some very fundamental things that Paul wants us to realize, which are made clear through 1 Corinthians 4:7: "For who maketh thee to differ from another? and what hast thou that thou didst not receive? now if thou didst receive it, why dost thou glory, as if thou hadst not received it?"

The first is that all of us are different: "For who maketh thee to differ from another?" We do not all have the same propensities, the same talents, or the same gifts.

Secondly, everything that we are and everything that we have in life is a gift from God. "And what hast thou that thou didst not receive?" A person cannot acquire the gift of singleness or the gift of married life. Rather, they are given to individuals by God.

Finally, we should not pretend that our gift from God is something that we attained for ourselves: "Now if thou didst receive it, why dost thou glory, as if thou hadst not received it?" We should recognize that all we are and possess is a result of God's grace and be grateful for our gifts, rather than judging others.

Christ's Tasks for Individuals Are Not All the Same

Christ recognized that there are tasks that He had for some people to complete that He could not impose on others. Not all Christ's words nor His commands are to be equally applied to everybody. There are those, of course, which are common to all such as the ability to think. But the ability to understand complex mathematical concepts, for instance, is not for all.

When the Lord said in Matthew 19:11, "All men cannot receive this saying, save they to whom it is given," He was speaking of marriage. He had told His disciples that if anyone puts away his wife except for fornication and marries another, he commits adultery. And whoever marries a spouse who has been put away with the stigma of adultery, he himself is stigmatized as an adulterer. The common idea at that time, as is so prevalent today, was, why not be able to change spouses when one wants to? Why does it have to be only for the reason of adultery?

Then the Lord went on to tell His disciples about some people having the ability to be eunuchs and others not. But being a eunuch is not something to be imposed on anybody or something to be grasped at in an attempt to become more holy. It is a gift of God. Therefore, the Apostle Paul in 1 Corinthians 7:7 expands the teaching of Christ presented in Matthew 19:11.

Moral Uprightness Is an Absolute Injunction, Not a Matter of Choice

Paul, of course, is not giving license for immorality—for anyone to claim that he or she does not have the gift of remaining sexually pure. Moral uprightness is an absolute injunction of the Scriptures. Paul says in 1 Corinthians 6:13, ". . . the body is not for fornication, but for the Lord; and the Lord for the body." And in verse eighteen he says, "Flee fornication. Every sin that a man doeth is without the body; but he that committeth fornication sinneth against his own body." Paul says in 1 Thessalonians 4:3, "For this is the will of God, even your sanctification, that ye should abstain from fornication."

Seeking God's Perfect Will for Our Lives

It therefore behooves each one of us to find out first what God expects and wants us to accomplish in our lives individually. He has a particular task for each one born into this world.

Then we must examine very carefully whether or not this task can best be accomplished within the realm of the single or married life. It is not wise to live in an evidently unnatural state.

God, nevertheless, may not provide a marriage partner in spite of the fact that a person desires to marry and believes that marriage is the best medium through which he or she can accomplish God's calling in life.

Perhaps we should add here that in the divine order of life, God did prepare a mate for each person. This conclusion can be drawn from the fact that births are almost equally divided between male and female. However, with the entrance of sin into the world, God's original plan for man was frustrated. The results of sin, that is war, sexual perversion, and even death by accident or sickness, cause the sexes to be unequally balanced. The effects of sin are always like the ripples on the water, spreading out its grief and heartache to encompass more and more wherein we must all suffer, both good and bad.

Nevertheless, continence is an absolute; there can be no excuse for violating it. Within marriage, one must remain with his or her own individual spouse. Outside of marriage, it is possible to abide without any sexual expression since God promises to give the necessary grace for the circumstances that He permits. The same apostle said in Philippians 4:13, "I can do all things through Christ which strengtheneth me." And one of these things is a pure and uncompromising life which is spoken about in verse eight.

God, the Direct Source of Our Gifts

Paul says, "Every man hath his particular or private gift *of* God." That preposition translated "of" in Greek is *ek*, indicating the origin or source of the gift and referring to it as of a primary, direct and immediate source, that being God.[1] Therefore, the ability to remain single and accomplish God's will is a direct gift of God. A person cannot acquire that instinctive ability to refrain from marriage by his own efforts or through rules imposed upon him by others, although he can be an overcomer. As Paul says in Philippians 4:11, "Not that I speak in respect of want: for I have learned, in whatsoever state I am, therewith to be content." While a person may not be able to choose his own preferable state, he can rest assured that God can give contentment in whatever state He permits or directs. This is a *chárisma* or "gift" coming directly from God, says the Apostle Paul in 1 Corinthians 7:7.

Remember this in thinking of gifts: the initiative is always taken by the giver and not by the receiver. God knows when the special enablement of His grace is needed for you to be content in such a state as He permits. He will take the initiative when a person has done his duty in recognizing God's activity in his life.

Recognizing differences in individuals is what Paul actually meant when he closed this verse with the phrase "One after this manner, and another that."[2] Let us each be what God made us to be and not otherwise.

---

[1]This is in distinction from another preposition, *apó*, which marks the secondary, indirect, mediate origin while *ek* denotes the primary, direct, ultimate source; and yet another preposition, *hupó*, denotes the immediate, efficient agent.

[2]In the Greek text this is *hós mén hoútōs hós dé hoútōs*: *hós*, "he who;" *mén*, "on the one hand;" *hoútōs*, "thus, in this manner;" and then *hós*, "he who;" *dé*, "on the other hand;" and *hoútōs*, "thus."

15

THE UNMARRIED AND THE WIDOWS

I say therefore to the unmarried and widows,
It is good for them if they abide even as I.
—1 Corinthians 7:8

From verses eight through twenty–four Paul treats the situations concerning special groups in the congregation in Corinth. The first such group is the unmarried ones, whether these be virgins who have never been married or widowed persons.

His remarks here are actually the conclusion of what he has said before. That is the meaning of the particle *dé*, which is correctly translated "therefore." From the general principles, he now comes to specific instructions and recommendations.

Do Not Remain Unmarried if
It Is Not God's Specific Gift

One of the general principles he has enunciated is that no one should remain unmarried if he does not have that specific, God–given ability to do so and providing God brings about circumstances whereby he can be married. If you are not meant for a life of celibacy, and God brings into your life a partner, go ahead and get married, he says. Don't ever pretend that God wants you to stay unmarried while He has not really given you that *chárisma*, or gift, to remain unmarried.

Paul's personality certainly enters the whole discussion. He speaks as an apostle, but he does not suggest that what he is saying are words that he directly received from the Lord Jesus Christ.

In verse six he says, "But I speak this."

In verse seven he says, "I wish," *thélō*, translated "I would," expressing a personal desire without expressing the necessity of its imposition.

And in verse eight he says, "I therefore say." The verb that he uses, *légō*, expresses reasonable thought on his part. He knows what he's talking about; what he says is not arbitrary.

The Unmarried Ones

The general group which he is addressing now he calls the unmarried, the single.[1] This term includes anyone who is not married, be it a virgin never married, a widow or widower, or a divorcee. It occurs only in this chapter in verses eight, eleven, thirty–two, and thirty–four.

The conjunction *kaí*, "and," connected with "the widows"[2] introduces one of the groups in the general category of the unmarried ones. Paul does this to put special emphasis on the widows. His special mention of widows has mixed in it a certain amount of compassion toward them because, after all, they became widows and suffered grief not because of any fault of their own, but because God saw fit to take their husbands from them. They are widowed because of an act of God. We could therefore translate this verse thus:

"I therefore say to the unmarried ones, and particularly to the widows." It would be unfeeling for anyone to tell such widows that their widowhood and singleness is a bad state to be in. Since it is a state which was directed or permitted by God, it cannot be bad. Therefore Paul admonishes that they may consider it as a good state because it has been permitted by the Lord.

No Compulsion for Widows to Stay Unmarried

Paul is not promulgating a compulsion that such widows should stay unmarried. He says, "It is good for them *if* they abide even as I." If they have to stay as widows, God will give them the necessary strength to live a moral life and not to constantly burn with the desire that they should be married. If they decide to stay in this state of singleness, there is nothing wrong with it as long as they exercise continence and are not unduly preoccupied with the desire to marry. The Apostle Paul is not demanding that they should remain single, but if they decide to remain single as he also had done, it is perfectly all right, he says.[3] Paul readily assumes that some of the widows will remain unmarried and others will marry. There is no moral value in either state. As in his own case, he is sure that as long as the personal decision is to remain unmarried, God's grace will be sufficient for that state.

When Paul says, "Even as I," he affirms the fact that he was unmarried, and as his decision was voluntary, so the decision must be voluntary when it comes to widows and other unmarried persons. He infers, of course, that celibacy was a gift. By implication here, he also infers that those unmarried persons or widows who are certain that they have this God–given gift are free to remain in that choice. It is interesting to note that the verb *meínōsin*, "if they abide," is in the aorist which implies a decision to be reached at the time that he was writing. This decision could be altered without any scruple of conscience that one has been unfaithful to a vow. Paul's advice is personal, and he offers it only for those who can receive it. All that Paul is saying here is that at given times and for certain persons, marriage may be wisely avoided, and this is all that he means to teach.

First Corinthians Chapter Seven Is Not a Complete Treatment of Marriage

Another thing that we must remember is that this chapter is in answer to specific questions and is not a total treatment of the subject of marriage. There may have been other points which to his mind seemed equally important, but since his advice was not sought on those, he passed them by. Under no circumstances could his words be interpreted as implying that marriage was a morally inferior condition. As expressed in other epistles, Paul saw in marriage the most perfect symbol of the union of Christ and the Church. But since unmarried men were most likely to be available and free for the work of Christ, therefore he could wish it were possible, though he knew it was not possible, that all unmarried men should remain unmarried.

---

[1] *Agámois*, the dative plural of *ágamos*, from the negative *a* and *gámos*, "marriage."

[2] *Tais chērais*, the dative plural of *chēra*, "widow."

[3] The verb *meínōsin*, "they abide," is in third person plural, first aorist subjunctive of *ménō*. The aorist tense implies a voluntary decision to remain single.

16

MARRIAGE PROVIDES THE ONLY MORAL EXPRESSION OF THE SEXUAL INSTINCT

But if they cannot contain, let them marry: for it is better to marry than to burn.—1 Corinthians 7:9

Man's sexual drive is an instinctive, God—given part of his human nature which is meant, however, to be controlled by man himself. We use the word "man" in a generic sense as referring to both man and woman. The same rules apply to both. Man is not permitted to enjoy greater liberty in the expression of his sexual instinct just because it may be stronger than it is with some women.

The Sexual Instinct Can Be Controlled

In 1 Corinthians 7:8 the Apostle Paul expressed the opinion that it is good for the unmarried ones and widows to remain as he was, unmarried. Once Paul himself took the decision to remain unmarried, he determined to keep his sex drive under control. Such control should be exercised by all those whose decision is to remain unmarried.

In 1 Corinthians 7:9 Paul proceeds to deal with the case of those who find it impossible to control themselves. He says: "But if they cannot contain, let them marry: for it is better to marry than to burn."

The word "contain" refers to those who have put power or government over their desires.[1] This verb, *egkrateuomai*, is used twice in the New Testament, here in 1 Corinthians 7:9 and in 1 Corinthians 9:25.

Man Must Not Lower Himself to the Level of an Animal

The body of man as personalized by his soul and in which he holds a common trait with animals has inherent in it a sex drive which naturally seeks expression. There is nothing wrong with the presence of the sexual instinct itself. God put it there for a purpose. The natural man in the New Testament is called the "soulish" man, as in 1 Corinthians 2:14, "But the natural man receiveth not the things of the Spirit of God: for they are foolishness unto him: neither can he know them, because they are spiritually discerned."

The Greek word translated "natural" is *psuchikós*, derived from *psuché* which is the nonmaterial element in man which leads him to express his instincts as if he were no different than an animal.

This is why our Lord in delineating the conditions of discipleship in Luke 14:26 said, "If any man come to me, and hate not his own life also, he cannot be my disciple." That word translated "life" in the Greek text is *psuché*, the same as the word "natural" in 1 Corinthians 2:14. It refers to the animal instinct in man, one of these being the sexual instinct. It should come under the control of the Spirit of God which activates the spirit of man and tells him the prescribed confines of sexual expression. The natural man expresses his lust toward anybody and at any time, and thinks that there is nothing wrong with it. When man expresses his instincts without proper spiritual thought and control, he lowers himself to the level of an animal.

The Redeemed Child of God Must Still Live in a Body Susceptible to Sin

Man's body and its personalizing soul do not constitutionally change when a man becomes a believer in Jesus Christ. Paul in Romans 6:6 calls his body the body of sin: "Knowing this, that our old man is crucified with him, that the body of sin might be destroyed, that henceforth we should not serve sin." The word translated "destroyed" in the Greek means inactive or useless.[2] A believer, knowing that his body is still susceptible to sin, must crucify it or render it inactive. As the body of Christ experienced pain and suffering on the cross and was made subject to His Spirit, so man's old body and nature must experience subjection to his spirit. When this takes place, then the body of sin, in other words, the body that is yet susceptible to sin—doing something that it ought not to do or not doing what it ought to do—is rendered inactive.

In Romans 6:12 the Apostle Paul says: "Let not sin therefore reign in your mortal body, that ye should obey it in the lusts thereof." Man's body, even after he becomes a believer, is still a mortal body subject to sin, sickness, and finally death. Man, in spite of the experience of the new birth, does not acquire a new body constitutionally different from the body of the unbeliever.

Man experiences the weakness of the flesh even in his regenerated state. Paul acknowledged this in Romans 6:19: "I speak after the manner of men because of the infirmity of your flesh: for as ye have yielded your members servants to uncleanness and to iniquity unto iniquity; even so now yield your members servants to righteousness unto holiness." The word translated "infirmity" is the Greek word *asthéneian*, which means "lack of strength" it also is used repeatedly in the New Testament to indicate sickness. The believer is infirm or weak in his flesh. This weakness is due to the presence of sin in us and around us. Victory is possible against the power of sin, but we must never live under the illusion that sin does not lurk in us and all around us and its object is to cause us to fall. The easiest prey of Satan is the person who thinks it is impossible for him to fall into sin.

Control Over Our Natural and Sinful Nature

A single person, whether never married or a widow or widower, may have a struggle in controlling his or her sexual instinct as long as he or she lives. Romans 8:10, however, indicates that the believer can have victory: "And if Christ be in you, the body is dead because of sin; but the spirit is life because of righteousness." This is a very unfortunate translation. The preposition translated "because of" in Greek is *diá*. On many instances when it is followed by an accusative such as *hamartían*, "sin," it could be translated "because of." In this instance, however, it should be translated "as to" or "in respect to" sin and "in respect to" righteousness.[3] If Christ is in us, Paul says, the body will be dead in respect to sin. And on the other hand, if Christ lives in us, He has control over our sinful nature through the spirit which is life in respect to righteousness. Righteousness here refers to God's legitimate right over us.

One thing that Paul wants us to realize when we feel the impact of our sexual instincts is that they are very real. We must never pretend we are all "spirit" and no "body," all "spirit" and no "soul." We are both until the day when, in God's own timetable, our bodies will also be redeemed even as our spirits are now. Paul speaks of the redemption of our bodies in Romans 8:23, and then again in First Corinthians chapter fifteen, where he delineates the time of this redemption to be at the time of the resurrection of our bodies when corruption will be replaced by in-corruption, dishonor with glory, sickness with power, and when our natural body (*psuchikón*) will be replaced by a spiritual body (see 1 Cor. 15:42–44).

Self–Imposed Continence in the State of Singleness

This continence or control that the spiritual man must exercise over his natural body is self–imposed. The verb *egkrateuontai*, "contain," is in the present indicative which indicates that this conti-nence or control over the body is not something that God stamps on a personality, but it is some-thing that is imposed upon man by his own spirit as energized by God's Spirit. We can never excuse ourselves by saying that God did not give us the necessary control over our bodies.

If for reasons other than personal choice a man or a woman has to stay single, God's grace is suffi-cient to enable that person to exercise the necessary control over his or her sexual desires. Did Paul have a struggle with his body? Anyone who has read Romans chapters six and seven knows that he did. Paul did not remain single because he had no struggle with his sexual instinct, nor did he remain single just for the sake of remaining single. He re-mained single because he knew that in his case it was the best way for him to accomplish God's call-ing in his life. He never, however, gave vent to his sexual drive. It was within his power to marry, and apparently there was no reason why he could not marry. As long, however, as he could control his sexual appetite and have victory and joy in such control in the accomplishment of the purpose that he had set for his life, he stayed single.

We must never make sex the end of life. If it is within our power to get married and if it will enhance our ministry we should do so, especially if we recognize that the struggle over our sex instinct really hinders us from accomplishing our purpose in life. There is no allowance for a person to give vent to his sexual desires outside of marriage.

"But if they cannot contain, let them marry." In reality the Greek text does not say "if they cannot contain," but "if they do not exercise continence or control." The verb being in the present indicative indicates continual exercise of continence. If they do not continuously exercise control over their sexual appetite, they are not permitted to resort to prostitution or fornication. The expression of such instincts by Christians is permitted only within marriage.

In fact, Paul gives an indirect commandment: "Let them marry."[4] In other words, the Apostle Paul says that the only way for such people to give vent to the sexual instinct is within marriage.

The Sexual Expression Is Not Just for Child Bearing

This verse is a clear indication that coition is not to be exercised only for the procreation of the race, in other words, to have children; but is for the proper and permissible release of sexual desires. Whereas it is wrong to engage in sex outside of marriage, it is perfectly legitimate within marriage.

Marriage Is Not Mere Cohabitation

The verb *gamēsátōsan*, "let them marry," is in the aorist tense, which indicates a once and for all act at a definitive time. This indicates that marriage is not a mere cohabitation with a mate, but is an official commitment implying a permanent joining together into one life.

In the second part of the verse, Paul gives the reason why it is better to marry than to stay single. The word "better" in Greek means "more excellent" or "more profitable."[5] Again Paul speaks of the voluntary state of singleness in which, however, man finds it extremely difficult to cope with his lustful nature. It is better to marry than to burn, he says.[6] The meaning here is to burn or to be fired as it were with unchaste desires. To burn means to have constant thoughts and desires for sexual expression. The verb is in the present infinitive indicating a man or a woman being constantly plagued by such unclean desires. Again, as in the first part of the verse, the verb *gamḗsai* is in the aorist infinitive which indicates the act of getting married versus the state of burning with unchaste desires. Such a state of constant desire for the fulfillment of one's sexual appetite can be devastating to a person's spiritual life. The single person, therefore, must be on the alert in avoiding scenes and situations whereby the sexual instinct is aroused. It is foolish to pretend such desires do not exist or to think oneself fireproof in its presence. The only alternative to this state is marriage.

But for the woman who has no opportunity to marry, there must be a strong dependence upon and trust in God. Perhaps this is why, in most cases, God created women with a less easily–aroused sexual drive than men. The mind feeds the body, and as one allows improper thoughts and stimulants to enter, the desire grows and may eventually overwhelm the individual. Who has not heard the illustration of the camel who wanted only to warm his nose within the tent? Of course, before long, he managed to get his whole body inside forcing its tenants out of their protected environment to perish in the cold.

---

[1]*Egkrateúontai*, which is the present indicative form of *egkrateúomai* made up of the preposition *en*, meaning "in," and *krátos*, "power, government."

[2]*Katargēthē* from *katargéō* is derived from *katá*, an intensive, and *argós*, which means inactive or useless.

[3]Parkhurst, John. *A Greek and English Lexicon to the New Testament* (London: 1769; AMG Publishers, 1980), p. 128.

[4]*Gamēsátōsan*, a verb, is the third person plural, first aorist imperative active of *gaméō*. This is an indirect imperative in

the third person. Direct imperatives are given in the second person either singular or plural.

[5]*Kreísson* is from *kreísōn* which is an irregular comparative from *krátus*, "strong."

[6]*Puroústhai* is from *puróō* from *púr*, "fire."

17

CHRIST'S COMMANDS AND PAUL'S AMPLIFICATIONS

*And unto the married I command, yet not I,
but the Lord . . .* —1 Corinthians 7:10

Paul is now speaking to a different group of people, the married ones who are believers in the Lord Jesus Christ.

He speaks of those who are unable to sexually control themselves, saying that it would be better for them to marry instead of to burn with sexual desire, it does not necessarily follow that they are directly connected. Verse ten stands rather in contrast to verse eight and not verse nine.

Verse eight says: "I say therefore to the unmarried and widows. . . ."

Verse ten says: "And unto the married I command. . . ."

It cannot be inferred, therefore, that those who are married have married simply because the sexual instinct was so hot within them that its satisfaction was the only motive for marriage. He speaks rather to those who have followed the natural, pre-scribed course of marriage in line with the admoni-tion of Hebrews 13:4: "Marriage is honorable in all, and the bed undefiled."

Paul recognizes two main groups. First, those who are unmarried and who should be in full con-trol of their sexual desires and not engage in illicit sex. That is how he lived, and if he lived that way, it is possible for others to live as he lived. But the state of singleness, as we have seen, is not a manda-tory state. It is a way of life that one may or may not choose, but one in which he will find the grace of God sufficient.

Marriage for the Christian Continues to Be Valid Even if Contracted in the State of Unbelief

Secondly, those who are in the married state Paul designates with the Greek participle *gegamēkósi*,[1] referring to those who at a particular time in the past exercised their decision to enter into a mar-riage contract. He does not refer to those who are living together in a common–law relationship. Such are really not married.

From what he says in verse twelve, we can with certainty arrive at the conclusion that both husband and wife are believers. It makes no difference whether or not they were believers when they were married. They are now believers. The marriage con-tract between a man and a woman, though carried out in a state of unbelief, does not become null and void when either one or both become believers. Even as the constitutional makeup of a human body does not change when someone becomes a believer, so the marriage contract is in no way affected by the state of a spiritual change in either one or both of the spouses. A husband and wife who were married as unbelievers cannot, after they come to know Jesus Christ, claim in any shape or form that due to their new faith their marriage is dissolved. It is still binding

In the same manner, Paul is speaking of those who were formerly heathen and became Jews. If they were married as heathen, the adoption of their Jewish faith did not annul their marriage. In the same manner, if at the time they were Christian believers but had married as heathen or as Jews, their new faith did not affect their marital status. Marriage is indissoluble, no matter what one's personal faith was at the time of marriage. In spite of the fact that a man and a woman may decide to marry without any reference to God and acknowledgment that marriage is a union which God brings about, it does not mean that such a marriage is not bonded together by God. The decision is binding either in the context of God's blessing or in the absence thereof. God does not decide marriage for anybody. It is a man and woman's own decision.[2] The Lord Jesus clearly stated in Matthew 19:6, "What therefore God hath joined together, let not man put asunder." God is not the one who makes the choice, but He does confirm the choice that a man and a woman make to marry as husband and wife. If God made the actual direct choice, then He could be held responsible for the failure or success of such a marriage.

God's institution of law does not guarantee His approval of the existence of a certain state. Man sinned and fell. As a result of that fall, he himself has to cope with a mortal and corruptible body and an environment which is also corruptible, both of which are consequently groaning for their liberated state (see Romans 8:19–28). If God did not create law in order to control man in his sinful state, conditions would be chaotic both in the universe and in man's personality. In the same manner as God instituted law in an attempt to regulate sinful man and sinful creation, so God instituted the law of marriage to control the existence and perpetuation of family life which is the basis of human order and government. Thus man chooses to marry, and God makes the marriage lawful, the two partners being held responsible by God to live together for life no matter what the circumstances were under which they were married.

Paul thus speaks concerning those who were at that time married irrespective of the circumstances under which they were married. Their present state, however, was the state of faith regardless of their spiritual condition at the time of their marriage. Since this group that he now discusses is contrasted with the group he introduced in verse eight, "the unmarried ones," and since the married ones in verse ten are now Christians, therefore it can be safely deduced that those he refers to as "the unmarried ones" in verse eight are also believers.

Divine Command Transmitted Through Apostolic Authority

Paul exercises his apostolic authority when he says, "I command."[3] This is the er term used in Greek for military commands (Acts 4:18; 5:28, 40; 16:23). In using this term to show his apostolic authority, he wants to indicate that this is not an arbitrary enactment but a pressing injunction. He uses this term elsewhere for the same purpose (1 Cor. 11:17; 2 Thess. 3:12 and 1 Tim. 1:3 and 4:11). This term was used of Christ when He sent forth His disciples (Mark 6:8; Acts 10:42).

In order to give weight, however, to this injunction, he adds, "Not I, but the Lord." Paul without any hesitation places what the Lord said as a commandment which he himself as an apostle is under obligation to transmit, even as an inferior officer transmits the command of a superior one. He never wants to give the impression that his authority is the same as the Lord's. Christ's authority is one and apostolic authority is another, and the authority of an ordinary believer is yet another. Specific authority was granted to the twelve apostles in Matthew 10:7, 8. We have, on the other hand, in Matthew 28:19 an indication that total comprehensive authority was given by the Father to the Lord Jesus Christ to exercise on earth and in heaven. "All power is given unto me (not unto you) in heaven and in earth," the Lord Jesus said to His disciples. And yet it was the apostles and the disciples who were going to be proclaiming the gospel after the Lord Jesus was to ascend to heaven.

The Apostle Paul wanted to make absolutely sure that no one thought that this was a commandment that emanated from himself. Having come from the Lord Jesus Christ, its authority was far higher than if it came only from Paul.

Nor did the Apostle Paul want to appear to the Corinthians as a "super apostle," as undoubtedly there were some in Corinth who pretended to be so as indicated by 2 Corinthians 12:11. These apostles Paul calls *hupér lían*. Although in this word appears as one in the Textus Receptus, yet in most Greek manuscripts it appears as two words, *hupér*, which when used in conjunction with an accusative as here, means "above in dignity" as in Matthew 10:24 and Philippians 2:9, or "above, beyond, more than" as in Matthew 10:37, 1 Corinthians 4:6 and Galatians 1:14. The other word is *lian*, an adverb meaning "very much, exceedingly, very." These apostles, obviously, were those who presented themselves to be far above the other apostles by claiming authority beyond the common apostolic authority.

Paul did not want to present himself as a super apostle with super authority. In the matter of marriage, he had his own preference in staying single. He did not want to impose his way of life on others, and this is why in this general passage he is so careful in specifying that his injunction now is not his own, not affected by his own human preference, but is a direct injunction from the Lord which he is passing on to mankind.

Such clear distinction is always advisable when we deal with problems that deeply affect the lives of others. We must make clear to them what is Christ's command, what is apostolic advice, and what is personal advice. Let us beware lest we make our own personal viewpoint to appear as if it were something coming directly from Christ or the apostles.

Paul Never Refuted the Commandments of Christ

Another impression that the Apostle Paul wanted to give was that he himself never took issue with the commandments of Christ. He was careful to transmit them intact, but whenever they needed amplification in their details, he was willing to give such amplification as he does earlier in this chapter in the case of the marital relationship between a husband and wife in verses five and six. Thus we have a general principle that we shall do well to remember. The amplification of a detail never annuls the general principle. Whatever we find in the epistles cannot be anything more than an amplification of the truth that is found in the gospels. The apostles were duty–bound to transmit that which Jesus Christ came to proclaim with divine authority.

Especially in Corinth there were those who were doubting the fidelity of Paul to the words of Christ, thinking that he was propagating doctrines and practices that emanated from himself. This is why in 1 Corinthians 14:37 he says: "If any man think himself to be a prophet, or spiritual, let him acknowledge that the things that I write unto you are the commandments of the Lord." This is a clear assertion that nothing that the Apostle Paul ever promulgated was in conflict with the Lord's teaching. If we conclude it to be so, we are mistaken about the interpretation of the words of Christ or those of His apostles.

The Apostle Paul was aware of the fact that in this chapter he was going to deal with some details in the matter of marriage and divorce. He wanted to make clear, however, that his answers to these detailed questions which may have come to him in letters from the Corinthians (1 Cor. 7:1) were subject to the general principles promulgated by the Lord Jesus on the subject. Paul did not need to restate these general principles enunciated by the Lord. They stood then and still stand today, and Paul himself could not contradict them.

In Matthew 5:32 and 19:9 the Lord made it clear that a spouse has the authority to dismiss an unfaithful husband or wife. Paul's elaboration on the subject in First Corinthians chapter seven cannot contradict that. When Paul says, "Let not the wife depart from her husband," he does not mean to go over the head of the Lord Jesus making this more absolute than the

Lord made His word that it was permitted for a wife to put away her husband if that husband committed the sin of fornication or adultery. Paul did not need to repeat what the Lord said as an exception to this rule.

In fact, the Lord Himself did not repeat that exception of fornication as authority for releasing one's spouse in Mark 10:11 and Luke 16:18. The absolute is qualified when the specific exception has been made elsewhere, and that exception is to be understood when only the general rule is spoken about without the exception. The Lord did not have to repeat the exceptive clause at all times when He spoke about the dismissal of one's spouse nor did the Apostle Paul have to repeat it. Both the Lord and the Apostle, and we also, should put the stress where it belongs: that there should be no dismissal of one's life partner. This is the teaching which must be stressed loudly and clearly, and the exception should be given as a footnote so to speak. Yet, we must never pretend that the exception is not there and is not valid, even if it was mentioned only twice. What has been stated even once by the Lord must be taken for granted as being valid.

---

[1]Dative plural masculine perfect active participle of *gaméō*.

[2]This is clearly shown by the active voices of the verbs in verse nine: *gamēsátōsan*, "let them get married," and the aorist active participle of verse ten: *gegamēkósi*, "those who

are married," indicating those who decided to marry each other and are now in the state of matrimony.

[3]The Greek is *paraggéllō*, from *pará*, an intensive, and *aggéllō*, "to tell."

18

SEPARATION

. . . Let not the wife depart from her husband.
—1 Corinthians 7:10

The commandment which the Apostle Paul is transmitting, "Let not the wife depart from her husband," is an indirect one given as an infinitive. Paul does not speak directly to such women, but he indicates what should be done in case one is confronted with a situation where such action is conceived of as humanly desirable.[1]

The verb "depart" in this verse means to separate or to sever (in the passive with middle meaning, "to separate oneself"). This verb (*chōrízō* in its active voice) would mean to set someone else or something else apart from oneself. However, as used by Paul in 1 Corinthians 7:10, 11, 15 in connection with the marital relationship, it means to separate oneself from one's spouse.[2] It is action that is taken by the individual whose effect returns upon the individual. The object is oneself and not the partner as the case is with the active verb *apolúō*, "to dismiss," used consistently in the pertinent Gospel passages on divorce (Matt. 5:31, 32; 19:3, 7–9; Mark 10:2; Luke 16:18). Therefore, the verb *chōrízomai*, "I separate myself," affects only the person who takes the action. The verb *apolúō*, however, being an active verb, affects the spouse. I separate myself (*chōrízomai*) and I dismiss my spouse (*apolúō*).

"To Dismiss" to Be Free to Marry Another

The verb *apolúō*, "to dismiss," in all the gospel passages has inherent in it the desire on the part of the one who dismisses his or her spouse to marry another. The Lord clearly taught that one could not dismiss a spouse unless that person was guilty of infidelity. If this were not the case, the Lord commanded that a legal certificate of divorce be granted the innocent party to absolve that partner of any stigma from having been dismissed. If the dismissing spouse did send away a partner for any reason other than fornication, that one is commanded to give the innocent spouse a certificate of divorce. God's commandment in the Old Testament was that one who was dismissed for fornication was to be stoned to death. Therefore, we conclude that the verb *apolúō* means to dismiss for no reason of infidelity.

Separation for Reasons Other Than Sexual Infidelity

The verb *chōrízomai* is used when the other spouse is not guilty. In this case, one may not separate himself from his spouse primarily to marry another but because he may want to live alone by himself or herself.

Such temptation may come, for instance, upon a highly spiritual person who comes to the conclusion that his or her partner in marriage does not possess the same spirituality or does not share the same call, and therefore he or she considers separation really to please God. The motive of this separation is really much higher than the motive of *apolúō*, dismissing one's wife.

Take, for instance, two Christians. One of them feels called to become a missionary, but the other does not share the same calling. The Apostle Paul says that it is not permitted for the one who feels that God is calling him or her to become a missionary to separate from his spouse in order to accomplish even such a high goal.

Another case may involve a believer, particularly a woman, who feels she is not treated in a Christian manner by her husband and who does not enjoy sweet spiritual fellowship with him because their ways of life are so divergent. Such a Christian woman is not permitted to leave her husband simply because he does not share either fully or partly in her philosophy of life and commitment to Christ.

The reason Paul mentions only a wife separating herself from her husband is because the wife, being the weaker spouse, may often be mistreated by her husband or may be forced into sexual activity such as would be considered by her as perverse.

How Absolute Is the Commandment: "Let Her Not Separate Herself"?

How absolute is this commandment of Paul in such particular cases? This is a detail and a particular situation on which the Scriptures give very little guidance. It is difficult to know why the Scriptures do not elaborate on such an important area that affects so many couples today, and we believe in all history. I would suggest that those who are directly affected and must make a decision consider two things:

The first is that such a decision belongs to the person involved, and since the Scriptures are silent on it, we must not be too rash to criticize or to condemn. Each one of us must take the attitude, "But by the grace of God, there go I."

The second basic concept to remember is that each one is going to give an account for himself or herself for the decisions that they may make that are outside the prescribed, detailed instructions of the Scriptures.

A Spouse's Responsibility to Her Own Body When That Body Is Defiled by the Partner

Each person has a responsibility towards himself. The Apostle Paul in Romans 12:1 definitely commands: "I beseech you therefore, brethren, by the mercies of God, that ye present your bodies a living sacrifice, holy, acceptable unto God, which is your reasonable service."

Our Lord permitted an innocent party to separate himself or herself from a sexually unfaithful spouse for this very reason. One spouse, being a chaste believer, cannot be required to become voluntarily adulterous by submitting to an adulterer. A spouse, of course, is permitted to do so, but in such cases, what he or she considers to be the lesser of two evils is to be preferred. When I give my body to my unfaithful spouse, I disregard God's commandment in keeping my own body clean. The same Apostle Paul writes to the Corinthians: "I have espoused you to one husband, that I may present you as a chaste virgin to Christ" (2 Cor. 11:2). Writing to young Timothy he says: "Keep thyself pure" (1 Tim. 5:22).

At the time when a spouse faces an unchaste partner, there is the choice of either submitting to unchastity and thus committing fornication or preserving one's chastity. The choice is not for that which is best for the individual, but that which is the lesser of two unavoidable evils. In such a case, a woman can choose to stay with her husband and submit herself to his sexual desires, but she will then be allowing her body to become part of an unchaste person. The same dilemma, of course, can be faced by a husband toward his wife. There is also the possibility that the innocent spouse may live with an unfaithful partner and abstain from sexual relations on mutual agreement. The innocent spouse is never under obligation to dismiss the unfaithful one. It is a matter of personal choice.

The Apostle Paul in speaking of homosexuals in Romans 1:24 says, "Wherefore God also gave them up to uncleanness through the lusts of their own hearts, to dishonor their own bodies between themselves." In marriage, a sexually unfaithful or deviate husband has no right to force his sexually faithful wife to submit to his sexual desires, or vice versa. She, however, can choose to submit, but in choosing to do so, she chooses between two evils. She voluntarily causes her body to be defiled but obeys the command of Paul to stay with her husband.

When a chaste wife chooses to continue in the marital relationship, she may be considered to be following the example of Christ who, having no sin of His own, allowed Himself to become sin for the sake of the sinner.

A faithful spouse who decides to stay with an unfaithful one for the sake of the Lord Jesus Christ and perhaps for the sake of the children whose lives may suffer more by a separation than otherwise, must remember the injunction of Paul in 1 Corinthians 13:3 "And though I give my body to be burned, and have not charity, it profiteth me nothing." One cannot live with an unfaithful spouse and just pretend love. Love and concern must be real in spite of the spouse's sin. If the defilement of one's own body can be avoided, this lessens the evil. If it cannot be, then the decision belongs solely to the person involved.

Is Mistreatment Valid Reason for a Wife to Leave Her Husband?

But what about a case when a woman is cruelly mistreated and beaten by her husband? There is much to be questioned about a person who thus treats his wife but claims to be faithful to her. Most probably, cruelty toward one's wife is a sure indication of unfaithfulness toward her. It is not possible to love and mistreat a person at the same time.

There is, however, a further consideration in the case of cruelty toward one's spouse. The Lord not only commanded that one should not commit adultery but also that one should not kill. Mistreatment is the first step to murder. Is the Christian supposed to submit to someone who comes to her with murderous designs? The Lord never permitted selfish vengeance. He taught that one who is angry with his brother without cause shall be in danger of hell fire (Matt. 5:22). Paul taught that the husband is expected to love his wife even as Christ loves the Church (Eph. 5:25). But when the Lord said, "Love your enemies," He did not mean that we should permit them to continue in their sinful ways but to do everything in our power to win them to His way, even if that means suffering or inconvenience on our part.

If, however, the other person shows murderous tendencies toward us, then another implied standard of the Lord, that we should love ourselves, takes over. In other words, we must do everything we can to preserve ourselves as His children and His stewardship. The fundamental commandment of God reiterated by Christ is in Matthew 19:19: "Thou shalt love thy neighbor as thyself." A spouse is certainly one's neighbor. The measure of one's love for himself should be the measure of his love for his spouse. Therefore if a person neglects his duty toward his spouse, he is neglecting his duty toward himself. Allowing a spouse to do whatever evil he or she wants is permitting the perpetuation of the state of evil which our Lord never implied in His injunction to love those who hate us or oppose us. Loving a person is doing everything that one who really loves should do in order to change the character of one in sin. That sometimes may be achieved by restraining the evildoer and sometimes by turning the other cheek. By allowing the perpetuation of the evil done by anyone through action or inaction on our part has never been promulgated by Christ or any of His apostles. Therefore, the attacked spouse must decide what action to take to bring about the change in the marital partner. Allowing that partner to unscrupulously commit atrocities, and perhaps eventually murder, is never loving a spouse as he or she loves himself or herself.

Indiscriminate subjection to cruelty is tantamount to suicide. It is allowing oneself to be killed, and this is the perpetration of murder. Therefore, a married person who is faced with the problem of a spouse who is murderously inclined toward her must make the personal decision of allowing the possibility of murder to be committed against her self or to remove herself from such possibility. The decision is the individual's, and whatever decision is made should be the lesser of two evils.

All that has been said applies also to a man, or the husband, separating himself from his wife as Paul in verses twelve and thirteen reverses the order. Paul is first presenting the wife here because the practice was that the wives were the more likely to separate themselves from their husbands because of the untoward behavior of their husbands. The same order is followed by our Lord who, in Matthew 5:32 and 19:9, mentions only the husband dismissing the wife as this was a common practice by Jewish men. It is the wife who is presented as the innocent victim. When, however, we come to Mark 10:12, the wife is mentioned first because in this case Gentile Christians are concerned. In this instance, the Lord presents the wife taking the action of dismissing her husband.

Sending One's Spouse Away—*Aphíēmi*

There is yet a third verb that is used in this whole discussion of marital separation, *aphíēmi* from *apó*, "from," and *híēmi*, "to send," which actually means to send someone away from oneself.

It is interesting to note that this is the word that expresses forgiveness in the New Testament. When God forgives, He separates our sins away from us. When we forgive someone, we do not disregard his sins, but we do everything in our power to see that his sins are removed from him. In God's forgiveness, man experiences not an overlooking of his sins (*páresis*, Rom. 3:25, wrongly translated as "remission"), but *áphesis*, a redemption from the guilt and power of sin. The person who is truly forgiven is no longer guilty or given unto sin, but is considered by the One who forgives to be innocent and with no guilt. We must remember this important aspect of the meaning of *aphiēmi* in its use in the context of marital relationships in 1 Corinthians 7:11–13.

The picture presented to us here is that of a spouse dismissing or putting away a wife or a husband. This is the only portion of Scripture (1 Cor. 7:11–13) where the word *aphíēmi* is used in connection with marital separation.[3] In general, the word means to leave anything, to free oneself therefrom, to let alone. When God forgives a sinner based on genuine repentance, He sends away from him his sins and He sets him free. Back in the Old Testament in Leviticus 16:21, we find Aaron laying his hands on a live goat and confessing the sins of Israel. He then sends away the goat, bearing their sins, into the uninhabited wilderness. To forgive also means to set one free having proven himself or herself not to be under judicial sentence.

Dismiss—*Apolúō*

The verb *apolúō* is used in the same manner as the verb *apallássein* is used in Luke 12:58, Acts 19:12 and Hebrews 2:15. The meaning is "to liberate" as Hebrews 2:15 clearly indicates. In Acts 19:12 it is used with the meaning "to withdraw," and in Luke 12:58 "to escape." For this reason we conclude that *apolúō* as *apallássō* implies the dismissal, liberating, withdrawal, or escape of a person, not in spite of his being guilty of an offense, but because there is no offense.

Thus the verb *apolúō*[4] in its use in the Synoptic Gospels, and consequently the Pauline epistles, infers that the person is dismissed not because the dismissed one was formerly guilty and given merciful consideration and let go, but in spite of the fact that that person was innocent and the dismissing one is guilty, unless specifically spoken of otherwise. This dismissing in the Old Testament, which the New Testament has reference to, was done privately since doing it publicly could only be a declaration of the guilt of the dismissed one.

This word *apolúō* is used in Matthew 1:19 in regard to what Joseph was planning for Mary when he found out that she was pregnant. He "was minded to put her away (*apolúsai*) privily."

He wanted to release her from her obligation to himself, to set her free. But why did he want to do it privately? Because he must have had doubts either way. Had he put her away (*apolúō*) publicly, it would have been his confirmation of his thought that she was guilty. That he was going to do it privately would have been out of consideration that she, after all, may have been telling the truth that she was innocent of having been with another man. In merciful consideration, he wanted her simply to be declared free of her obligation to him.

In the case of Pilate releasing Jesus or Barabbas, the same word is used (Matt. 27:15, 17, 21, 26). It was he who was to be considered innocent who could be released and the guilty one who was to be crucified. The releasing depended on the declaration of innocence.

When Paul was being tried as a criminal for Christ's sake, Agrippas said to Festus: "This man might have been set at liberty (*apolelústhai*)" (Acts 26:32). If so, Paul would have been declared innocent and set at liberty.

Related closely to *apolúō*, "to release as innocent," is the verb *aphíēmi*. The difference, however, is that the former leaves open the possibility of actual innocence, while the latter, *aphíēmi*, is often used in combination with propitiation or atonement involving forgiveness. In fact, the word *aphíēmi* is used throughout the New Testament to indicate forgiveness. God forgives because Christ paid the penalty for sin in His own blood on condition that man repents of that sin. Hence there is the abrogation of the divine claims upon man. It is deliverance from suffering divine punishment because Christ suffered it for us.

Now how does the use of the verb *aphíēmi* affect our interpretation of 1 Corinthians 7:11–13? Let us take each instance.

The last phrase of 1 Corinthians 7:11 states "and let not the husband put away his wife."

That verb *aphiénai* (present infinitive active of *aphíēmi*) is not the same as *apolúsai*, "to dismiss." If it were, it would mean that the husband dismisses his wife. He orders her to go. The translation "put away" gives room for such misunderstanding.

Separate Oneself—*Chōrízomai*

Here in 1 Corinthians 7:11, we have the case of a wife who wants to separate herself from her husband (*chōristhénai*). This, Paul says, should not be done. Christ had previously said that the only reason a wife could separate would have been on the grounds of her husband's fornication. But this is not the case under discussion by Paul.

What should be the attitude of a husband who realizes that his wife may want to separate herself from him? May he encourage her to go? He has no right to send his wife away, but neither should he encourage her to leave on her own. He should change in himself anything that is causing friction in the marriage and, at the same time, assure his wife of his love and dedication to her. In love, he can seek closer cooperation on the part of his wife. In this case, there is not sufficient guilt on the part of either to merit separation, either entirely voluntary on the part of the wife or if encouraged by the husband. The husband should endeavor to maintain the marriage.

This passage indicates that such a husband does not initially want to marry another, nor does his wife want to leave him because he is an adulterer. But he may have allowed some little things to build up into resentment on the part of his wife. Don't let such things, Paul advises, develop into a wall of desired separation on the part of the wife. A husband should take the initiative to prevent the departure of his wife from him and to restore the marriage.

Aphíēmi is an active verb whose action affects its object and therefore is different from the verb *chōrízomai*, "to separate myself." It is not actually separating myself, but allowing my spouse to separate from me. The wife is said to separate herself from her husband because usually, in biblical times, the house belonged to the husband, and a woman's only alternative was to leave on her own accord and separate herself.

Aphíēmi, however, is spoken of in verse eleven, "And let not the husband put away his wife." In this instance, it is the wife that leaves, but she is forced to do so by her husband. In verse twelve Paul says, "But . . . if any brother hath a wife that believeth not, and she be pleased to dwell with him, let him not put her away."[5] The verb here refers to the man, a believing husband who has an unbelieving wife. Again, it is the wife that is let go, not on her own, but on the action of her husband.

In verse thirteen we read: "And the woman which hath an husband that believeth not, and if he be pleased to dwell with her, let her not leave him."[6] In this instance, the unbelieving husband does not want to go, in which case, the believing wife should not let him go just to be free of him.

We shall examine in detail these verses as we come to them.

The item that distinguishes the verb *aphíēmi* is that the one spouse does not allow the other to go. To put it positively, the believing spouse does everything that he or she can in order to influence the departing partner to stay. This applies whether the wife is a believer married to a believer as in verse ten, whether the husband is married to a believing wife as in verse eleven, or whether the wife who is a believer is married to a husband who is an unbeliever as in verse thirteen.

---

[1]In this verse, what is translated as "depart" in Greek is *chōristhénai*, first aorist infinitive passive form with middle meaning of the verb *chōrízō*, from *chōrís*, which means "separately, by itself, apart."

[2]*Chōrízomai*, passive voice with middle meaning.

[3]In order to differentiate from the other words, *apolúō*, "to dismiss," and *chōrízomai*, "to separate oneself," we should translate *aphíēmi* as "to send or put away." The ancient Greek writer Herodotus uses exactly the same word in the phrase "to put away a wife" *gunaíka aphiénai*, in the infinitive.

[4]The basic verb is *lúō* which means "the freeing of those in prison, the opening of things that are closed, the loosing of fetters." The verb *apolúō* is made up of the preposition *apó* which means "from" and the verb *lúō*. It therefore means to release from the attachment that bound another to oneself. *Lúō* is the opposite of *déō* "to bind." Therefore *apolúō* is releasing somebody or something from a binding relationship to oneself.

[5]The verb here is *aphiétō*, third person singular, used as an indirect imperative.

[6]The verb is exactly the same as in the previous verse, *aphiétō*.

142

19

WHEN A SPOUSE SEPARATES UNJUSTIFIABLY FROM A MARITAL PARTNER

But and if she depart, let her remain unmarried, or be reconciled to her husband: and let not the husband put away his wife.—1 Corinthians 7:11

A little background is necessary in the understanding of this entire passage. In Corinth there were many Jews; however, the city was under the jurisdiction of Roman law. Residing in Corinth were Jews married to Gentiles, and Jews and Gentiles married to Christians. When Paul came and preached the gospel in Corinth, some spouses believed in Christ while others did not resulting in many mixed marriages, not because they began as such, but because belief occurred after marriage.

One of the main principles Paul establishes in this passage is that marriage is marriage, no matter whether the parties are Gentiles or Jews, believers or unbelievers.

Legally Right but Morally Wrong

It was so easy, however, for the Christian community to be affected by civil or state law, even as it is today. Christians may think that because the civil law permits divorce that that is adequate justification to proceed to divorce one's spouse. One may be led astray by something that may be legally right to do, but morally wrong. Through civil law society has often established moral standards which do not agree with scriptural standards. In Corinth, Paul was establishing the scriptural standards by which marriage should be regulated. Since we live in a similar multi–ethnic and multi–cultural society and the judicial system is totally non–religious, it is so easy for us to be affected by the laws of the land and to try to justify what the law permits as morally correct just because it is permitted by the courts.

The Roman state law and custom which prevailed in Corinth permitted either party, regardless of the religious background, to take the initiative in dissolving a marriage.

Because, however, society at the time was divided into those who were free people and those who were slaves, there were certain state laws that pertained to each society. Marriages, for instance, between slaves had no legal standing. Slaves were never influenced nor were they under the impact of civil law because they were not considered members of civil and recognized society.

Paul makes reference in 1 Corinthians 7:21 to the state of the slave: "Art thou called being a servant (slave)? Care not for it: but if thou mayest be made free, use it rather." From this we understand that there must have been a number of slaves who had become Christians and were part of the church in Corinth. In spite of the Roman attitude toward these slaves and their lack of legal marital status, the same principles that Paul promulgates in this chapter held for them as well. The permanence of the bond of marriage within Christianity which Paul stresses applied equally to them.

Therefore, Paul's instructions regarding marriage apply to all, whether Jews, Gentiles, slaves, or believers, whatever the background.

In verse eleven Paul introduces a hypothesis. He begins with the hypothetical word *eán*, "if." The first part of verse eleven really constitutes a parenthetical statement. Here is how the construction should be viewed:

"Let not the wife separate herself from her husband. (But even if she be separated, let her remain unmarried or else let her be reconciled to her husband.) And that a husband send not away a wife." A wife is not to separate herself from her husband or, actually, as the Greek text has it, from *a* husband (*apó andrós*). And a husband should not send away a wife. In each instance it is the wife that leaves, but in the first instance she separates herself on her own volition, and in the second instance she is let

145

go because of her husband's wish or disinterest in maintaining the marriage.

If a Wife Separates Herself

Now to the parenthetical statement: "But even if she (the wife who decided to separate herself from her husband) separates herself or if she be separated, let her remain unmarried, or else let her be reconciled to her husband."

As a woman can separate herself from her husband, so of course a man can separate himself from his wife. This instance, however, is not mentioned here in view of the fact that the woman's position in that culture was always inferior. The departure of a husband is only mentioned in verse thirteen, and in that instance he is an unbeliever. Or perhaps Paul meant to imply that a believing husband married to either a believing or an unbelieving wife ought not to leave her.

In a same way that a man, however, can cause his wife to separate herself from him, so a wife can cause a husband, especially if he is an unbeliever as in verse thirteen, to separate himself from her. Neither Paul nor Christ implied that the woman has any less rights than the man and vice versa.

Paul Does Not Advocate Separation

Paul does not advocate separation, but assumes that there will be such cases and therefore he decides to give some guidance concerning these situations. It is the same when the Lord declares punishments for sinful acts. He does not advocate the sinful acts, but He does impose certain rules to govern these, otherwise total anarchy would prevail.

"And even if she be separated," or better, "if she separates herself."[1] The reason for her separation is not given, whatever that may be. Paul addresses a certain hypothetical situation as having become reality. Whether we take the meaning of this subjunctive as passive or active really does not make much difference. If we take it as passive, it would indicate that a cause other than herself makes her to separate herself. If we take it as middle, then she herself without any obvious cause decides to separate herself. In either case, whatever Paul says is appropriate in its application.

We are not told whether the husband that this wife leaves is a believer or an unbeliever. The assumption, however, that he is a believer is valid since in verse thirteen Paul presents the case of a believing wife not leaving an unbelieving husband.

"Let Her Remain Unmarried"

That the wife has not separated herself on the grounds of her husband's infidelity there is absolutely no doubt. In such a case, Paul would not contradict the Lord by saying that she should remain unmarried because if the reason was infidelity, then she, being the innocent party, would be free to remarry according to Christ's teaching.

The reason for this wife's separation from her husband must be other than the husband's unfaithfulness. If such is the case, Paul implies here, she should not remarry. And also if she is the one who is guilty, she must not remarry according to Christ's teaching. Nevertheless, usually guilty spouses separate themselves or send away their wives for the purpose of remarrying and disregard the moral wrong.

That this wife is a believer also there is no doubt. She may be one of many women of all ages who, in a moment of disgust and despair in view of her husband's behavior, decides to leave him. She may have taken that first step for self–protection, or it may be that the first step was due to selfish motivation. Paul does not state the reason for her leaving, and so whatever we say is only conjecture. Whatever the reason may be, if it is not due to her husband's adultery, she should refrain from a second marriage. "Let her remain unmarried."

If she is a true believer, she will ask of God in prayer to perform His miracle in the life of her husband and change him if he is an unbeliever, or if he is a believer, change his attitude toward her. It is as if Paul is saying here, "Don't give up so easily on people, and especially on your own life partner. As God exercises longsuffering toward us, we ought to exercise longsuffering toward our marriage partner." God's fellowship with us is not due to the fact that we are pleasant to live with, but rather that we need Him. We must not continue in marriage only when it is pleasant, but also when it is necessary, when our partner needs us.

If this wife has left her husband for a reason other than adultery, Paul says, "Let her remain unmarried, or be reconciled to her husband." She is not at liberty to marry another. If she, of course, manufactured reasons for leaving her husband for the express purpose of marrying another, then she is the guilty party and she is the adulteress.

Such a wife should exercise great caution lest she act thoughtlessly and on the spur of the moment, perhaps leaving her husband and then trying to rationalize her action for the purpose of remarrying. Such an attitude cannot be scripturally justified. The only choice for the woman who has left her husband for reasons other than his infidelity is for her to remain unmarried or to be reconciled to him. She cannot at will break the bond of marriage. All this applies likewise to the man who decides to leave his wife.

The Apostle Paul very clearly in this verse states that no spouse who has separated from his or her partner for reasons other than the partner's infidelity can marry another.

The Options of the Faithful, Forsaken Partner

There is one aspect of this whole situation, however, which the Apostle Paul does not mention: is the unjustifiably deserted husband in a marriage between Christians free to remarry? If his wife remarries, yes, he is free to remarry for even though she had not committed adultery at the time she left him, she did do so when she remarried.

But we have no clear guideline as to what the deserted husband or wife is supposed to do if the partner has not remarried. If there is evidence, however, that the one who took the first step of desertion has fallen into immorality, even if he or she has not married, it is the same as adultery or as if the second marriage had taken place. Desertion alone is not liberty to remarry if both parties are believers. If one does, he or she clearly disobeys God's Word. Of course, such disobedience is indirectly and originally due to the action of the spouse who separated herself or himself and may have some mitigating merit in the day of the judgment of believers. The deserted spouse in this instance is clearly the victim of the sin of another. God can certainly give grace to bear the consequences of the sins of others which fall squarely on us, but it behooves us to pause and carefully consider whether we are doing all within our power to maintain a loving and harmonious relationship with our partner.

Indirect Guilt of the Deserting Spouse

It is quite likely that a wife who leaves her husband without scriptural reason for divorce finds that he has decided to remarry. Does that then leave her, the deserting partner free to remarry? By the letter of the law, yes, but her motive for desertion which caused her husband to fall into the sin of remarriage will one day be revealed and judged accordingly. Rationalization of motives can be agonizing to the conscience. They cannot in the end escape God's judgment.

How we should watch, therefore, those desertions with the motivation of leading one's spouse to remarry so that the other may be free to remarry. This, in reality, is compounded sin. God will judge those whose motives have been to act in such a way as to create a situation which would justify a questionable action.

King David did not actually murder Uriah the Hittite himself. But he did arrange the circumstances so that the man would be killed in battle, and God and mankind ever since have held King David to be directly responsible for Uriah's death (2 Sam. 11; 12).

Efforts to Reconcile Must Be Made by the Deserter

What did the Apostle Paul mean when he wrote that a woman who leaves her husband for any reason other than immorality on his part should not marry again but be reconciled to him? The verb used here means to change a state of enmity between persons to one of friendship.[2] In the passive form, of course, it means to allow that reconciliation to be brought about by another upon oneself. The meaning here is in the middle although the form is passive.

This verb proves that the woman must take the initiative to reconcile herself to her husband whom she deserted, and refers to the particular time in which this can be accomplished. It may take repeated efforts on her part until such time as she succeeds to break the enmity that exists between her and her husband. Since this verse really applies to both husband and wife, whoever decides to separate from the other, it is primarily the one who separates who must make the effort to reconcile herself or himself to the spouse. This reconciliation, however, could not take effect if the departing spouse decided to remarry.

This is why Paul's admonition is to remain unmarried and to make every effort toward reconciliation. The Apostle Paul implies that in any separation, there should be no hurry to remarry or even to consider remarriage.

The basic consideration should rather be how the departing one can reconcile himself or herself to the deserted spouse. That it is possible to be reconciled is implicit in the aorist tense that is used.

There are, of course, cases where such reconciliation is impossible, but in these cases then it is the duty of the one who left to stay unmarried in order that the door may be kept open for a restored relationship. No child of God should harden himself or herself to the point of thinking that such reconciliation is impossible. This is equal to saying that God's Holy Spirit cannot or will not be able to work in someone's life. Who are we to predetermine the movement of God's Spirit?

The verb used by Paul in the expression "or *be reconciled* to her husband" is *katallagḗtō*, the indirect imperative of *katállassō*, "to reconcile oneself to someone." This verb, however, implies guilt on the part of the one whose duty it is to be reconciled to the other person. We must therefore view the deserting partner as one who bears guilt for leaving.

If the deserted partner is not a fornicator, but one who is so cruel that he is likely to perpetrate a sin greater than fornication, the harming and possibly killing of his wife or children, then it is the duty of the wife to separate herself and, if there are any, the children from him. In my opinion, such a protective desertion can hardly classify the deserter as guilty.

That is not the situation envisioned by Paul in this verse. It is the situation of a nonjustifiable desertion. It is what we would call today incompatibility. If a marital partner deserts the spouse because they just cannot get along or because he or she considers the other incompatible, that classifies the deserting partner as guilty and consequently one who should return and be reconciled to the other partner. One just cannot leave one's mate for reasons other than the infidelity of the partner or criminality and feel innocent about the desertion. A husband or wife may not be all that one desires, but this is no justification for leaving one's mate.

Iit is possible for an innocent spouse to depart when it comes to saving one's life or one's children from cruelty on behalf of the deserted partner. The picture then is that of an innocent partner waiting for the guilty spouse to repent so that a reunion may be effected. However, such cruelty in a marriage partner is often linked with sexual immorality in which case the innocent spouse is permitted to re-marry. This is not the eventuality that Paul speaks about here, i.e., that of a deserting spouse leaving an innocent partner.

Forgiveness Between Christian Spouses
When Neither Is Guilty of Infidelity

The last part of verse eleven says: "And let not the husband put away his wife." This actually should be read as if the parenthesis which is the previous state-ment in this verse did not exist.

Here is the thought: "Let not the wife depart from her husband . . . and let not the husband put away his wife." What is in between is in parenthesis and supposes the situation of a wife who actually sepa-rates herself from her husband.

The first admonition of Paul is that the wife should not separate herself (*chōristhénai*) from her husband. This action is taken entirely on her own without any necessary sexual guilt on the part of her husband which led her to depart. Not, of course, that there cannot be the case of desertion by an innocent spouse of a guilty partner which is justifiable. Paul cannot handle all eventualities simultaneously.

The verb used in verse eleven translated "put away" is *aphiénai* which is, as we examined already, "to send his wife away" by his own act, either directly or indirectly. Even if the wife is to blame, but the blame is less than infidelity on her part, he has no right to send her away. A husband is not to send away his wife but to forgive her and attempt lovingly to prevent her from deciding to go on her own. As God forgives us by sending His Son to suffer for us, so we must suffer in order to see the faults of our own wife removed and redeemed by our own actions. Paul says to the believing husband, "Don't do anything in the first place to make your wife go away, to separate herself from you, and even if she has faults, don't tell her to go because of her faults, but rather do everything that you can to redeem her and to love her into staying with you."

The passage in Matthew 5:24, ". . . first be reconciled to thy brother . . ." uses *diallássomai* (or *dialláttomai*). It is the only place in the New Testament that this word is used. It refers to the dispute, not between a guilty and non–guilty man, but between two Christian brothers who have quarrelled. It is impossible that the total guilt rests only with one. Whenever two brothers or sisters in Christ have a disagreement, neither one can bear the entire responsibility. Fault lies with both parties although it may be in varying degrees. One of them must take the initiative, Christ says, and that should be the one who goes to the altar to worship since he is apparently the more spiritual of the two. He is to go to his brother who he knows may have something against him. He may be in the wrong in the first place because his brother has something against him, but he, as the more spiritual, ought to help the less spiritual who may be in the bond of resentment. With the word *diallágēthi* we are to understand that in the case of dispute between brothers, the blame cannot be placed entirely on one.

Estrangement From and Reconciliation to God

All through the New Testament, wherever the verb, *katállasō* or *katallássomai*, is used (Rom. 5:10, 2 Cor. 5:18–20) in relation to our being reconciled to God, it is not because both God and we are guilty for our estrangement one from the other. It is we who deserted God and not He who deserted us. Therefore, it is we who must come to God to be reconciled to Him, acknowledging our sin and shortcomings and seeking His forgiveness.

---

[1]The verb in Greek is *chōristhḗ*, the third person singular first aorist subjunctive passive with the middle meaning of *chōrízō*.

[2]*Katallagḗtō*, third person singular, second aorist imperative passive of *katallássō* from *katá*, an intensive, and *allássō*, "to change, to alter."

20

WHEN A CHRISTIAN IS MARRIED TO AN UNBELIEVER

But to the rest speak I, not the Lord: If any brother hath a wife that believeth not, and she be pleased to dwell with him, let him not put her away. And the woman which hath an husband that believeth not, and if he be pleased to dwell with her, let her not leave him.—1 Corinthians 7:12, 13

The Apostle Paul dealt in 1 Corinthians 7:8, 9 with those Christians who are unmarried or widowed. In verses ten and eleven he dealt with married Christians. Now, in verses twelve and thirteen he deals with a Christian believer who may be married to an unbeliever. He covers this last category with the all–inclusive "But to the rest."

Corinth, the Scene of Resultant Mixed Marriages

When the Lord Jesus dealt with the matter of divorce, He referred primarily to Jewish couples who were married under the Old Testament law. There was no reason at that time for the Lord Jesus to deal with the case of mixed marriages. This, as we mentioned previously, later became a very live issue in Corinth because upon hearing the Apostle Paul's preaching of the gospel, there were those who turned to Christ from both Jewish and Gentile backgrounds. Although Paul could exercise no apostolic authority over either the non–believing Jewish or the heathen partner in marriage, he could influence the Christian.

Opinions Ought to Be Given and Received Only as Opinions

The first thing that Paul finds himself under obligation to make clear is that what he is going to say he did not receive actually and directly from the Lord Jesus. This is why he says: ". . . speak I, not the Lord." The verb that he uses, however, is *légō*, which means a word which has deliberate thought behind it. This gives us an insight into what we as servants of Christ must do in cases where we do not have a direct commandment in the Word of God. We must thoughtfully and carefully consider what we speak, but we must also very definitely qualify what is our word and what is the word of Christ. In our case, we have the word of Christ and the word of the apostles, that is to say, the entire Scriptures. Admittedly, there are many questions that are not treated in the Scriptures in specific detail. Therefore, in giving guidance to those over whom we have spiritual responsibility, we must bear in mind, of course, the general principles of Scripture although they do not always contain details and specifics.

It must also be borne in mind that when we speak on subjects concerning which the Scriptures are silent, we must not in any way make others believe that our word is equal to apostolic injunction. There is always the word of Christ, the word of the apostles, and finally the word of fallible disciples of Christ who may err in our interpretation. I wish to make clear that whatever I have said in this book which is outside the specific word of Christ or the apostles must not be taken with any authority that does not belong to it. I have asked the Holy Spirit repeatedly to guide me in the understanding of His Word and the interpretation thereof. There are some situations that I have dealt with that are not directly covered in the Scriptures, and I want these portions to be considered as only my personal opinion.

No one in this day can speak as Paul did in 1 Corinthians 7:17: "But as God hath distributed to every man, as the Lord hath called every one, so let him walk. And so ordain I in all churches." The word for ordain is *diatássomai* which means "to set in order, to command." He did not allow anyone to question his apostleship (1 Cor. 9:1).

No Sanction for Initiating Mixed Marriages

In no way can the words which Paul speaks in these verses be construed as giving sanction to mixed marriages. A believer must marry a believer. If he doesn't, he is deserving of the consequences of his disobedience. In 2 Corinthians 6:14, 15, Paul was very clear in regard to this question: "Be ye not unequally yoked together with unbelievers: for what fellowship hath righteousness with unrighteousness? And what communion hath light with darkness? . . . or what part hath he that believeth with an infidel?"

Paul begins with the Christian brother, and again presents the case as a supposition: "If any brother hath a wife that believeth not, and she be pleased to dwell with him, let him not put her away." The first thing that is concluded by this verse is that the marriage stands as valid. These two apparently were married when they were both unbelievers. One, however, the husband, came to know Jesus Christ. His wife did not receive Christ and did not follow the example of her husband.

Indeed the words of Christ may then be realized: "Think not that I am come to send peace on earth: I came not to send peace, but a sword. For I am come to set a man at variance against his father, and the daughter against her mother, and the daughter–in–law against her mother–in–law. And a man's foes shall be they of his own household. He that loveth father or mother more than me is not worthy of me: and he that loveth son or daughter more than me is not worthy of me" (Matt. 10:34–37). In Luke 14 we find the wife included (Luke 14:26).

It is clear that the teaching of the Lord is that a believer cannot put his wife or any other relative in the same category as Christ Himself. He is above all human relations. Therefore, implied in the commandment of Christ is the thought that a Christian husband cannot betray his Lord in order to please his unbelieving wife. The Lord must come first. When a spouse becomes a believer and puts Christ first, the marriage partner is not loved less, but more. A believer in Christ distinguishes between his or her love for Christ, who is God, and for the marriage partner or for any other human relative.

A Believer Cannot Break the Marriage Simply Because of the Unbelief of the Spouse

What is to happen if the unbelieving wife or husband is unwilling to respect the faith of the Christian spouse? Again, there is no specific instruction in the Word of God. If the unbelieving spouse is sexually unfaithful to the believing partner, then the latter has Christ's permission to dismiss the adulterous spouse. This, however, is not because of the unbelief of the spouse, but because of his or her unfaithfulness to the believing partner. Divergence of faith alone is not suffcient reason for a believer to separate himself from an unbelieving wife and vice versa.

It is more likely that the unbeliever will dismiss the believer, but is very unlikely that in so doing the unbeliever would remain single and chaste. On the basis of the unbeliever's sexual infidelity then, the believing spouse may remarry.

**Believing Partners Are Obligated Only If Their
Unbelieving Spouse Is Willing to Live With Them**

Observe that Paul says: "If any brother hath a wife
that believeth not." It does not say, "takes a wife,"
but "has a wife." The marriage took place prior to
the husband coming to know Jesus Christ. How does
one face a situation that is not the direct result of his
disobedience in marrying an unbeliever, but comes
as a result of his obedient faith in Christ and the resistance of his wife to believe?

His continuing to live with her as her husband is
based on a condition to be fulfilled by her: "And she
be pleased to dwell with him." The verb translated
"be pleased" means "to think well together with another, to consent, to agree together."[1] It does not say
that she has to follow him in his faith, but simply to
find pleasure in living together with him as a wife.
She should find pleasure "to dwell with him." The
word for "dwell" means to live together in the same
house.[2] This, of course, gives us to understand that
living under the same roof, they live together as husband and wife. This indicates that she is willing to
perform the duties of a wife and he is willing to perform the duties of a husband. There is no question at
all as to what should be the believer's attitude toward an unbelieving wife. She is his wife, and he
must find pleasure in living with her as her own
husband, and if she agrees, then he should not send
her away.[3] This means that the believing husband
should not do anything to cause the unbelieving

wife to leave him. There is no question at all about the obligation of the Christian husband to stay with his wife as long as there is willing agreement which naturally makes the marriage compatible.

In verse thirteen Paul reverses the case and presents a believing wife who has an unbelieving husband: "And the woman which hath a husband that believeth not, and if he be pleased to dwell with her, let her not leave him."

In both instances the word translated "unbeliever" is *ápiston*, "without faith," which does not refer in any way to sexual immorality, but rather to one who disbelieves the gospel of Christ, an infidel (1 Cor. 6:6; 2 Cor. 6:15). The condition in this instance also is the consent of the unbelieving husband to live in the same house and perform the duties of a husband. In that case, the believing wife should not send the unbelieving husband away. Again, the verb is exactly the same, *aphiétō*. A believing wife should not do anything to cause an unbelieving husband to leave her. I would add that an unbelieving spouse should rather endeavor to win his or her unbelieving spouse to Christ through an example of a loving, Christian attitude.

---

[1]The word translated "be pleased" in Greek is *suneudokeí* from the conjunction *sun*, "together with," and *eudokéō*, "to think well," which is derived from *eu*, "well, good," and *dokeō*, "to think."

²*Oikeín* is the infinitive of *oikeō*, from the substantive *oíkos*, "a house."

³The verb again here for "send away" is *aphiétō*, third person singular present imperative active of *aphíēmi*.

21

HOW IS AN
UNBELIEVING PARTNER
SANCTIFIED?

For the unbelieving husband is sanctified by
the wife, and the unbelieving wife is sanctified
by the husband . . . —1 Corinthians 7:14

In this verse Paul delineates the spiritual reasons why a believing spouse should continue to live with an unbelieving partner with whom marriage was consummated before the belief of the one.

The Unbeliever Can Be Influenced for Christ

Besides the fact that a marriage continues intact and does not bring shame on the name of Christ by its breakup, there is a further advantage to the continuation of such a marriage. The unbelieving partner dwells under the same roof as the believing partner, and as long as there is contact, there is hope that the unbelieving one will turn to faith in Jesus Christ. The primary concern should not be the difficulties which a believing spouse may encounter in living with an unbelieving partner, but rather the prospect of winning the unbelieving one to Jesus Christ.

This influence with the hope of winning the unbelieving partner to Christ is expressed by Paul with the verb "is sanctified." Verse fourteen does not begin as the English translation has it, "For the unbelieving husband is sanctified by the wife. " It begins with the verb *hēgíastai*, "is sanctified." The same is true with the next clause, "And sanctified is the unbelieving wife by the husband." This verb is in the third person singular perfect indicative passive of *hagiázō*, "to separate, to set apart or sanctify," from a common to a higher or sacred use or purpose. A perfect tense indicates that this setting apart is a present state of being which had its beginning at a definitive time in the past.

Remember that even animals and inanimate objects used in the furnishing of the temple, such as bowls and lavers, were sanctified, or set apart, for spiritual purposes. (See Ex. 13:2 and Lev. 8.)

The decision of the believing spouse to accept Christ as her Lord and Savior automatically sets the unbelieving partner apart. The believer has her husband with her to influence for Christ which she would not have the privilege of doing should she leave. The passive voice of the verb indicates that this setting apart has not really come upon the unbeliever by himself, but is the result of the believing spouse. It is the faith of the believing spouse that brings about this separation of the unbelieving partner from an unholy atmosphere into a holy one.

The Believer's Consent to Live With an Unbelieving Spouse

The translation says: "For the unbelieving husband is sanctified by the wife." The preposition translated "by" in Greek is *en*, the literal meaning of which is "in." When this preposition is used with a dative as the case is here, it means "on account of" or "by means of." What the Apostle Paul is saying here, then, is that an unbelieving husband is set apart on account of his believing wife.

"Is Sanctified" Refers to an Already Accomplished Fact

The perfect tense of the verb indicates that this is not a condition that is yet to be achieved, although a believing spouse must do everything for her unbelieving husband in the prayer and hope that he will come to know Jesus Christ. The translation of this statement, therefore, ought never to be thought of as meaning that the unbelieving husband is to be sanctified on account of the wife. He is already sanctified, that is set apart for special and direct spiritual influence.

To Sanctify Indicates Purity

The verb "to sanctify" does not merely mean to set apart, but to make holy, to separate from sin. It is derived from the noun *hágios*, which is made up from the negative *a*, "without," and *gé*, "earth." It means someone who is separated from earth. It indicates purity. In this instance, when the entire discussion is about purity of body and the preservation of the sanctity of marriage, we can conclude that the word must mean moral uprightness.

Not all unbelievers are morally corrupt in their sexual relationships, and should the Christian mate depart, most likely sooner or later, the unbeliever would either fall into fornication or remarry, thus becoming an adulterer. Thus the departing believer would indirectly contribute to his moral downfall. Many a husband or a wife who may be unbelievers are very faithful to their spouses. When such is the case, it is then the duty of the believing spouse to remain with the marriage partner who may be an unbeliever. The obligation of the believer to stay with the unbeliever is predicated on the sexual faithfulness of the unbeliever since one of the duties of the believer is not to allow the defilement of one's body which is the temple of the Holy Spirit. Of course, it is also the duty of the believer to weigh the situation from every possible angle, such as the resultant effect on the children or the church or the community or generally the cause of Christ, before she leaves her immoral husband. But the believer is not required to stay with an unbeliever who does not promise to abstain from fornication.

What the Apostle Paul therefore is saying in this verse is that, by virtue of a believing spouse and her consent to live with him, it is taken for granted that he has already set himself apart for her alone. For if the unbelieving spouse does not do this, then the believing one has the right to refuse to live with the unbeliever. The choice may be otherwise, however, if the believer so decides.

Sanctification in This Context Means Abstaining from Fornication

The word "sanctified" here must not in any way be construed to mean living faith in Jesus Christ. It is true that in the New Testament sanctification is the result of living faith in Jesus Christ. But it also means abstaining from fornication. Paul in 1 Thessalonians 4:3, 4, 7 says: "For this is the will of God, even your sanctification, that ye should abstain from fornication: that every one of you should know how to possess his vessel in sanctification and honor; . . . for God hath not called us unto uncleanness, but unto holiness."

Sanctification here is clearly identical to a conduct conformed to the ideal attitude or standing of the Christian. It is described as the state of abstinence from fornication. It is the ability of a man to possess his own vessel, that is to say, his body, in a condition of hallowedness and honor in contrast to one of lustful passion. Paul therefore maintains that such moral conduct is possible by an unbeliever who consents to live with a believer who, by virtue of the believer's faith, would not consent to give his or her body to uncleanness. Thus, Paul's remarks are very true that an unbelieving husband is made sexually moral by means of, or because of, his believing wife. He knows perfectly well that her faith requires her to keep her body pure.

It is to these same Corinthians that Paul wrote: "Know ye not that your bodies are the members of Christ? Shall I then take the members of Christ, and make them the members of an harlot? God forbid. What? Know ye not that he which is joined to an harlot is one body? For two, saith He, shall be one flesh" (1 Cor. 6:15, 16). Then in verse nineteen he says: "What? Know ye not that your body is the temple of the Holy Ghost which is in you, which ye have of God, and ye are not your own?" A believer's body is not his own. It is Christ's. How then can a believer lend that body to a husband or a wife who would defile it because of his or her sexual sin? It is therefore the believer's privilege that in the consent to allow an unbeliever to continue a marital relationship, he or she can require chastity on the part of the unbeliever. If that requirement is not met, then the believer is free to choose whether to stay or not.

The importance of the believer's chastity is actually what the Lord had in mind when He gave permission to a believer to leave an unchaste partner and to remarry. One must bear in mind that even above the marital relationship, there is the relationship of the believer to his or her Lord. That the choice must be made by the individual believer is the thesis of Paul. But in the exercise of that choice, there must not be any ulterior motive of simply serving the desires of self and the flesh.

Sanctification Which Is the Result of Justification in Christ

This state of sanctification for the Christian is definitely presented as the direct result of his justification before God by and through Jesus Christ. Paul says in 1 Corinthians 1:30: "But of him are ye in Christ Jesus, who of God is made unto us wisdom, and righteousness, and sanctification, and redemption." Who is he speaking about? "Jesus Christ crucified, who is unto the Jews a stumblingblock and unto the Greeks foolishness" (1 Cor. 1:23). He is the believer's justification. Here the thought is not of sanctification as a process, but as a status into which a man is brought by God's act on condition of faith. This is seen in 1 Corinthians 6:11, "And such were some of you: but ye are washed, but ye are sanctified, but ye are justified in the name of the Lord Jesus, and by the Spirit of our God." If we look at verse nine, we shall find out that among other things these believers were formerly adulterers. They became sanctified or "chaste" in Christ. Every Christian as such has been put into a virtual or implicit state of purification by the blood of Christ from his sinful past, and becomes consecrated to God's holy ends in the same experience of faith which ushers him into the state of justification.

171

These are, indeed, but different aspects of one and the same spiritual fact and are produced by the same divine means, both objective and subjective.

Limited Sanctification (Abstaining From Fornication), the Result of Being Married to a Believer

In the case, however, of an unbeliever, his sanctification is limited, and it is not for the sake of pleasing God but for the sake of pleasing his wife and remaining faithful to her. In such a case, a believing partner is under obligation, according to the Apostle Paul, to stay with the unbelieving spouse. The unbeliever's sexual morality, however, must not be interpreted as the result of living faith in Christ as is the case with the Christian believer. He is still *ápistos*, "without faith" in Christ, an unbeliever.

It is very clear, therefore, that this state of sexual sanctification is not a state to be achieved by the unbeliever but is due to his marital relationship with a believer. It is being set apart from moral impurities, to be influenced for Christ, and to be used by God in caring for his or her spouse who is part of the body of Christ.

22

THE EFFECT UPON
THE CHILDREN

. . . Else were your children unclean; but now they are holy.—1 Corinthians 7:14

Paul proceeds to set forth the effect on the children of the union of an unbelieving spouse with a believing marital partner. "Else were your children unclean; but now are they holy." This does not mean that a believing spouse should consent to live with an unbelieving spouse only when there are children. The basis of the continuation of the marital relationship has already been established and that is the sexual sanctification of the unbeliever. Children are a consideration, but they should not be the only consideration. After all, a spouse may believe and there may not be any children as a result of that marriage. This clause is introduced by the conjunction *epeí* from *epí*, "upon," and *ei*, "if." This implies a condition, and it could be translated "for then" or "for else," or "for otherwise." What is the result of the decision of a person who has believed after marriage and has consented to live with the unbelieving spouse? If they have children, the effect on the children can be very beneficial. Otherwise, Paul says, your children would have been unclean, but now they are holy.

It is evident that the word "holy," *hagía*, here stands in definite contrast with unclean. This is a further indication that the meaning of the word "sanctify" in this verse refers to a state of being set aside. Because of the believing father or mother, the children, instead of being otherwise unclean, are now holy.[1] The unbelieving spouse has already become sexually sanctified or sexually chaste in the believing spouse. The second effect of such a marriage is that the children are now holy, while otherwise they would have been unclean. When a believer is obedient to Christ and His commandments, the results are felt upon his or her mate and offspring, just as the summer shower spreads its blessings upon all within its reach.

What Does Unclean Mean?

What is the meaning, however, of the word "unclean"?[2] As used here the word does not mean sexually unclean. We must remember that both marriage partners of whom Paul is speaking probably came from a heathen or non–Christian background. What were their religious practices in that particular culture? In the apostolic period the word "unclean" referred to that which was considered ceremonially unclean or unatoned. In the sixth chapter of Second Corinthians, Paul speaks about heathen idol worship. In First Corinthians chapter eight, he speaks about the sacrifices made to these heathen idols. All that is connected with idolatry and the sacrifices to idols he calls in 2 Corinthians 6:17, "the unclean thing."

Observe what the conclusion of his discussion about the non–participation by the Christian in any idolatrous practices is in 2 Corinthians 7:1: "Having therefore these promises, dearly beloved, let us cleanse ourselves from all filthiness of the flesh and spirit, perfecting holiness in the fear of God." Such practices are called filthiness from which we must cleanse ourselves.

The tenth chapter of Acts deals with the gospel coming to a Gentile by the name of Cornelius. He was considered unclean simply because he was a Gentile, a non–Jew, and certainly up to the time that Peter met him, a non–Christian. When Peter met him and the others at Caesarea, he said: "Ye know how that it is an unlawful thing for a man that is a Jew to keep company, or come unto one of another nation; but God hath showed me that I should not call any man common or unclean" (Acts 10:28). By this he implied that Cornelius was unclean.

The Jews believed that any contact with a non–Jew was an act of betrayal to their God which made them unclean. The two words that we find together translated "common" and "unclean" (Acts 10:14, 28; 11:8; Rom. 14:14) stand as the opposites of *hágios*, "holy." The direct opposite of *akáthartos*, "unclean," and *koinós*, "common," so called because it was of common practice, is *katharós*, "clean," and *hágios*, "holy." Both of these positive words refer to the Levitical ritual of theocratic cleanliness as opposed to those practices of idolatry which are called common and unclean. This is made clear in Hebrews 9:13: "For if the blood of bulls and of goats, and the ashes of an heifer sprinkling the unclean, sanctifieth to the purifying of the flesh."

It is evident therefore that the word "unclean" in 1 Corinthians 7:14, referring to the children of former unbelievers, means children who were brought up in the practices of the worship of idols. It refers to children estranged from the fellowship of the true God because of their parental connection with idolatry. When one of these two idolatrous parents becomes a Christian, it is then the duty of the Christian parent to remove the children from heathen idolatrous practices and separate them unto the worship of God. Therefore, the word *hagía*, "holy," referring to the children belonging to one believer and one unbeliever, does not mean saved but rather separated unto the worship of the true God.

There is no guarantee that the children of believing parents will necessarily be saved, but they do have a far better opportunity to be exposed to the gospel and to the true worship of God than otherwise. Every Christian parent must remember this privilege that he or she is to grant to his or her offspring. Personal sacrifice in marriage becomes truly worthwhile when one remembers the benefits that may ensue for one's children. What a terrible grief of heart it would be for a Christian parent to know that his or her children are spiritually lost just because he or she was unwilling to make the necessary sacrifice to maintain the marriage and decided rather to take the easy way out.

---

[1]Observe that the verb that is used here is *estí*, "they are," in the present tense, and not in the perfect tense as with the verb *hēgíastai*.

[2]*Akátharta*, which is the neuter plural of *akáthartos* from the negative *a*, "alpha," and *kathaírō*, "to cleanse."

23

WHAT IS A BELIEVING SPOUSE SUPPOSED TO DO WHEN THE UNBELIEVING SPOUSE LEAVES?

But if the unbelieving depart, let him depart.
A brother or a sister is not under bondage in
such cases: but God hath called us to peace.
—1 Corinthians 7:15

In Corinth there were many couples whose life became problematic because one of the two accepted the gospel preached by Paul and by others and became a Christian. The Christian spouse ought to continue to love, and love even more and more sincerely, the unbelieving partner. As long as the unbeliever consents to live with the believer under the same roof and to set himself apart for the exclusive conjugal relationship to his spouse, the believer husband or wife should continue in the marriage.

If the unbeliever, however, is not separated unto chastity for his believing spouse, the latter has the freedom to leave him even as if he were a believer who proved unfaithful. Sexual unfaithfulness, the Lord taught, is the only reason for the innocent party in marriage to leave the guilty one if he or she wishes. It is not necessary to do so, but if the faithful partner does not do so, then she is like her Lord and becomes sin for her husband's sake who is a sinner. Of course, she may at the same time suffer the consequences of her husband's sin even unto death.

A Believing Spouse Abandoned by an Unbelieving Partner Is in a Situation Beyond His or Her Control

It is conceivable, however, that when one of the two marriage partners becomes a Christian, the one who remains a non–Christian may decide to leave the Christian partner. The believing spouse actually can do absolutely nothing to prevent this. What is the believer supposed to do in such a case?

This is what is dealt with by 1 Corinthians 7:15. "But if the unbelieving depart, let him depart." The word for "unbelieving" is exactly the same word used in verses twelve through fourteen. It is in the masculine, but it is used generically and would refer also to the unbelieving wife.[1] The word *ápistos*, "unbeliever," does not refer, of course, to sexual infidelity, but to a person who stands in contrast to the one designated as a brother in verse twelve, and which ought to also include a sister.

Here we have a Christian brother or sister and a non–Christian spouse. The non–Christian spouse does not base his desertion of the wife on the sexual infidelity of the latter. For the simple reason that the wife has become a Christian, he decides to separate himself from her. In such a case, the Christian wife can do absolutely nothing to hinder this. This is why the Apostle Paul says, "If the husband, the unbelieving one, separates himself, let him separate himself."[2] Apparently, he separated himself on the news of the conversion of his wife to Jesus Christ. Implied may be an effort on the part of the converted Christian wife to win him to her Lord, but he would not respond and he keeps himself separated from her. The middle voice indicates that he is responsible for his own act of separation and the continuation of it. Paul says, "Let him keep himself separate."[3]

God is no man's debtor, and He has told us in Mark 10:30 that anyone who has suffered thus for Him shall be rewarded a hundredfold. Although the experience may be traumatic for the believer, God has promised His grace to be sufficient and His healing in due time.

Divorce as We Understand It Today Is Equivalent to the Ancient Bill of Divorcement

In the Scriptures, actually, legal divorce as we know it today is not discussed. The equivalent to a legal divorce is what Christ called the bill of divorcement or the divorce certificate spoken of in the Old Testament. When separation occurred, the legalization of the dissolution of marriage was taken for granted. The only reason why the Lord Jesus insisted that such a bill of divorcement should be given to the innocent party was for the purpose of declaring the one dismissed as innocent and, therefore, available for remarriage without the one who marries the divorcee being stigmatized as an adulterer or an adulteress. The dissolution of the marriage, however, occurred by the mere desertion of one of the two marriage partners.

Is the Deserted Spouse Still Under Bondage?

When an unbeliever in this way separates himself or herself, then the believer, Paul says, "has not been placed in bondage in such circumstances." The King James Version has it: "a brother or a sister is not under bondage in such cases." This clause in Greek begins with a verb, "is not enslaved."[4]

The slaves in the ancient world were not considered to be men, but dead men or beasts. They were in a worse state than cattle. They were of no standing in the state. They could not own anything. They were not entitled to the rights and considerations of matrimony, could be separated from their mate at the whim of their owner, and had no relief in case of adultery. They could be sold, transferred or pawned as goods. The verb *doulóō* therefore means "to reduce to the state of such slavery, to be enslaved or be in bondage."

The implication of the use of this verb is that, in reality, marriage is a state in which the two partners agree to become slaves one to another in a good, voluntary sense. Our Lord has already told us that there is only one reason for breaking this slavery commitment, and this is the unfaithfulness of one's spouse. Now the Apostle Paul says that if the unbelieving spouse leaves the believer, then the slavery of the bond of marriage does not exist anymore. This is saying negatively what could be expressed positively as such a believer becoming free to make a choice.

The King James Version translates *dedoúlōtai* with a present tense, "is [not] under bondage." The present tense, however, does not really render the meaning of the perfect tense *dedoúlōtai* which means that when the Christian spouse was deserted, from that moment on he or she was free from the marriage bond. The responsibility is not the Christian spouse's, but the unbeliever's choice which the believer cannot change.

Desertion Equal to Adultery

In reference to the unbelieving husband or wife, desertion is understood to be equal to adultery. In the case of adultery, however, on the part of either an unbelieving or a believing marriage spouse, the innocent partner is free to leave and remarry. The

183

same is true with the deserted Christian spouse irrespective of the fact that the deserting unbeliever does or does not commit fornication. It is very unlikely, however, that an unbeliever would desert a believing spouse and not engage in fornication or proceed to remarry. Desertion by an unbeliever can, therefore, be viewed by a deserted believer as adequate reason for the declaration of the freedom of the believer from the marriage bond. Speaking of infidels, it is good to remember what Paul says in 1 Timothy 5:8: "But if any provide not for his own, and specially for those of his own house, he hath denied the faith, and is worse than an infidel" (*apístou*, exactly the same word as in 1 Cor. 7:15).

In essence, there is a difference between an adulterous spouse and a spouse that deserts the marriage partner. In the case of adultery, the innocent spouse can forgive and continue to live with such a spouse. In the case, however, of desertion, the possibility of maintaining the marriage is erased. The only hope remaining is that the one who has deserted may think it over and return to the abandoned spouse. In such a case, the deserted believer must take the spouse who has abandoned him or her back. If infidelity exists, the deserted Christian spouse may refuse to take him back. The hope of the return of the spouse who leaves a partner is what prompts judges today to delay the granting of an official divorce.

What is the meaning of the words "in such cases" in the phrase "A brother or a sister is not under bondage, in such cases"?[5] By implication, of course, this refers to the deserting husband or wife. The deserted spouses are no longer bound to their partners once they have been deserted.

Peace Is Possible Even in Abandonment

But why does Paul add at the end of this verse: "But God hath called us to peace"? The preposition which is translated "to" is *en*, meaning "in." Therefore, a better translation would be: "But God has called us *in* peace." To be deserted by one's husband or wife is a very traumatic experience. But no matter how traumatic it is, it is possible for that one's peace to be preserved. The believer's peace is not primarily derived from or dependent upon a husband or a wife but upon Jesus Christ Himself. It is well for any believer who is going through such an experience to remember the words of Christ in John 14:27: "Peace I leave with you, my peace I give unto you: not as the world giveth, give I unto you. Let not your heart be troubled, neither let it be afraid." It is this peace of Christ to which Paul refers.

The basic reason for the desertion in this particular case is the fact that one of the two spouses has accepted the Lord Jesus Christ as Savior and Lord. The fact that it is God who has called us believers makes it clear that the verb for "hath called," *kaléō*, is a technical term in the New Testament for the process of salvation.[6] It is tantamount to "but God saved us to live in peace." Although we may be deserted by even our spouse, this cannot destroy the peace that we have received because we are in Christ. "I will never leave thee, nor forsake thee," He promised in Hebrews 13:5.

Being in Christ means being at peace with God despite our circumstance. When a Christian is forsaken by a non–Christian spouse, one should find great comfort in the fact that this has come about as a result of one's living faith in Jesus. It is good to remember that the union with Christ has brought about an eternal marriage which has become the reason for breaking an earthly marriage. A person who goes through such an experience can truly say with Paul: "For I reckon that the sufferings of this present time (even desertion by my own husband or wife) are not worthy to be compared with the glory which shall be revealed in us" (Rom. 8:18).

---

[1]The text actually does not have the word "husband," but it is understood because *ho ápistos* is in the masculine and it means "the husband, the unbelieving one."

[2]The same verb is used as in verses ten and eleven: "If the husband, the unbelieving one," *chorízetai*, third person singular present indicative middle of *chorízo*, "to separate." The present indicative means that he keeps on separating himself or that he maintains the state of separation.

[3]*Chorizéstho*, is the third person singular, present imperative middle of *chorízo*, "to separate."

[4]*Ou*, "not," *dedoúlotai*, is third person singular perfect indicative passive of *doulóo*, from *doúlos*, "a slave."

---

[5]The Greek is *en*, "in," and *toís*, plural neuter dative of the definite article *ho toioútois*, "such things, circumstances, or cases."

[6]*Kékléken*, is third person singular, perfect indicative active of *kaléō*, "to effectively call."

24

GRIEVING OVER A LOST OPPORTUNITY TO SAVE YOUR SPOUSE

For what knowest thou, O wife, whether thou shalt save thy husband? Or how knowest thou, O man, whether thou shalt save thy wife?
—1 Corinthians 7:16

The grief experienced by the believing spouse who is deserted by an unbelieving spouse for no other reason than that one has become a Christian is mitigated by the abundant peace that Jesus Christ gives. This is how Paul concluded verse fifteen.

The natural outcome, however, of such a separation is the loss forever of the opportunity to lead the unbelieving party to Jesus Christ. How often, in such cases, the reaction of the believing partner is best expressed with the regret: "I wish he hadn't left, because I am sure that he would have come to know Jesus Christ had he stayed."

In answer to that very frustrating question, the Apostle Paul answers with a question in verse sixteen: "For how do you know, O wife, whether you will save your husband? Or how do you know, O husband, whether you will save your wife?" The verb know here is the Greek *oídas*, (second person singular of *oída*), referring to an intuitive knowledge. It is no use blaming yourself for something that you really couldn't know whether or not would take place. The only way to find out is to wait and see. Even had you lived your lifetime in the bond of marriage, you still may not have had the privilege and pleasure of seeing him saved. Of course, a deserted marital partner must at all times continue to pray in faith believing that God can still save the departed, unbelieving spouse.

What Does It Mean to Be Saved?

The verb "shall save"[1] means to save from sins, that is to say, from the guilt (Luke 7:48, 50), dominion, and eternal punishment of them (Matt. 1:21). This salvation takes place or commences when Christians are, through the operation of the Holy Spirit, put into a state of salvation in this present life. (See Luke 7:50; 1 Cor. 15:2; Eph. 2:8; 2 Tim. 1:9; Titus 3:5; 1 Peter 3:21.) Those who embrace the gospel as in Acts 2:47 are called "the saved ones," (*hoi sōzomenoi*), "those who are being saved," that is, those who followed Peter's advice to be saved (v. 40). For someone to be saved is to repent of and turn from his or her sins and to become a believer in Jesus Christ, to become a Christian.

In the Scriptures, however, we learn that it is not man who saves man, but God through Jesus Christ. It is He who is the Savior. No believing wife or husband can save their marital partner. They can only lead such a one to the Savior, but whether that one will accept the Savior or not is a matter entirely of his own will and the energy of the Holy Spirit.

The reasoning that the Apostle Paul is following here is: "You don't know whether you shall save your unbelieving husband, even if he lived with you all his life. Therefore, let not his departure destroy your peace in Christ. God can still save him, even away from you. Don't blame yourself for something that you cannot help and that you cannot effectively bring about."

What Paul says about the deserted wife, he also says about the deserted husband who is a believer. "Or how do you know, O husband, whether you shall save your wife?"

It was Paul who also wrote in Ephesians 2:8, "For by grace are ye saved through faith; and that not of yourselves: it is the gift of God." Man cannot save himself or anyone else. It is good to remember this when we feel frustrated about the resistance of some of our closest relatives to the gospel. This, however, should not diminish our vigor in witnessing and in desiring to lead others to salvation. But to save them ourselves, we cannot. We must pray and commit their salvation to our precious Lord and

Savior whose love and concern for them is, in reality, far greater than ours.

---

[1]In Greek it is *sōseis*, second person singular future indicative active of *sōzō*, "save." The verb is derived from *sōs* or *sóos*, "safe."

25

BE SATISFIED WITH YOUR GOD–ORDAINED LOT

But as God hath distributed to every man, as the Lord hath called every one, so let him walk. And so ordain I in all churches.—1 Corinthians 7:17

One of the most devastating experiences in life must be to be deserted by one's marriage partner. The case under discussion in Corinth was the acceptance of the Lord Jesus Christ by a former heathen unbeliever. On his conversion, the unbelieving spouse forsook him. Evidently, the believer had a sincere desire to lead his spouse to the Lord Jesus Christ, but he now felt he had lost the opportunity forever.

It is only natural when a person is found in such a state to cry out: "Why did this happen to me? Is this what I get for having believed on the Lord Jesus Christ and desiring to follow Him?" 1 Corinthians 7:17 is an answer to this perplexing state of mind of a believing husband or wife whose spouse has left him or her.

What Paul says from verse seventeen through verse twenty–four actually pertains to his advice for a Christian to patiently accept God's providence whatever that providence is. It is not easy for any husband or wife to be forsaken for the reason of being a Christian. And yet, this must be included as a situation encompassed by what Paul says in Romans 8:28: "And we know that all things (including being forsaken by your spouse) work together for good to them that love God, to them who are the called according to his purpose." "Good" here is continuing to be found in the peace of God and in drawing even closer to God.

God's Concern for the Individual

Verse seventeen begins with the Greek expression *ei*, "if," *mé*, "not," which could be better translated "only," taken with *hōs*, "as." "Only as God distributed to every man," or better still, "to each man."

That which is translated "every man" in Greek is *hékaston* which refers not to the totality of humanity, but to the individual as distinct from others. This word occurs also in 1 Corinthians 7:7 which would be better translated: "But each man (*hékastos*) hath his proper gift of God" and Galatians 6:4. As we experience sorrow and desertion in our lives because of our faith in the Lord Jesus, there is danger in coming to the conclusion that the Lord does not care about us as individuals. This Paul wants to dispel. God, he says, has personally handed down your lot to you as an individual. You are not a number, one of a multitude; your experience is not the product of chance. God knows and He cares, and what takes place in your life is either a product of His directive will or His permissive will.

God does not deal with humanity as a whole, but with individuals within humanity. You and I are parts of the puzzle that God puts together, each one individually fashioned to fit in a particular place. The individual experiences of our lives don't make sense sometimes, but when they are in the hands of God and He places them correctly into their proper place, they form the total picture for which He is responsible.

The Direct Action of God

The state in which each believer is found is related to God's direct activity in his life. Paul says, "Only as God distributed to each one."[1] I believe that Paul wants to impress the deserted Christian spouse with the assurance that what happened to him or to her was not the product of blind circumstances, but it was the direct action of God. The part that has been given to this Christian believer is a part that was given directly by God. How can one complain when he realizes God's direct activity in his life?

The whole philosophy here is that the Christian ought to take that part that God gives him and use it to His glory. Take that musical instrument that God puts in your hands; play the low notes on it as well as the high notes. This is the verb that is used also in Romans 12:3, "hath dealt." We shall do well to ponder that verse: "For I say, through the grace given unto me, to every man that is among you, not to think of himself more highly than he ought to think; but to think soberly, according as God hath dealt (here we have the same Greek verb *emérisen* in the aorist indicating that God apportioned or distributed at a particular time) to every man the measure of faith." Even the faith that we have, whether that faith may refer to our dependence upon God or His enablement to accomplish things in life, is measured out to each one of us by Him.

The Call of God

In the second clause of 1 Corinthians 1:17: ". . . as the Lord hath called every one." Again, that which is translated "every one" is the Greek *hékaston*, exactly as in the previous clause. Each one as an individual God called.[2] The distribution of each person's lot in God's providence took place at a particular time as if it were a gift of God handed down by Him. But when it comes to the effective call of God unto salvation, it really makes no difference when the Lord called that person, but what really is of importance is his response to that call and his present standing in the Lord.

Observe that in the first clause it says, *ho Theós*, "the God," referring to the One who distributed to each one his particular lot in life; but in the second clause it is *ho Kúrios,* "the Lord." The first refers to the Father, and the second obviously refers to the Lord Jesus Christ. The Father distributes the circumstances of life, and the Lord Jesus saves or effectively calls from sin.

Called for a Definite Purpose

In this instance, however, the verb *kaléō,* besides the meaning of "effectively call unto salvation," has the meaning of calling a person for a definite purpose. It could be said that the word is a synonym of *select* or *choose.* Here it was because of the exercise of living faith in the Lord Jesus Christ that this situation has arisen in which a Christian spouse has been forsaken by a non–Christian partner. Even in that particular circumstance, the Lord Jesus has a definite purpose. The verb itself implies the calling of an individual that he may hear, come, and do that which is incumbent upon him or that which the Lord has designed for him. The purpose for which a Christian is called, and it is Christ Himself who calls, implies a special relationship between the Caller and the called one in the accomplishment of the Caller's purpose.

When Deserted by a Spouse, Keep Going

Then comes Paul's admonition to one whose lot is that of a forsaken husband or wife: "So let him walk."[3] The present tense indicates continuous walking which here is used figuratively for Christian activity and behavior and living.[4] The verb refers to the opposite of despair or just giving up and becoming morose about a situation that has developed. Paul says, "Keep going and accomplish that which God wants you to accomplish in and through the circumstance that He has apportioned to you."

The conjunction "so" in the phrase "So let him walk," may be misunderstood as providing the conclusion of what Paul has been saying. In Greek, to make it clear, it is better to translate it "thus, in this manner," (*hoútō*). But Paul does not tell us in what specific manner. It refers to the acceptance of the lot that God has distributed to the deserted spouse and the discovery of what the Lord wants to accomplish through it, and then pressing right ahead to accomplish it. Indeed, one of the greatest difficulties in our lives is not the acceptance of God's providential lot for each one of us, but the discovery of how He wants us to use that lot and the discovery of the purpose that it is meant to accomplish.

Paul's Message Applies to All Churches

Paul is concerned lest the Corinthians would take his directives and complain that they applied only to them. For this reason he adds the last clause in verse seventeen: "And so ordain I in all churches." Again, what is translated "so" is the Greek *hoútōs*, "thus, in this manner." What he is saying to them, in other words, applies to all the churches. The term "churches" here, of course, applies to local

congregations that either he himself or others established. It is not a rule, in other words, that pertains
to only one local congregation, but to all. We can,
therefore, safely take it as a rule for today.

Paul here asserts his special apostleship and the
right that this office gives him to command all the
churches. His concern is the smooth and Christlike
function of each local church. He recognizes that
the marital status of the believers in the church is a
very important part of the life of the church. Every
one of us, as we behave in our marital relationships,
should consider how our actions and our behavior
affects the church of Jesus Christ in our individual
location and also the church of Jesus Christ at large.
It cannot but be affected by our marital behavior.

The word that is translated, "I ordain," is not
what we understand in the religious sense as meaning to invest with ministerial or sacerdotal func-
tions or to introduce into the office of the Christian
ministry.[5] It is actually equivalent to issuing an
edict as in Acts 18:2, to give official instruction as
in Acts 23:31; 24:23. Church order was his apostolic prerogative. In 1 Corinthians 9:14 Paul says,
"The Lord ordained," (*diétaxen*, "commanded").
He is referring to one of the special orders of the
Lord Jesus in His address on sending out the disciples recorded in Matthew 10:10 and Luke 10:7. We
have detailed instructions of the Apostle with reference to the collection in 1 Corinthians 16:1 and the
regulation of questions of worship in 1 Corinthians

11:34. This verb can be considered as part of the apostolic office (1 Cor. 16:1).

---

[1]The verb translated "distributed" is *emérisen*, which in the King James Version is translated as a perfect, but in reality it is the first aorist indicative active of *merízo*, from *merís*, "a part." The difference between the aorist and the perfect is that in the aorist we see God's action at a particular time which permits a particular situation in the life of a specific believer. The perfect would indicate rather the result of that action, the circumstance in which a believer is found.

[2]The verb translated "hath called" is *kékleke*, third person singular perfect indicative active of *kaléo*, "to effectively call unto salvation." The perfect tense here is contrasted with the aorist of *emérisen*, "distributed."

[3]The Greek is *peripateíto*, third person singular, present imperative of *peripatéo*, from *perí*, "about," and *patéo*, "to walk."

[4]See also Romans 6:4; 8:1, 4; 2 Cor. 10:2, 3; Gal. 5:16; Eph. 5:2; 1 John 1:7; 2:6, etc.

[5]It would have been better translated "I command," *diatássomai* from *diá*, an emphatic preposition, and *tásso*, or *tássomai*, "to order, to command, to place in its right place."

26

SHOULD A CHRISTIAN REVOLT AGAINST HIS CIRCUMSTANCES WHEN CHRIST COMES INTO HIS LIFE?

Is any man called being circumcised? Let him not become uncircumcised. Is any called in uncircumcision? Let him not be circumcised.
—1 Corinthians 7:18

It is evident that Paul moves on from the discussion of those who were non–Christians and became Christians and as a result of their belief in Christ, suffered the breakup of their marriages. Paul in the previous verses suggested that a Christian whose unbelieving husband consents to live with the new believer should not terminate the marriage. Based on the teaching of Christ, the only valid basis for which a Christian could break a formerly contracted marriage is the infidelity of the spouse. But even at that, the Christian may decide to stay on as a faithful partner to an unfaithful spouse, but in such a case, the believer disobeys God's commandments in that he or she gives his or her body unto uncleanness. A Christian spouse in such a case has to decide which of the two is the lesser evil, taking all circumstances into account.

Paul has, however, presented the case of the possibility of the unbelieving spouse deciding to desert the believer thus breaking the marriage. In such a case, the believer is free to remarry. The effort should be made, of course, for reconciliation, but if such is impossible, then the believer is free from the contract of marriage.

Circumstances Are Not Always Changed When One Becomes a Believer

There emerges one basic problem from this total discussion: When Christ comes into the life of a person, that person is inwardly changed, and the peace of God comes into his heart. His attitude toward life is completely changed. There is one thing, however, that Christ chooses not to do as He changes the individual believer, and that is He does not simultaneously or consequently change the circumstances in which that believer lives. The Lord may sometimes do this, but sometimes He may not. In many instances, when one marriage partner receives Christ, then the other follows, and then if there are children in the family, they, too, receive Christ and the whole family is saved and the circumstances become quite different. However, this is not always the case.

While Christ brings peace into the human heart, that peace may become the very basis of outward conflict between husband and wife, between relatives, between employer and employee, between master and servant, between teacher and student, etc.

What the Apostle Paul says in 1 Corinthians 7:10–16 is a series of guidelines in the attitude of the Christian in the matter of marriage. Paul declared in verse seventeen that God is a sovereign God and that He distributes the circumstances of life variously to each individual. The commandments that Paul gives are primarily of concern to the local church. Certain decisions, however, for one's private life must be made by the individual according to the measure of faith and grace given by Jesus Christ. His grace and provision of faith, however, are always sufficient for each individual to make the right decision. As a result, God can never be blamed for our wrong decision as if He did not grant us sufficient or appropriate faith and grace. These individual decisions, however, do affect the life of the Church and this is the basic concern of Paul as an apostle.

The Example of Circumcision

Now in verses eighteen through twenty–four, the Apostle Paul gives two illustrations which provide parallel circumstances to that of marriage. As someone may become a Christian believer and by that his marriage is affected, so there may be those who perhaps were formerly Jews and were circumcised, or they may have been Gentiles and were not circumcised. Then suddenly, they become Christians. What should their attitude be toward a situation that is the result of their previous religion or culture? Paul wants to give certain guidelines to help Christians face the circumstances of life that they cannot help and which God does not necessarily change.

Paul asks in the eighteenth verse: "Was someone called who has been circumcised?"[1] Undoubtedly this must have been a Jew, since circumcision at that time was the mark of being Jewish, and now he has become a Christian. It was through God's sovereign grace that this Jewish individual was led to saving faith in Jesus Christ. What must he do with the mark of the Jewish religion, that is, circumcision? Here Paul uses a word referring to uncircumcision that is not used anywhere else in the New Testament.[2] It relates to an operation which sought to create a new foreskin on Jews who had become Gentiles or Hellenistic Jews. This was an endeavor to cover the fact that they were Jewish in order to escape persecution or ridicule in the public baths or games. So Paul says that if you have become a Christian and you have been circumcised, don't try to become uncircumcised—"Let him not become uncircumcised!"

He then gives the opposite example: "Has someone been called in uncircumcision?" Thereafter the negative command: "Let him not be circumcised."

The conclusion of all this is Paul's advice: "Remain as you were when God called you unto salvation and you became a Christian."

---

[1]This is expressed by the verb *eklḗthē*, third person singular first aorist indicative passive of *kaléō*, "to effectively call unto salvation."

[2]It is an indirect negative imperative: *mḗ*, "not," *epispásthō*, the present imperative of *epispáō* from *epí*, "over," and *spáō*, "to draw."

27

THE MEANING OF CIRCUMCISION IN THE CONTEXT OF GOD'S COMMANDMENTS

Circumcision is nothing and uncircumcision is nothing, but the keeping of the commandments of God.—1 Corinthians 7:19

Paul is referring to the period of time in which he was writing. He could have left out the verb "is"[1] in which case, without a verb, this would have meant that there never was a time when circumcision was anything. On the contrary, there was a time in the Old Testament that circumcision had much meaning.

In Genesis 17:10–14, circumcision is identified in relation to the covenant made with Abraham (see Acts 7:8). At that time, circumcision signified the mercy of God to man, and only derivatively, the consecration of man to God. Circumcision, therefore, at that time was a token of the work and grace whereby God chose out and marked men for His own. Those who became members of the covenant were expected to show it outwardly by obedience to God's law expressed to Abram. The relation between circumcision and obedience remains a biblical constant (Jer. 4:4; Rom. 2:25–29; compare with Acts 15:5; Gal. 5:3). Circumcision, in reality though, was only an outward sign and did not necessarily guarantee the obedience of the heart (Deut. 10:16; Jer. 4:4; 9:25; Rom. 2:27).

Circumcision Was a Sign for a Specific Period

The New Testament doctrine is that circumcision should be taken only as a sign, and without obedience it becomes uncircumcision (Rom. 2:25–29). This is exactly what 1 Corinthians 7:18, 19 teaches—that the outward sign fades into insignificance when compared with the realities of keeping the commandments, faith working by love (Gal. 5:6), and a new creature (Gal. 6:15). Nevertheless, the Christian is not at liberty to scorn the sign. There was a time that God required it, and it indeed had significant meaning at that particular period in God's timetable. But insofar as it expressed salvation by works of the law, the Christian must shun it (Gal. 5:2ff), yet in its inner meaning he needs it (Col. 2:13). Consequently, there is a "circumcision of Christ," the "putting off of the body (and not only part) of the . . . flesh," a spiritual transaction not made with hands, a relation to Christ in His death and resurrection, sealed by the initiatory ordinance of the new covenant, baptism of those who believe and are initiated into the body of Christ even as circumcision was an initiation into Israel (Col. 2:11, 12). Christians, as a result, are the circumcision (Phil. 3:3).

Circumcision Had Ethnic, Regional, and Chronological Limitations

It is interesting to note that the first two clauses of verse nineteen contain the verb *esti*, "is," but the last phrase has no verb. "Circumcision is nothing, and uncircumcision is nothing." Paul is speaking of the particular dispensation of grace. However, when it comes to the last statement of verse nineteen it reads, "But the custody (keeping) of God's commandments." There is no verb in this last statement. This refers to the commandments of God that had no ethnic, regional, or chronological limitation in their application and importance. It is evident from what Paul is saying here that circumcision was one of those commandments of God which was restricted as to its application and duration.

Commandments with General and Permanent Value and Application

What does Paul mean when he says: "But the keeping of the commandments of God"? First of all, since there is no verb in this phrase indicates the permanence of the value of God's commandments. What is to be understood, however, is the opposite of *oudén*, "nothing," which was used in relation to the circumcision and uncircumcision. Circumcision and uncircumcision are nothing, Paul said, but this does not mean that we should take the commandments of God in general as being of no value. It is not always correct to take a commandment that was given at a certain period of history and apply it to all periods of history. This is so especially if it was a specific commandment that had its purpose in place and time.[2]

Commandments with Intrinsic Value and Commandments to Test Obedience

The command, for instance, which God gave to Adam and Eve not to eat of a certain tree can be said to be an *entolé*, a particular command. It may have seemed of no intrinsic value to the first man and woman. Why, after all, should God give authority to mankind to partake of the fruit of all the other trees in the garden and not of this particular one? There are certain commandments that God gives that have intrinsic value in them because of the inherent good that may result for man as he obeys them. But there are also commands that God gives primarily to test man's obedience. All throughout history, God has given both types of specific commands so that the disobedience might have been without excuse.

At a certain time in history God gave the command for the Jews to be circumcised. This was a particular command relating to Jews only, but it did not mean that if others followed the Jews in their obedience to this command, it displeased God in any way. For Gentiles to be circumcised is not considered by God as wrong doing. Nor do Jews today, according to the Scriptures, have to be uncircumcised if they are Christians. Circumcision was for the identification of the nation of Israel. Therefore, circumcision was a specific command for a limited time without permanent value, but it had to be obeyed simply because it was a commandment of God.

We learn from this that there are commandments that are of permanent value and not specific but which test man's obedience at each period in the history of mankind. The abrogation of a specific commandment given for a specific people for a specific time does not cancel out God's commandments in general.

It is to be noted also that there is no definite article in front of the word *entolón*, "commandments," in the genitive plural which indicates that Paul refers to the commandments of God in general without any specific application as to which ones they are.

It is also interesting that the genitive *Theoú*, "of God," does not have the definite article. Because it does not have the definite article, it can be taken as commandments given by God the Father, God the Son, and God the Holy Spirit. The phrase *entolón Theoú*, "commandments of God," is given in the most general terminology possible referring not to the specific commandments that the Father, the Son or the Holy Spirit have given at any time, but referring rather to the obedience to God demanded at particular times in history.

In the discussion in Matthew 19:7 and Mark 10:3 concerning the giving of a bill of divorcement, when referring to an unjustifiable divorce, the verb *entéllomai* is used. This refers to the specific command that God gave through Moses. In John 8:5, referring again to the specific commandment given through Moses for a woman caught in the act of adultery and deserving of stoning, the same verb is used. These were *entolaí*, commandments of God that were specific for regulating a special situation. The Lord Jesus confirmed the validity of the first, that is to say that if a spouse dismisses a partner for a reason other than adultery, that spouse should give the dismissed partner a bill of divorcement so that he or she may be free to remarry. The Lord, however, remained silent as to the deserved fate of the marriage partner who was guilty of adultery. Nevertheless, although specific commandments are confirmed or abrogated, or silence is kept about them, does not mean that the commandments of God in general ought to be disregarded. Such commandments are inherent in the concept of God's justice in declaring the innocent or forgiven free and in applying proper punishment on the guilty. They are of value at all times. That is what the

Apostle Paul means by this phrase, "But commandments of God are important to be kept."

Guardians of God's Specific and General Commandments

Not only must we recognize that God has given commandments which are important for the time that they are imposed and for the people to whom they apply, but God's commandments in general in their particular application are very important and we must be their custodians. The word that is used in the King James Version, "the keeping," in Greek is *térēsis*, which is derived from the verb *tēréō* which means "to keep" or "to watch, to guard" (see Matt. 27:36, 54; 28:4, Acts 12:6; 16:23; 24:23; 25:4, 21).[3]

It is interesting that in this verse there is no definite article in front of the word. The Apostle Paul is not speaking about *the* guarding of *the* commandments of *the* God, but he is speaking about guarding commandments of God. He is speaking about a general principle that God has given commandments which are important not only in relation to their external application but because they test man's obedience to Him. "If you love me, keep (*tērésate*) my commandments" (John 14:15), His Word says. We, as His children, are supposed to be the guardians of specific commandments that were given for specific people to be kept at specific times. However, we are also, and perhaps to a greater extent, to be guardians of God's commandments given to test man's obedience in the context of the circumstances in which God placed him.

Discerning the Circumstances in Which God's Commandments Apply

When this principle is applied to the commandments and guidelines in regard to the matter of marriage, divorce, and remarriage, we must recognize what constitutes God's commandments that are general, and we must guard these commandments. We must discern the circumstances in which they apply as, for instance, in Corinth in the case of a believer and an unbelieving spouse and also between two believing spouses. It is our duty to discern which general commandment of God applies to a specific situation, and we are then responsible for the guarding of the commandment applicable. Man can never abrogate God's eternal commandments.

---

[1]*Estí*, which is the third person singular present indicative of *eimí*, "to be."

[2]The word that Paul is using to indicate the commandments of God here is *entolai*, which is the noun derived from *entéllomai*, from *en*, "in, upon," and *téllomai* or *téllō*, "to charge, command," which is akin to *prostássō*, "to order." The word *entolé* refers, however, to a particular command (Matt. 22:36, Eph. 2:15, Heb. 7:5; 9:19).

[3]The substantive *tērēsis*, "guarding," is used only in Acts 4:3; 5:18, and in 1 Corinthians 7:19.

28

DON'T DISTURB THE MARITAL STATUS WITHOUT VALID REASON

Let every man abide in the same calling where-with he was called.—1 Corinthians 7:20

This verse really refers to the total discussion from verse eight on. It begins with the word *hékastos*, the same word used in verse seventeen meaning "each one individually." Each one is responsible for applying God's general commands in his own particular case.

In the case of Paul, he was called to be single and to accomplish his work for God in that state. He was keeping God's commandments to love Him with all his heart and to serve Him with full devotion as a single person. That did not mean, however, that everyone else must apply this as God's general command for service to Him in that state. There were others who would fulfill their own calling of God while being married. Some would fulfill that purpose of God in their lives as a believer maintaining a marriage to an unbeliever; or if the unbeliever departed, he or she would find God's will in that state, either by remaining single or being married again. And the same would apply in the matter of a widow or widower.

Should a Marriage Be Terminated When One Becomes a Believer?

Although the word *klḗsis*, "calling," from *kaléō*, is used in the epistles to refer to the effective calling of God unto salvation, it may also refer to the particular calling to fulfill a specific purpose for which God ordains an individual. In this instance, it refers to both. We have the case, for instance, of two unbelievers married together. God effectively calls one of them unto salvation. From that moment on, as a believer, he is also called to a particular purpose in life. That purpose may be to suffer with an unbelieving marital partner so that the unbelieving spouse may lead a chaste life and to Christ. This may be the most important thing God has ordained for the lifework of that believer. None of us has the right to question the motive of such a believer. On the other hand, for someone else it may be the accomplishment of other things for God through the consent that the believer would give when the unbeliever desires to leave him. The deserted believer may decide to stay single or to remarry, choosing that state which will be the better means of accomplishing God's calling in his life.

The verb is *eklēthē*, "he was called," in the passive voice which indicates that God has done this particular calling in the situation in which the believer is found. The King James Version translation is excellent indeed: "Let every man abide in the same calling wherein he was called." In other words, this is saying that in whatever situation you are found when God called you, stay there. If you are married, for instance, to an unbeliever, don't take your salvation as an occasion to terminate your marriage. The verb "abide"[1] implies that a person should stay where he is when God calls him unto salvation. He should not seek a change from the circumstances of his life, be those circumstances marital or cultural, as long as they do not entail compromise of the general principles of God in the believer's life.

This is to be understood by virtue of what Christ said in Matthew 5:31, 32, and 19:9 that anyone, believer or unbeliever, has the right to leave a partner in marriage who is an adulterer. The exercise of this right, however, is the individual Christian's option. Therefore, the admonition to continue in the state that one finds himself when he is saved is not without exception. We must know the commandments of God that apply to each situation. The believer must choose. If there is no valid reason for departing such as the insistence of the unbeliever to live in adultery, the believer must not disturb the marital status quo.

---

[1]The Greek is *menétō*, the third person singular imperative of *ménō*, "remain, abide, stand firm."

29

ON BECOMING A CHRISTIAN, ONE SHOULD NOT BECOME AN INSTANT REVOLUTIONARY AGAINST HIS STATE OF BEING

Art thou called being a servant? Care not for it . . .
—1 Corinthians 7:21

In this verse, Paul goes on to give a further illustration as to what a slave is supposed to do when he becomes a believer. There were, it seems, a number of such slaves in the Corinthian Church. The Greek text has it as follows: "If you were a slave when God saved you."

Now we can really substitute that word "slave" with any state in which one is found when God came into that life through Jesus Christ. As He saved the unregenerate soul, He also put into his or her heart a sense of direction for a life of service and the desire of a specific accomplishment for Him. That is all inherent in the verb *eklēthēs*, which refers not only to the call unto salvation but also to the purpose of a new life in Christ. The moment that one is called of God unto salvation, if one had been a slave, he or she did not cease to be a slave as far as the external relationship was concerned. The new child of God became free inwardly, but continued to be a slave outwardly. There should be no immediate revolting against the natural state of being in one's political setting.

A slave, when saved, must not become an immediate revolutionary. This does not mean that he does not desire external freedom as he has experienced freedom from the chains of sin. A believer should desire freedom, but at the same time must exercise wisdom and circumscribe the limitations of his immediate freedom for the gaining of his ultimate freedom.

By applicaton to the marriage situation, we could say that Paul implies here that a new believer should not attempt to break his bonds of marriage to his unbelieving spouse.

In what is translated as "care not for it,"[1] the imperative is not direct as the English would imply, "don't you care," but rather has the meaning "let him not care."[2] The *melei*[3] is an impersonal verb which means "to toil or labor" whether in body or mind. It shows care or concern. It is projecting oneself into the future and living the consequences of the future based on a present situation and therefore disturbing one's peace of mind in the here and now. Worry would be an apt description.

Paul speaks of a slave who is saved. He immediately projects himself into the future and into situations in which he will be found by being a slave and at the same time a Christian. What shall I do, he worries, if, as a Christian, my master asks me to do something which is contrary to the freedom which I have found within my heart having believed on the Lord Jesus Christ?

The fear created in the human heart, the Apostle Paul says, over the danger of the possibility of future compromise should not predominate. Paul wants believers to avoid present distress over possible future situations. God is able to give grace to face each situation which may arise as a result of someone being saved and being in a position which he has no power to change and from which God may not provide an escape.

---

[1]The Greek phrase is *mē soi melétō*.

[2]Third person singular present imperative of *mélei*.

[3]The verb, *mélei*, is usually followed by a dative of the person caring as in this instance, *soi*, as also in Matthew 22:16 and Mark 4:38. It is related to another compound verb, *metamélomai*, usually translated in the New Testament "to repent" which, however, has to be distinguished from *metanoéō*, which latter verb means to change one's mind as to his sin and character and to change direction. *Metamelomai* is made up of *metá*, "after," and *mélomai*, "to be concerned," from the imperfect *mélei*. The word *metamélomai* means to show concern after seeing where an action has led and then regretting

the action"; not, however, because of the wrongness of the action, but because of the consequences of that action, as in the case of Judas (Matt. 27:3). *Metamélomai* (Matt. 21:29, 32; 27:3; 2 Cor. 7:8; Heb. 7:21) therefore means to regret the consequences after an action has been perpetrated. *Mélei* could therefore have the same meaning.

30

DON'T BE FATALISTIC IN ACCEPTING A SITUATION, BUT ACT CIRCUMSPECTLY TO CHANGE IT

. . . But if thou mayest be made free, use it rather.—1 Corinthians 7:21

Lest any person may misunderstand Paul's position and think that a Christian ought to be indifferent and fatalistic in accepting adverse circumstances without any endeavor to change the situation, his advice to slaves in the latter part of verse twenty–one was, "But if thou mayest be made free, use it rather." A better translation of this would be, "But if you are also able to become free, use it rather (this ability)."

Slaves could be freed in several ways at that time. A master could leave it in his will that he desired all or any one of his slaves to be set free, and compliance with this was mandatory. Even while a master was alive, he could express his generosity by freeing a slave either as a gesture of gratitude or as a matter of reward for the faithfulness of the slave.

God's Providence Is Involved in Our Present Disappointing Situations

One of the first things that the Apostle Paul wanted to impress upon the Corinthians was that the setting of our circumstances in life, be it sociological standing, educational achievement or vocation, is not of our own making entirely. God did have a bearing on it in His divine providence. The constant use of the verb *eklēthē*, "was called," gives us to understand that it is God at all times who does the calling.

One's position in life, be it high or low, rich or poor, free or bound, belonging to the Jewish race or the Gentile, a heathen or a Christian, is not entirely of a person's own making. The sense of personal responsibility must not go beyond its limits. It must, however, assume the responsibility of opportunity within the context of life that God permits to each one.

God's witness in man's heart in varying degrees (John 1:9) is available to all, but only a few receive it. How great a revolution this new relationship with God in and through Christ, when accepted, can bring about in one's life. On believing on Christ, a person enters into the circle of Christ. He cannot by force or personal persuasion, but only by the grace of God being accepted by others, bring friends or family into the circle of Christ in which he is found. The thesis of the Apostle Paul is that while a believer is in Christ and maintains his relationship with Christ, he simultaneously is in the world and must reconcile himself to that very basic, realistic fact. Even a casual reading of Christ's prayer for His own in John 17 would provide an interpretation of what Paul is saying in this verse; namely, that the believer is in the world and yet not of the world. He cannot, because he is in Christ, become totally disassociated with all his past. Listen to our Lord praying in verse fifteen: "I pray not that thou shouldest take them out of the world, but that thou shouldest keep them from the evil."

This is the spirit the Apostle Paul is teaching throughout this seventh chapter of 1 Corinthians. The marital relationship should be maintained when one is transformed from a worldly person into a believer, and he should not succumb to evil related to it for which he bears personal responsibility. One of the greatest things to understand in Christianity is the limitation of personal responsibility and the responsibility of God in the manifestations of His providence.

Let us look at our state of being in our relationship with our national, religious, and cultural background, and especially in our marital status, and consider it a calling of God. Let us never believe that things just happen. Our circumstances are not the products of chance, but the products of providence. We are where we are, we are what we are, and we do what we do by God's divine directive and providence. We should consider His providence as the best opportunity to exercise our personal responsibility in answer to the call for a personal relationship with God in and through Christ. There is, in other words, a horizontal environment from which we cannot escape and to which we must be reconciled without the exercise of personal evil. It is that personal evil for which we are held accountable.

There is, however, a vertical relationship with God which no environment can or should be permitted to influence. This is the thesis of the Apostle Paul. He does not teach us to be fatalistic, but rather to wait upon the Lord to bring about the ultimate change in circumstances and to behave prudently every step of the way. He says to the Corinthians— keep your occupation; continue to be married to the same person after you are saved; if you are a slave, continue to serve the same master until such time as the Lord gives you an opportunity to change your status. The Apostle Paul is not advocating that a Christian's primary goal should be a change for better circumstances in life.

What Is Good for the Believer in Christ?

We must, however, be very careful in evaluating what is really good for us in this life. All too often, we have a basic misunderstanding of that which is good. Good for man is not what he thinks is good for him if it estranges him in any way from a proper relationship with God. For a man to double his income may or may not be to his ultimate advantage. If the doubling of his income would detract from his relationship with and dependence on God, then that would not be good for him. Health is not always good for man. If, in the enjoyment of health, one's personal relationship with God is adversely affected and diminished, health is a curse and not a blessing. What we are or what we have should never be made an end in itself, even our marital or celibate status. These are all means to an end, and that end in the Christian's life should be a closer walk with God, for ultimately that is the only thing that will bring joy and satisfaction in his life. Not even the maintenance of marriage can be considered the end in itself, but only a means to an end. This is exactly what Paul is teaching here. If by remaining single, I can better reach that end, then I will remain single. If I can reach the end which God purposes for me by being married, then so let it be. Any change that I may desire or work for in my life must be viewed primarily as to its effect upon my personal relationship with God. All else must be made subservient to that one basic consideration.

Situations That Are Dishonoring to the Lord

Paul did not teach that when a person becomes a believer, he could continue in a state dishonoring to Christ, but rather that he should exercise a sense of personal responsibility. This is demonstrated by what happened when Paul preached the gospel in Ephesus. There were in Ephesus, as Luke calls them in Acts 19:13, "certain of the vagabond Jews, exorcists," those who were casting out evil spirits from people and who undoubtedly performed other so–called miracles. These, however, after hearing Paul preach, thought it good to dress their activity in the mantle of Christianity, and presumptuously began to declare that what they were doing was being done in the name of Christ. God's Word says they "took upon them to call over them which had evil spirits the name of the Lord Jesus."

Now, some of these magicians were genuinely saved. Did they continue to be magicians and healers and exorcists? No. We read in verse nineteen: "Many of them also which used curious arts brought their books together, and burned them before all men: and they counted the price of them, and found it 50,000 pieces of silver." Apparently, exorcists made a great deal of money, and they continue to do so today. Benefiting from the suffering and desperation of others is part of their profession. But these new converts did not continue in the same profession. So let us not misunderstand the words of Paul in First Corinthians chapter seven as implying that disregard and maintenance by the Christian of a questionable, preconversion relationship is always proper. It is only proper if it is not in disobedience to God's commandments in His Word and does not adversely affect the individual's personal relationship with his Lord.

Maintaining a Marriage with an Unbeliever

With regard to marital relationships, this is exactly what the word "sanctified" means in 1 Corinthians 7:14. A man or a woman, a husband or a wife who becomes a Christian, with a clear conscience may not choose to live with a spouse who is an adulterer and who would cause the believer's body to be defiled by virtue of the marital relationship. A Christian spouse should do his utmost to maintain the marriage and win his or her mate away from such sinful practices. However, the believer may leave the unbeliever because the believer, in order to maintain the chastity of the body which is the temple of Christ, should not become one with an adulterer.

Every man or woman who is saved must consider whether remaining in the same relationship, profession, or state would cause him to violate his very basic faith. He cannot always escape his environment. What, for instance, can a person who becomes a believer by listening to a radio broadcast emanating from outside his own country do to escape a totalitarian regime in which he is found, whether that regime is totalitarian politically or even religiously? He is bound by his environment. Then he must accept the principle of "inasmuch as lies within you," and exercise personal responsibility for the things that do lie within his power. He can rely on God for intervening in such a way that God Himself, with the believer's own cooperation, may provide a way of escape or a way of victory in the midst of adversity.

What a believer, however, can change in his vocation or environment so that it may be more congruent and beneficial to his relationship with God, he must do. A prostitute who is saved by Christ cannot continue in her prostitution. A drug trafficker cannot continue in that vocation after he is saved.

In the matter of marital relationship, Paul says that when a worldly person becomes a believer, the believer must maintain the marital relationship as long as the unbelieving spouse has the desire to continue and, at the same time, pledges his fidelity to the believer. If the unbelieving spouse does not pledge that fidelity, then it's a matter of personal decision by the believer as to what he or she should do. He or she can either stay on for the sake of Christ and compromise his or her body, becoming one with an adulterer, or separate from a marital spouse who wants to continue living in sexual or other kinds of sin, perhaps even crime. I once spoke with an infamous man who was won to the Lord by his prison guard. His faithful, believing wife did not desert him, but labored in prayer for years for his salvation.

Using Our Ability to Change a Situation
When God Gives the Opportunity

Keeping in mind Paul's train of thought throughout this entire seventh chapter of First Corinthians, we must interpret the second part of verse twenty–one as follows: "But if you are also able to become free, rather use it." This means that, if possible, use your ability to become free. (Paul, of course, is referring to the newborn Christian who was found in slavery. He was not in any way advocating that upon conversion the new Christian should immediately seek freedom from his or her marital partner.) The difficulty in the interpretation of this verse is the absence of the object of the verb "use." In fact, in Greek the last two words of this verse are *mállon,* "rather," and the verb *chrésai.*[1] Together they mean appropriating or using an available opportunity. Actually, the only logical object of this verb is the entire previous statement which Paul makes, "But if thou mayest be made free," then use that ability. This ability depends on the opportunity that God's providence makes possible.

Paul, however, is not referring in this phrase to a passivity toward circumstances, but an active realization of any opportunity that may be available for one who is a slave to become a free person. Paul does not condone slavery nor recommend satisfaction in being a slave, but if it is a circumstance of life that cannot be helped, then it must be accepted, and that without bitterness. The Lord Jesus repeatedly spoke of the relationship of His disciples to Himself as that of servants to their Lord—*doúloi* (Matt. 10:24, John 13:16). At the same time, He stressed the inadequacy of this figure. None of the twelve disciples was a slave. The disciples were emancipated, so to speak, and admitted to higher privileges of intimacy (John 15:15).

Paul's message here must be understood in the context of the fact that at that time churches were often established on a household basis and the membership of these churches included both masters and servants. A perfect example of this is found in Paul's letter to Philemon where he speaks of the church in his house (v. 2) and of Onesimus, his servant (v. 16). In fact, this is why the Apostle Paul brings this illustration in conjunction with that of marriage. As in the same household, a newly converted marital partner may be considering whether he should continue to live with the licentious nonbeliever, so in the same household there may be a slave who has become a believer who must consider his attitude toward a master to whom he is bound. Even as a Christian spouse should endeavor to preserve the marriage relationship with a non–Christian spouse, so must a slave who has become a Christian continue in his relationship with his master. The first and immediate responsibility after salvation, as Paul indicates in Ephesians 6:5–8 and Colossians 3:22, is that slaves please God by their faithful service. When it comes to a relationship of both slave and master being Christians, then Paul intimates in 1 Timothy 6:2 and Philemon 1:11 that the fraternal bond with a believing master should be an added reason for faithful service on the part of the slave. On the other hand, the responsibility of a Christian master toward a believing slave is that recommended by Paul to Philemon toward Onesimus (Phile. 1:8–17). The fraternal sentiment shared by Christians should prevail over the relationship of servant or slave and master (Phile. 1:16). Masters are admonished to treat their slaves with restraint (Eph. 6:9) and strict equity (Col. 4:1).

The fact is that household slavery, which Paul is referring to here and which is the only kind referred to in the entire New Testament, was generally governed by a feeling of good will and affection. This is implied by its figurative use in the "household of God" (Eph. 2:19). The Apostle Paul brands the institution of slavery as part of an order that was passing away and advises that if a slave had the opportunity to be emancipated, he should use that opportunity.

---

[1]Second person singular, first aorist imperative of *chráomai*, which is perhaps derived from *cheír*, "hand," and which may have been at one time *cheiráō*, meaning "to lend, furnish as a loan, or to put into another's hands." That is the verb that is used in Luke 11:5 where a traveler came and knocked at the door of a friend at midnight and said to him, "Give me three loaves of bread." That word "give me" is *chréson*. We shall discuss the verb in its passive form with middle meaning as we discuss 1 Corinthians 7:31 in which it occurs again in this chapter: "And they that use this world, as not abusing it: for the fashion of this world passeth away." Suffice for now to state that the meaning of this imperative *chrésai*, "use," in 1 Corinthians 7:21 can be to take into your hands or appropriate such an opportunity to become free.

31

FREEDOM IN SLAVERY AND SLAVERY IN FREEDOM

For he that is called in the Lord, being a servant, is the Lord's freeman: likewise also he that is called, being free, is Christ's servant.
—1 Corinthians 7:22

The opposite parallel which Paul presents here of a free man voluntarily becoming a slave is almost inconceivable. Therefore, in order that the parallels may follow each other as in the case of a circumcised one becoming uncircumcised and the uncircumcised becoming circumcised, Paul presents not a supposition in verse twenty–two, but a fact: "For he that is called in the Lord, being a servant, is the Lord's freeman: Likewise also he that is called, being free, is Christ's servant."

In verse twenty–one, he told the slave that if he is a slave when he becomes a Christian not to show undue concern about his future. If he at any time has the ability to become free, he should use that ability and opportunity. And then in verse twenty–two, he reminds the believing slave that, in reality, inwardly he is not a slave but he is a free man, "For he who was called in the Lord as a slave is the Lord's freed man," or liberated man.

Outward Circumstances Cannot
Steal Inner Peace

When a slave becomes a Christian, he may continue to be outwardly a slave, but inwardly he is liberated in Christ. In reality, a Christian slave should no more consider himself a slave but rather a free man in Christ. External circumstances diminish in importance when considered in the context of eternity. It doesn't, of course, follow that a Christian slave should not try to change the outward circumstances, but he should not be so overly concerned about them as to disturb his inner peace, for as Paul says in the fifteenth verse, "For God has called us to peace." That inner, peaceful relationship to Christ should never be disturbed by the circumstances which we cannot help but which God may permit us in some way to alter in the future. The slave should never allow the future possibilities of his freedom to rob him of his present peace even in slavery.

Paul wanted the Corinthian slaves to realize that the important thing was not what they were when the gospel came to them, but what they had become. The slaves in the Lord are called the freed or liberated men of the Lord. The Lord is the One who brought about their spiritual freedom. The Greek word translated "freed man"[1] means a man freed from slavery; not born free, but made free through the intervention of the Lord. By implication, since this is an illustration only of the marital question, Paul implies that a Christian married to a non–Christian is experiencing the freedom of the Lord in spite of his being bound to a non–Christian. The outward relationship should in no way detract from the inner relationship.

A State of Real Freedom Is Impossible

The second part of verse twenty–two speaks of a non–slave who nevertheless, because he is in the Lord, is a slave of Jesus Christ: "Likewise the free man who was called is a slave of Christ." The word for "free man" in this clause is not *apeleútheros*, but *eleútheros*, referring to a person who never was in bondage to anyone in his life. Such a person, when he is in the Lord, is actually a bond slave of Christ. In essence, Paul is saying here that no one can really be free in this life. A person is either a slave of sin or a slave of Jesus Christ. Independence is impossible. As the Lord Jesus said, "No man can serve two masters." But service to one or the other is unavoidable. So whatever a person's state in life is, it is good to remember that if he is a Christian, he has an inward freedom which no one can take away. In fact, a slave in Christ is freer than a master without Christ. Liberation from the guilt and tyranny of sin is a far greater blessing than external, political, or social liberation.

For the believer, any circumstance that is external is tolerable. A Christian in any binding circumstance or distress can say: "For I reckon that the sufferings of this present time are not worthy to be compared with the glory which shall be revealed in us" (Rom. 8:18). A Christian slave should not consider it beyond his status to respect a master, even as a spouse who is a believer respects his or her spouse who is an unbeliever. If both slave and master are Christians, then in one aspect they are on the same level; they are both equal at the foot of the cross although socially they are unequal. However, this should not make the slave anxious and the master arrogant. There is freedom in slavery and there is slavery in freedom.

---

[1]*Apeleútheros*, made up of the preposition *apó*, "from," and *eleútheros*, "free."

32

LET US NOT SELL OUR GOD–EARNED FREEDOM TO ANY MAN

Ye are bought with a price; be not ye the servants of men.—1 Corinthians 7:23

Whatever the condition of man prior to coming to the Lord, God considers him of inestimable value, whether he be a sinner in freedom or a sinner in bondage. The Lord Jesus would not have given His blood for something that was worthless. That is exactly the message of comfort that Paul wanted to convey, especially to the believers who may still be in a state of external slavery. You are so precious to God, Paul said, that He gave His Son who shed His blood for you. You were purchased with a price. As we enjoy our freedom in the Lord, we should never forget the price beyond measure paid for it by Christ.

The second truth that the Apostle wanted to convey, especially to those who were slaves and had been made free by Christ, is that since their spiritual freedom was acquired by the same payment of the blood of Christ, therefore in that respect they are all alike and of the same value to God. God paid the same ransom for the redemption of the slave as for the free man.

The Price Paid for Freedom

What is translated "you were purchased"[1] in Greek comes from the root word *agorá*, "marketplace." The verb means "to buy," as in Matthew 13:44 and 14:15, etc. It is applied to our redemption by the precious blood of Christ as we find not only here but also in 1 Corinthians 6:20 and Revelation 5:9.

Adolf Deissmann, in his fascinating book, *"Light From the Ancient East,"* gives an account of the inscriptions found on the wall of the temple at Delphi which show the nature and ritual of a slave's redemption in ancient times. One way in which a slave might become free was by the slow and painful accumulation of money to purchase his freedom. When the amount was sufficient for the price of his ransom, it was paid by the slave into the treasury of the temple of a heathen god. Then he and his master went together to the temple, and the priest, in the name of the god, paid the price over to the master. Thus, the master was considered to have sold his slave to the god. He received full payment for him, and gave him his discharge. Now the slave belonged no more to his master, but was the property of the god. He had changed owners and gained freedom by the change.

Paul, in expanding and adapting to the Greek world the Lord's saying about ransom, was admirably meeting the requirements and the intellectual capacity of the lower classes. For the poor saints of Corinth, among whom there certainly must have been some slaves, he could not have found a more enlightening illustration of the past and present work of the Lord. A Christian slave of Corinth, going up the path to the Acrocorinth about Eastertime when Paul's letter arrived, would see towards the northwest the snowy peak of Parnassus rising clearer and clearer before him; and everyone knew that within the circuit of that commanding summit lay the shrines at which Apollo or Serapis or Asclepius, the healer, bought slaves with a price, giving them their freedom. Then in the evening assembly the letter from Paul lately received from Ephesus was read, and straightway the new Healer, Jesus Christ, was present in Spirit with His worshippers. He gave them freedom from another slavery, redeeming with a price the bondsmen of sin and the law. And that price was not pious fiction in which a man had to gain his redemption out of the hard–earned pittance of a slave, but it was a free gift, paid for by Christ Himself.

The slave had to go back to his daily drudgery and degradation, but he found in this gospel message of the cross rest amidst all his labor, and comfort even amid cruel usage. What other service could gall him now? He already belonged to the true and living God.

The word translated "price" in Greek is *timḗs* (genitive of *timḗ*), which in this context means "the value or price of a thing, a sum of money given for it which it is worth" (as in Matt. 27:6, 9; Acts 4:34; 5:2, 3; 7:16, as compared with 1 Cor. 6:20; 7:23).

There is, however, a difference between the freeing of a slave and the freeing of a slave of sin. A slave could save his own money and bring it to the temple and pay for his own freedom, whereas man cannot pay for his freedom from sin. It was necessary for Christ to pay for it.

A Slave's Freedom Required Sacrifice Also

The freedom of the slave was not considered complete without a sacrifice. Within or in front of the temple stood the altar. There, the master and the servant and the priest stood while the sacrifice was offered in token that the transference of ownership was real and effective. This is true as to our spiritual emancipation. "Christ our passover is sacrificed for us" (1 Cor. 5:7). Here we do not have the sacrifice made by man for himself, but the sacrifice made by God for man.

In the third place, the slave's freedom was often attested to by witnesses, and was then frequently inscribed upon a stone. In the New Testament, we find frequent allusions to the attestation of our freedom. In Romans 8:16 we read, "The Spirit itself beareth witness with our spirit, that we are the children of God." There is divine attestation in regard to ourselves that we are now bought by God and belong to Him. It is a testimony written down like the old imperial inscriptions. "Rejoice," says Christ, "that your names are written in heaven" (Luke 10:20), as He tells of the great emancipation which makes His followers trample Satan's power beneath their feet.

A Person Freed by Christ Ought Not to Enslave Himself to Any Man

The consequence of that purchase of our souls by Jesus Christ should be that which Paul commands in the latter part of verse twenty–three: "Be ye not slaves of men." If we were bought at a definite time and with a definite price, we do not belong to ourselves, and consequently we have no liberty to sell ourselves now to someone else. This indicates that there will be men who will try to enslave us to themselves.

It seems that man is not satisfied in belonging just to God. He wants a human leader to whom he can claim allegiance. The Apostle had previously spoken in this epistle (1:12, 13; 3:4–9) with great grief and strong disapproval of the fact that so many in that church were almost exclusively partisans of individuals who had ministered to them the Word of God—one of this person, another of that. On this account, they appeared almost to forget their common Lord, whose servants they all were, so much so that instead of the unity of the Spirit and of faith, they were in danger of being split up into various factions. So great was the burden of this care upon Paul that even here, although he is speaking about another subject, he returns to it again and cries out to those who, released from the law, were called to become the children of God. As such, they ought to remember that, being bought with such a price, they should not again become the servants of men.

We should seriously take Paul's warning to heart against self–imposed bondage. We must not trade our freedom in Christ for slavery to any man, no matter who he is. It is a pity that this enslavery to men shows even with the names that we have selected to be called, not as Christians, but as belonging to this and that spiritual leader of the past. These should have their place in our respect, but we should under no circumstances become their slaves and be known as their followers. Doing so is betraying our freedom in Christ which has been purchased by such a great price.[2]

It is the Christian's direct responsibility to maintain his freedom in Christ, which was so costly. It is possible, even as the slave is free within but in bondage outwardly, that the believer may be free within and a slave outwardly, but this slavery is the one to which he succumbs himself. Our freedom, therefore, is asserted and renewed by us day by day, and we should beware lest at anytime we make ourselves the slaves of any man, and then we continue to be in bondage. We should allow no one to come between our Lord and us. In his epistles, Paul constantly complains that there were many false brethren who had come to spy out the liberty of God's children, only to lead them back into bondage. Among them were those who wished to impose the burden of the Old Testament law upon the Gentile Christians.

Peter understood such teachings by our Lord (Matt. 20:25, 26) and instructs in 1 Peter 5:2, 3 that the flock of Christ is not to be fed by dominion exerted over a people, but that pastors should be examples to the flock and servants of the church. They are to be stewards of the mysteries of God for the advantage and profit of those who wish to apply to the pure fountain, the source of all truth; namely, the revelation of God and His Son. One of our greatest dangers is not from those who hate the gospel, but from those who would enslave us to themselves and to their own doctrine and way of life and rob us of our precious freedom in Christ Jesus.

Paul's reason for bringing this subject into the general marital discussion is to emphasize that no one has the right to dictate to the believer what his marital status should be. This is a personal matter between each child of God and his Lord.

---

[1]*Ēgorásthēte*, the second person plural first aorist indicative passive of *agorázu*

²The command "be not slaves of men" is given with the verb *mḗ*, "not," *gínesthe*, second person plural present imperative of *gínomai*, "to become." Observe how most of the imperatives in this chapter are indirect, in the third person singular. In verse nine, "Let them marry," *gamēsátōsan*; "Let not the wife depart," *mḗ chōristhḗnai*; verse eleven, "Let her remain unmarried," *menétō ágamos*; "Let not the husband put away his wife," *aphiénai*; verse twelve, "Let him not put her away," *mḗ aphiétō*; verse thirteen, "Let her not leave him," *mḗ aphiétō*; verse fifteen, "Let him depart," *chōrizésthō*; verse seventeen, "So let him walk," *hoútō peripateítō*; verse eighteen, "Let him not become uncircumcised," *mḗ epispásthō*; "let him not be circumcised," *mḗ peritemnésthō*; verse twenty, "Let every man abide," *menétō*; verse twenty–one, what is translated as a direct command "care not for it" is really an indirect command, *melétō*.

We come to the direct command in verse twenty–one with the verb "use it," *chrḗsai*, when it comes to the utilization of the opportunity to become free. Paul wants us to more actively pursue that. And also in verse twenty–three, when it refers to not becoming the slaves of men, it is a direct command in the second person plural, *mḗ gínesthe*, which actually means, "Do not begin to be and continue to be slaves to men."

33

MAKE SURE YOUR CALLING IS OF GOD AND REMAIN IN IT

Brethren, let every man, wherein he is called, therein abide with God.—1 Corinthians 7:24

Paul addresses the fact that each believer is specifically called by God unto salvation and unto the performance of the task in life for which God has equipped him. Every believer bears the personal responsibility to do what God wants him to do and not be enslaved by others.

"Each one in that in which he was called," is how this verse literally begins. Consistently, Paul uses the word *hékastos* as in verse twenty, meaning "each individual one." The stress is not on the totality of the believers, but the individuals within that totality. Each one is distinct from the others.

No Christian Should Exercise Authority Over Other People's Marital Affairs

A common danger in Christianity has always been for one Christian to assume such leadership as to tell others exactly how to behave and what to do. Christians are not under the law of another, but they are under the law of Christ unto themselves.

Must We All "Fall in Line"?

This is exactly the subject of the Galatian Epistle of Paul. There were those who were insisting that all Christians should be circumcised. There are some spiritual leaders today who demand that those who serve God must be single. Even the opposite demand is wrong. It is in light of this general principle that the particular recommendation of Paul in 1 Timothy 3:2 concerning the bishop, that he should be the husband of one wife, be interpreted. It does not mean that he should be married, as if this were an inviolable requirement of a bishop, but rather that if he is married, he should be married to one woman. The same is repeated about the elders, equating the elders with the bishops in Titus 1:6. The same recommendation is given in the case of the deacons (1 Tim. 3:12). This, however, doesn't mean that all bishops, elders and deacons should be married, nor does it mean that they cannot be widowers, single, or remarried. Who remains single and who marries is a personal matter to be left to one's individual judgment and decision. In our Christian lives, we must always remember that any particular recommendation should not be made a general rule. What is recommended for one group in the Scriptures is not necessarily binding on another group. Therefore, we should never take a verse out of its context and build doctrine or a requirement for all Christians. We would happily observe a far greater unity among Christians if we exercised the principles which the Apostle Paul promulgates in this seventh chapter of First Corinthians—"Each one in that which he was called."

Man's Individual Responsibility before God

There is an extent to which a man does not bear the total responsibility for what he is and what he does due to circumstances and environment beyond his control. However, this is in no way an excuse to absolve ourselves of our personal responsibility to be what God meant us to be as individuals. It is never wise to compare ourselves with others or envy their positions. The preposition "in" (*en* in Greek) in this verse is very important. It implies a circle in which each one belongs, and if one endeavors to move out of that circle and into another, he will be moving into an environment for which he is unsuited, resulting only in frustration and ineffectiveness.

One's Calling Comes Only from God

The verb *ekéthē* is once again (1 Cor. 7:18, 20–22) in the passive voice which means "was called by God Himself." Spiritual leaders should never call upon others to be what they are. The matter of calling is something that belongs only to God and not to any human being no matter how elevated the position which he occupies. If our efforts and labor only end in failure and frustration, then perhaps we should examine ourselves and see whether our calling was of God or of man. Our calling must be of God in order to bring the joy that God meant to accompany it. Real success for a Christian comes in the assurance of and response to God's call, and not as a psychological puppet of a leader.

34

PERSEVERANCE IN ONE'S GOD–GIVEN POSITION

Brethren, let every man, wherein he is called, therein abide with God.—1 Corinthians 7:24

There is a slight difference between verses twenty and twenty–four of First Corinthians chapter seven which is not apparent to the English reader. Verse twenty says: "Let every man abide in the same calling wherein he was called." Verse twenty–four says: "Brethren, let every man, wherein he is called, therein abide with God."

"Calling" in Greek is *klésis*, which is a feminine noun. Therefore, when the relative pronoun is used, it is the feminine dative *hé*, referring to the particular calling itself. In verse twenty–four, however, the stress is not on the actual calling of the Lord, but on the position and state to which that calling has led the individual believer.[1]

In the life of the Christian there are two things to consider. One is the actual calling of the Lord, the wooing of His Spirit to enter into the Kingdom of

God, and then there is the position or state to which
a believer has grown. This is recognized by the
Apostle Paul. All believers are in Christ, but our positions within the circle of Christ are not all the
same. Our spiritual progress is the result of our obedience to Christ and the fulfillment of the conditions
that He has set to reach our appointed goal. What the
Apostle Paul is saying to the Corinthians here is:
"Stay where you are, or where you have managed to
come, which is the state of your achievement in the
circle of Christ. All Christians are equal at the foot of
the cross, but not all Christians are the same in their
ability to accomplish things for Christ. In that state
which you have achieved by the grace of God, stay,
and don't turn back and lose ground. Don't be lured
to a static position or to a retreat." This is the
Apostle Paul's admonition in verse twenty–four. In
the Christian walk, robust Christians move ahead.
There are Christians stationed all along the way of
Christ, and each one has a particular task to perform
wherever he is found.

In addition, there is a very important clause at
the end of this verse to which we shall do well to
pay attention. In English it is expressed with two
words: "with God." In the Greek in this context,
pará has the meaning of "near" rather than "with"
God. The thought implied is that as a Christian believer you may find yourself far ahead or far behind
other Christians. Your task may be something that
seems very important or perhaps very unimportant
in the walk of the Christian life. Don't be overly

concerned about it. Continue on and do what you are supposed to do; recognize the original calling of God in your life; don't worry that others are ahead of you or behind you, but have as your primary concern that you are near God.

On the Christian pathway, we may occupy different positions, but no matter what position we occupy, everyone of us can and should be near God, that proximity to Him made possible through our obedience to Jesus Christ. And it makes absolutely no difference, Paul stresses, whether we are married or unmarried when it comes to accomplishing our specific calling of God. The married ones should not look down upon the single and vice versa.

Paul has shifted in this verse from the direct imperative used in the previous verse, "Be not (*mḗ gínesthe*) slaves of men," to *menétō* "let him remain." This verse is in exactly the same form as the verb in verse twenty (durative present imperative) which means, "Let him abide" where he is already. Paul does not refer here to a new goal that the Christian ought to actively seek. He is warning him to be on his guard in his present state of freedom in Christ lest other Christians endeavor to enslave him to a life of legalism as indicated in verse twenty–three. He refers to a life of joy and satisfaction in the state and position that the believer's obedience to Christ has enabled him to achieve. He must not allow anybody to move him backward or hinder him from moving forward. He must stand firm. This does not mean he is to be static, but rather to be satisfied in his present achievement and position that God has granted.

---

¹To distinguish this, it is not the relative pronoun in the feminine dative that is used, but the relative pronoun in the neuter, *hō*. And in the second clause of verse twenty–four, again the dative neuter is used, *en*, "in," *toútō*, "this very position or state" resulting from the original calling of the Lord.

35

PAUL'S OPINION, NOT THE LORD'S COMMAND

Now concerning virgins, I have no commandment of the Lord: yet I give my judgment, as one that hath obtained mercy of the Lord to be faithful.—1 Corinthians 7:25

After admonishing believers to be content and abide in their God–given state, Paul turns his attention to the virgin Christians. The verse begins with the preposition *perí* meaning "concerning, about." This is the second time that this preposition is used in this chapter, verse one having also begun with *perí*. It therefore introduces the second large section of the answer which Paul gave to the Corinthians concerning their evident questions about marriage and its problems in Corinth.

The Corinthians apparently had asked Paul whether Christ Himself had left any directive concerning unmarried girls as to whether they should or should not marry. It is quite possible that there were some believers in Corinth who were teaching that the Lord had revealed answers to these questions directly to them. This seems to be a common error throughout Christendom. In many communities of Christians, there are those who believe or pretend that they have had direct revelations of God concerning specific situations, and they try to impose those views upon others. In their letter, therefore, it seems the Corinthian Christians inquired of Paul whether in reality he knew of any such commandments that the Lord gave concerning these matters. After all, he was an apostle and may have had more intimate and detailed knowledge of Christ's revelations. The believers in Corinth knew that Paul would be absolutely honest in telling them what the Lord really commanded and what he deduced from those commandments as the proper solutions to specific problems. And Paul is meticulous in stating exactly what was a commandment of the Lord and what was his own recommendation. In his honesty, he did not want anyone to be misled into believing that his personal opinion was a commandment of the Lord. When something was definitely commanded by the Lord, he states so as in verses ten and eleven. When the Lord was silent on a particular subject, Paul is honest enough to say so (vv. 12, 25).

Paul's honesty does not mean that what his words are to be disregarded by Christians as insignificant. The apostles in their epistles complement and supplement what Jesus said. They never contradict. They simply elaborate upon certain specific situations which were not dealt with by the Lord.

The general context, however, in which a statement was given must always be considered. It is no contradiction when in one set of circumstances the answer may be "yes," and in another set of circumstances the answer may be "no." We, as parents responsible for our children, many times would give permission for our child to do something in one set of circumstances that we would forbid at another time. If my child, for instance, wants to go out to ride his bicycle at midnight or at a time that he ought to be studying, I forbid it. If he asks, however, to ride his bike at a time that is proper for his physical exercise, then I permit it. That's exactly what the Apostle Paul is trying to do in his advice to the Corinthians. There are certain circumstances when it is good for a person to remain single, and there are certain circumstances when it is good for a person to marry. The situation determines the course of action.

Who Are the Virgins of Whom Paul Speaks?

To whom does Paul refer when he speaks of the maidens or the virgins? The Greek word is *parthénos* which can be either masculine or feminine. It is derived from *paratheínai*, "to lay out or set apart," and so alluded to the secluded life of virgins in Eastern countries and among the ancient Greeks.[1]

Two Hebrew words are translated "virgin" in the King James Version—*bᵉthūlāh* and *'almāh*. The first of these comes from a root word meaning "to separate," and is the common word for a woman who has never had sexual intercourse and is truly the equivalent to the Greek *parthénos*.[2] Therefore, the two Hebrew names for a virgin (to one or the other of which *parthénos* in the Septuagint most commonly answers) refer to their secluded, concealed mode of living.[3]

The Greek word *parthénos* in the New Testament means "a virgin, a maiden, a maid," as in Matthew 1:23, Acts 21:9 and 1 Corinthians 7:28. The word is used in reference to sexual morality, chastity, the fact that a girl has never known a man. It is spoken of the Church of Corinth, expressing Paul's desire to present her to Christ as pure from corrupt doctrines and practices as in 1 Corinthians 11:2. It is applied to believers in general, whether they be men or women, married or single, as unpolluted by idolatrous abominations as in Revelation 14:4.

While technically it could refer to both men and women in 1 Corinthians 7:25. However, the general context of verses twenty–eight through thirty–four and the fact that the word is used exclusively with the feminine definite article *hē*, to denote a female virgin, we must conclude that indisputably the word here is virgin maidens, referring only to women who are chaste and who have never known a man. This word must be distinguished from *agámois*, "umarried ones," used in verses eight and thirty–two to refer to men or women who, though they are not presently married, might have been married sometime before. When Paul wanted to refer distinctly to a virgin who was unmarried, as in verse thirty–four, he said: "There is difference also between a wife (*gunē*) and a virgin (*hē parthénos*, 'the female virgin')." Then he said, "the unmarried one," and that "one" is translated as the "unmarried woman" because the feminine article *hē* appears before *agámos*.

Fathers Used to Give Their Daughters in Marriage

Undoubtedly, then, Paul is speaking to virgin maidens who were chaste all their lives and whose fathers were wondering whether it was better for them to be given in marriage or to be kept secluded for the purposes of chastity. The entire passage has to be studied in the context of the custom that existed at that time, namely, that it was the father's responsibility to give or not to give his daughter away in marriage. This is expressed by the verb *ekgamízō* of verse thirty–eight translated, "he that giveth her in marriage." What Paul has to say, therefore, in this particular passage can be applied to our modern society only in a restricted way since usually today, except in some Eastern countries, it is not the father who gives away his daughter in marriage. Nowadays the daughters themselves select their own husbands and make up their own minds. Intrinsic, though, in the expression Paul's opinion as to what a Christian father should do are certain guidelines to be understood in the decision that present–day maidens themselves must make.

Paul's Counsel Concerning Virgin Maidens

Paul wants it very clearly understood as to what is the Lord's command, what is an apostolic command, and what is his opinion which he expresses without attributing to it apostolic authority. Paul wants his comments in verse twenty–five to be clearly understood as his own opinion, without the authority which Christ's commandments and apostolic commandments would entail. How very careful we should be ourselves to distinguish between what is divinely inspired Scripture and what is opinion and interpretation as we give it out.

The Greek word translated "commandment" in 1 Corinthians 7:25 is not the same as the one found in 1 Corinthians 7:19. In verse nineteen, reference is made to the known and declared commandments of God,[4] while in verse twenty–five it actually means to take someone or something and put that person or thing where it belongs. This word, when used in the Septuagint, means God's ordinances (Wis. 18:15; 19:6; the *Ordinances of the Ruler* in Wis. 14:17; I Ezras 1:16; Dan. 3:16; III Mac. 7:20).

What Paul Says About Virgins Is a Mere Directive, Not the Lord's Command

In the New Testament, the word occurs only in the writings of Paul, and always (except in 1 Cor. 7:25 and Titus 2:15) in the expression *kat' epitagén*, "according to the commandment." This refers to a directive by those in high office who have something to say and to which heed must be given. The verb is used in Mark 1:27; 9:25, and Luke 8:31 in the case of Jesus' strong command to demons. From the use of the word in 1 Corinthians, we have an indication that detailed norms of Christian conduct developed in primitive Christianity. The force and application of the word *epitagé* "commandment," depends on the person who gives it. It is so today; a directive receives its importance from the person who gives it.

Paul used the same word in the sixth verse of this chapter: "But I speak this by permission, and not of commandment (*kat' epitagén*)." This, in other words, is not a normative commandment. Paul did not want to be understood by what he was saying in verse five that he was making marital intercourse a general ethical requirement. This is why he adds in verse seven, "For I would that all men were even as I myself. But every man hath his proper gift of God, one after this manner, and another after that." Therefore in 1 Corinthians 7:6 as in 2 Corinthians 8:8, the "not by command" stands in contrast to the idea of an imperative. When Paul wants to assert his apostolic authority, he uses the verb *diatásso-mai* as in verse seventeen, inferring that he is giving a command that is general and applicable to all the churches. Here, distinctly, he is giving a mere *epitagé*, a directive which may or may not be obeyed.

Such would not have been the case if Paul was giving this directive as having been received from

God or Jesus Christ or if he had issued it as an apostle. He makes it clear, however, that this is not the case. As Paul advises Titus (2:15), there is an authority inherent in the opinion of a person because of who he is. Titus 2:15 says "These things speak, and exhort, and rebuke with all authority (*epitagē*). Let no man despise thee." The word translated "authority" is exactly the same word that the Apostle Paul used in 1 Corinthians 7:25. This is counsel which Paul gives not by apostolic authority or having received a directive from Christ. It is given only as a fellow believer and one who has genuine pastoral concern, one who was the spiritual father to the church in Corinth and who cares for the people there and how they conduct themselves. This counsel could be accepted, modified, or rejected according as each had been called of God to His purpose.

Paul Expresses an Opinion Which Is to Be Acted Upon Concerning Virgin Maidens

To qualify the meaning of *epitagē*, "commandment," that the person to whom it is addressed may or may not obey, Paul adds, "but I give an opinion as one who has had mercy conferred upon him by the Lord so that he may be trustworthy." The word that we have translated "opinion," and which in some versions is translated "judgment," is a Greek word meaning "to know, think, determine."[5] It is an opinion which one forms in examining a certain situation. (The word is also found in 1 Cor. 1:10; 7:40;

2 Cor. 8:10.) It is definitely related to the word *noús*, "mind," and generally means the capacity to form a judgment or exercise discernment in one's mind for the conduct that he should pursue.[6] Accordingly, what Paul is saying in 1 Corinthians 7:25 is that he has an opinion, *gnómēn*, which is not something that should be heard and put on a shelf, but something that should be received and acted upon voluntarily. It is as if Paul is saying to these Corinthians: "I don't have a directive from Jesus Christ, and I cannot give you an apostolic directive, but I am expressing an opinion which I hope will cause you to decide voluntarily to do that which I am suggesting." Paul is not presenting here to the Corinthian Church an opinion that he wants them to vote on and thus make it a church directive that all who are part of that church must obey. If he wanted to say this he would not have used the verb *dídōmi*, "I give," which in its basic meaning is "to give, to bestow or confer without price or reward. " Rather, he is saying: "Here's my opinion. It won't cost you anything, but I hope you will do what I am saying."

But if Paul's opinion was meant to be put to an examination and a vote by the members of the Corinthian Church, he would have used the verbs *eisēgéomai*, *eisphérō*, or *protíthēmi*, "to introduce, to bring into, or to present." The Apostle Paul did not ask and did not expect formal church acquiescence when he gave expression to his opinion as a fellow believer.

What a marvelous attitude Paul displays for any believer who is associated with a local congregation. A member may express his opinion but not ask or expect the other believers in the congregation to confirm his opinion and make it as a normative commandment for everyone to obey. There are many things that can be done or not done, and many opinions to be held or not held by believers in a local congregation without everybody necessarily toeing the same line. If Paul felt that as a fellow believer of the Corinthians his opinions could be either accepted or rejected, although he was hoping that they would move the Corinthian Church to the same dedication he experienced, how much more amiable should we be toward others.

The Path of Matrimony or Celibacy Is Not Strewn with Roses—It Requires God's Mercy

That Paul is not speaking forth a direct commandment of the Lord or does not issue an apostolic edict, he makes clear by the expression translated, "As one who has had mercy conferred upon him by the Lord."[7] He specifies that this mercy has been extended upon him from the Lord. It states that he placed himself under the source of mercy and he effectively received it. Here Paul is not speaking about grace, *cháris*, which leads a person to salvation and has to do with redemption. He is speaking of mercy, *éleos*, which relates to God's comfort, His compassion not for the character of a person in changing it, but for the state in which he is found as a result of a decision he has made. We are to be merciful toward others. We can see the unhappy consequences of their decisions and we must have compassion as we see them suffer those consequences. I cannot, as a believer, show grace to a drunkard, but I can show mercy to him. My mercifulness extends to the results of his being a drunkard. I cannot change his character, but I can take him somewhere and give him something to eat, alleviating the consequences of his sin.

In this passage, Paul tells us how he himself remained unmarried. That decision had certain definite results in his life, surely some pleasant and some unpleasant. For those unpleasant experiences or results of the single life, he has been experiencing the mercy of the Lord. What he states here is that the Lord can compensate for that which we forsake for the sake of that which we consider to be primary in our lives for His glory. Perhaps we can interpret this as saying that having been single all his life hadn't been a rosy path, but the Lord had been with him and had shown His compassion in all the inconveniences of the single life. In neither the single nor the married life can the path be in its totality all roses. Remember that the mercy of God is available to both the one who is single and the one who is married. As long as the Christian places himself or herself under God, His mercy is available in abundant measure to make up the minuses of any life resulting from a decison sincerely made which involves no compromise of the direct commandments of God and of the apostles.

Paul Claims Trustworthiness in the Expression of His Motive in Celibacy

The final two words of this marvelous verse in Greek are *pistós eínai*, "so that I be trustworthy." This would be a better translation than "so that I am trustworthy." It is the same word with which 1 Corinthians 1:9 begins speaking of God's dependability. Paul wasn't trying to boast that he was trustworthy, but in the expression of his personal opinion in the matters that perplexed the Corinthians, he wanted them to trust him. Opinions are usually disregarded unless the person who receives them considers the one who gives them to be trustworthy. Paul does not speak of his opinions as being trustworthy but of himself. When people believe in us, they will accept what we say as genuine. The word *pistós* can mean one who believes firmly and one who may be trusted. Paul was anxious not to prove his fidelity to Jesus Christ, but his credibility in the genuineness of his motive in giving this advice which came out of his own experience.

---

[1]This is a periphrastic translation of the perfect passive participle *eleeménos* of the verb *eleéō*, from *éleos*, "mercy." The verb means "to pity" in its active form and "to be pitied or to be merciful to" (*eleéomai*).

²See Parkhurst's *Greek and English Lexicon to the New Testament.*

³Metaphorically, it is used of groups of people, nations, and names of places, e.g., the virgin of Israel (Jer. 18:13; 31:4, 21; Amos 5:2); the virgin daughter of Zion (Is. 37:22); Judah (Lam. 1:15); Zidon (Is. 23:12); Babylon (Is. 47:1); Egypt (Jer. 46:11). The second word, *'almāh,* is derived from a root meaning "to be sexually mature," and refers to a woman of marriagable age who has not yet borne children although she may be married. It occurs seven times in the Old Testament and is translated "virgin," "maid," and "damsels." The Greek equivalent to *'almāh* is usually *neánis,* "a young woman," but in Genesis 24:43, speaking of Rebekah, and in Isaiah 7:14, *parthénos* is used. As a result, the Isaiah passage has been accepted since early Christian times as a prophecy of the virgin birth of Christ (Matt. 1:23), as it is indeed since Matthew 1:23 does not say *neánis,* but *parthénos.*

⁴Thus, in II Maccabees 3:19 are mentioned *hai katákleistoi tōn parthénōn,* "the virgins who were shut up"; that is to say, who went not out of their parents' houses due to virgin modesty and purity. Also, III Maccabees 1:18 speaks of *hai katákleistoi parthénoi en thalámois,* "the virgins that were shut up in the chambers."

⁵The Greek word is *entolé,* (singular of *entolaí*), while in 1 Corinthians 7:25, the word *epitagé* is used. This substantive is derived from the verb *epitássō,* from *epí,* "upon," or used as an intensive, and *tássō,* "to order, to appoint, to place in its particular category."

⁶*Gnōmē,* a substantive derived from the verb *ginōskō* or *gnóō.*

⁷The two words *noús,* "mind," and *gnōmē,* "opinion," are found in 1 Corinthians 1:10. It is clear therefore that *noús* and *gnōmē,* while connected, are nevertheless to be distinguished. *Noús* refers to the ability to think as a whole and form judgments, but *gnōmē* implies not mere opinion per se, but the direction and action toward which that opinion should lead a person. Hence, it is conviction, judgment, opinion, that moves

a person to do that which he believes he should do after having examined a certain situation. *Noús* could be said to be more or less subjective, while *gnómē* is a subjective mind that projects itself to the accomplishment of something.

36

WHEN CONTEMPLATING MARRIAGE, THINK OF THE CIRCUMSTANCES

I suppose therefore that this is good for the present distress, I say, that it is good for a man so to be.—1 Corinthians 7:26

Paul now proceeds to state his personal opinion as to whether a virgin maiden should be given by her father as a wife to someone, or should be kept as a maiden.

In our present society, and particularly in western society, such consideration must be made not so much by the father, but by the girl herself. Is it really better to marry or not to marry? This can only be answered by the individual woman. Marrying means adding responsibilities to oneself. It entails having a husband and probably children and exercising care and concern about them. How many times do we hear the statement, "I'm afraid to bring children into the world." As evil and difficulties abound, such feelings become more prevalent. It is a feeling of personal responsibility in bringing suffering upon the lives of others, and especially children. When our Lord spoke of the tribulation, He showed special concern for pregnant women. We read in Matthew 24:19: "And woe unto them that are with child, and to them that give suck in those days!" When one is married, there is natural concern for one's children. And Paul expresses this concern as one of the reasons why he himself decided to remain single, projecting it as a valid reason for other men and women to consider remaining single as he did.

What Factors Should Determine One's Decision to Marry or Not?

The considerations as Paul has expressed them until now are the following in order of importance:

1. *Ability to Be Chaste*
   If a person finds it natural to contain himself, then he may consider himself as a good candidate for celibacy. If he does not have this God–given ability to contain himself, then it is better to marry than to burn, as Paul has already stated.

2. *One's Goal in Life*
   Consider one's calling of God in life. Can it be best accomplished by being single or married? A Christian can be motivated to

sublimate his sexual instinct in his desire to accomplish what God has called him to achieve.

3. *The Particular Circumstances of Life*

Look around at the circumstances as they exist or as they may develop as a result of the state of matrimony in your own particular instance. Circumstances must be considered, and especially circumstances that one cannot help. Such were the circumstances existing at the time of Paul.

Exercising Hindsight, Paul Thought He Had Made the Right Decision to Stay Single

How would the wife of Paul, if he had had one, have felt in regard to the experiences that he went through as recorded in 2 Corinthians 11:23–30? He was in abundant labors, he was beaten, he was imprisoned, he was in danger of death, five times he received forty stripes save one, three times he was in a shipwreck, a night and day he spent in the deep, he was in many journeys, he was in perils of waters, in perils of robbers, in perils by his own countrymen, in perils by the heathen, in perils in the city, in perils in the wilderness, in perils in the sea, in perils among false brethren. He was weary. He experienced pain. He was often in hunger and thirst, often cold and naked. He often suffered from the internal strifes of the churches he established. As Paul thought back on his life, he decided that, after all, his foresight about not getting married was correct.

Actually 1 Corinthians 7:26 implies this: "I think I haven't made a mistake in staying single. Therefore, this is my opinion."

The verb that is used for "think" in Greek is *nomízō*, from *nómos*, "law." What the legislator thinks right and fit is established by law; hence it signifies "think, be of opinion." This verb is definitely related to the word *gnómēn*, "opinion," used in the previous verse. In that verse, Paul said, I give an opinion, and now he says, This is what I think to be right.

What does he mean by the pronoun *toúto*, "this"? He is referring to the state of celibacy for virgin girls. It cannot be taken, however, as the object of the verb "I think." It is rather the subject of the infinitive *hupárchein*, "to be." I think, therefore, says Paul, that this (the state of celibacy) is good because of the present distress, that it is proper for a person to be so.

It's interesting to note that in Greek what we have translated as "is" (*hupárchein*, the infinitive of *hupárchō*) refers to an existence or condition both previous to the circumstances mentioned and continuing thereafter. This is the same verb in the present participle used in Philippians 2:6 concerning the deity of Christ. The phrase, "being (existing) in the form of God," carries with it the two facts of the antecedent Godhead of Christ, previous to His incarnation, and the continuance of His Godhead at and after the event of His birth. It is used also in the same infinitive form in 1 Corinthians 11:18 as in 1 Corinthians 7:26. In the former it is translated in the King James Version as "there be." This indicates that there were divisions prior to the time that Paul was writing and at the time when he was writing. In 1 Corinthians 7:26 Paul says, "I therefore think that this is good"; in other words, the state of celibacy is good or has proven to be good before and after the circumstances of distress of which he's speaking. As he looks back, he can see justification for his forethought in remaining single, assuring the Corinthians that it was good before he made the decision, and it was good after he made it.

Why Paul Remained Single

Paul then proceeds to explain why it has been good for him to remain single: "because of the present distress." This is a unique expression.[1] The verb is used of the present in contrast with the past as in Hebrews 9:9 where the Revised Version correctly has "for the time *now* present," and not as the King James Version has it, "*then* present." It is used also in contrast to the future. (See Rom. 8:38; 1 Cor. 3:22 and Gal. 1:4.) In 1 Corinthians 7:26, the present distress is set in contrast to both the past and the future. In this way this participle agrees fully with the infinitive *huparchein* which refers to a past and a present condition. This distress of which Paul is speaking is not to be understood as the problems that may emerge as a result of the marriage itself. No one should look only at the difficulties of marriage which are inherent to it and reject it on that basis alone. If such were the case, marriage would be inadvisable for all. It is rather the intrinsic nature of life itself with its difficulties of all sorts apart from the bond of marriage that Paul is speaking about. There are difficulties prior to marriage, but because of marriage they are accentuated for then one has to face them not only as an individual, but with the added marital responsibilities.

This "present" distress of which Paul speaks stands in contrast to the future distress which he does not mention. No one should so project himself into the future and its difficulties that he is unable to consider marriage. When a person becomes obsessed about the future, he will never be able to do anything in the present. "Sufficient unto the day is the evil thereof," our Lord tells us. Thus Paul, through the use of this word, directs that we should not dwell too much on future difficulties but on the present situation as it exists. If present circumstances do not compel one to avoid marriage, then speculations over the future are not to prevent a Christian from considering marriage.

What is translated "distress" in Greek means necessity, a compelling force as opposed to willingness (as is found also in 2 Cor. 9:7 and Phile. 1:14).[2] In 1 Corinthians 7:26 it refers to distress and affliction not inherent to marriage, but independent of it.[3] Paul, speaking of the circumstances of life prevalent at the time he was writing, said it is hard to cope with the pressure which comes upon a person who faces difficulties beyond his ability to manage. His advice is to look at the present conditions of life and consider seriously your ability to face them. If you will be better able to face them in singleness, stay single. If you'll be better able to face them as a married man or woman, then proceed to marry.

In the last part of the verse he explains further the pronoun *toúto*, "this," of the previous clause, referring to the state of virginity and celibacy—that is good for a person, for man, so to be. He does not use the word *parthénon*, "virgin maiden," as he used in the previous verse because this is a general principle that can be applied not only to a virgin maiden, but to any single person contemplating marriage. Consequently, he now uses the generic word "man," or a person (*anthrópō*, the dative of *ánthrōpos*). The verb that he uses in this last clause (not *hupárchein*, as in the previous clause, but *eínai*, the present infinitive of *eimí*) refers only to a person's present state. In other words, he is to remain as he is without any consideration of the past, whether he was previously married or not. Paul in no way is referring here to an unfortunate past marriage.

[1]In Greek it is *enestósan*, the accusative singular feminine perfect participle of the verb *enístēmi* from *en*, "in, with," and *hístēmi*, "to stand, to be present or at hand, or to set in."

[2]*Anágkē* from the emphatic *aná*, and *ágchō*, "to constrict, bind hard, compress."

[3]It is used with the same sense in Luke 21:23; 2 Cor. 6:4; 12:10; 1 Thess. 3:7.

37

EXTERNAL CIRCUMSTANCES SHOULD NOT CAUSE ANYONE TO CHANGE HIS MARITAL STATUS

Art thou bound unto a wife? Seek not to be loosed. Art thou loosed from a wife? Seek not a wife.—1 Corinthians 7:27

Paul has already spoken in verse twenty–six concerning circumstances in life which a person ought to take into consideration when contemplating the important matter of marriage. It is good, he said, for anyone to remain as he is if marriage is going to add to his cares which, in turn, would hinder him from faithfully executing the purpose and goal of life to which the Lord has called him.

Paul then proceeded to elaborate on what he had just said in verse twenty–six in order to avoid any misunderstanding. He did not want anyone to say: "If circumstances are to be taken into consideration,

then the same situations can provide reasons to dissolve a marriage in which a couple had entered
without seriously thinking of the circumstances that
were present at the time." Paul wants to make one
thing absolutely clear through the intricate meaning
of the infinitive *hupárchein* of the first phrase of
verse twenty–six translated "is"—"I suppose therefore that this is good for the present distress." This
infinitive means actually not only the present situation in which a person is found, but also that in
which he was found in the past and continues to be
found. It is an already existing condition. He does
not refer to a new situation which may arise after
marriage, for there is none which would provide an
excuse for divorce excepting fornication on the part
of one of the marriage partners according to the
words of Christ in Matthew 5:32. Before marriage
occurs, a person has the right and the obligation to
examine the circumstances of his life, particularly
of his immediate environment and also the general
situation in which he is found. But there is no dissolving of the marriage after it has been instituted.

God Binds a Couple in Marriage

Paul speaks of being married as being bound.
This is why verse twenty–seven begins with the
verb *dédesai*[1] from a root word meaning "to fasten
by transposition or to tie with a chain or rope or
cord or the like." In this instance of 1 Corinthians
7:27, 39, as also in Romans 7:2, it means to bind or

oblige by a moral or religious obligation. Modern–day man is exactly right when he refers to getting married as "tying the knot."

The passive voice in which this verb is found indicates that this binding was not something that a person did by himself, but it is a binding that has come upon that person once he has given himself, or has been given, to marriage. In giving oneself to marriage, a person is giving him or herself to a binding or a chaining to another. It is not the individual himself who is performing the act of binding to another, but God who is making a single unit out of what had previously been two. The binding has been done by God Himself as the Lord Jesus taught in Matthew 19:6, and therefore man should not separate what God has joined together.

Personal Responsibility of One Marriage Partner to the Other

Paul does not use the verb in the second person plural (*dédeste*) which would refer to both parties of the marriage, but the singular, *"thou* art bound" (*dédesai*). This impresses the commitment upon each of the two partners of marriage to exercise individual responsibility toward the other. In marriage, each partner must have an overwhelming sense of personal responsibility toward the other. This binding cannot be broken by common agreement simply because the two partners decide in mutual consent that they are incompatible or do not love each other anymore.

It is true that one party in marriage may break the relationship as Paul already has discussed in verses ten through seventeen. A Christian spouse may be forsaken by an unbelieving partner. The Christian spouse should do everything possible in order to prevent this and to gain the vow of the unbelieving spouse to live faithfully with him or her without sexual deviations. But in the last analysis, the unbelieving and/or unfaithful partner might depart in spite of the believing spouse's efforts to the contrary, in which case the believing spouse has no choice. The believer has considered himself or herself bound to the marriage partner, and is not actually the one who has done anything to bring about the dissolution of the marriage. Marriage is like peace between nations. It depends to a great extent on the attitude of each one, but it cannot be preserved if the attitude of one is hostile. As Paul says in Romans 12:18: "If it be possible, as much lieth in you, live peaceably with all men." It is the same thing with marriage, Paul stresses in this verse. It is each partner's own personal responsibility as an individual to keep that marriage bond intact and to live together peacefully.

The Bond of Marriage Transcends Emotionalism

The necessity of keeping the marriage bond intact is not merely a feeling of obligation which would have been better expressed by another Greek word, *opheílō*, but rather the word *déō* which denotes necessity by virtue of the nature of things. Thus we find that this attachment in marriage is far greater than emotion; it is a necessity that is unavoidable, urgent and compulsory. It is mandatory to remain bound to your marital spouse whether or not you feel like it or whether or not you have a sense of obligation. There is no changing of the mind or claiming a lack of love which could constitute any basis whatsoever for the personal dissolution of marriage.

The Binding in Marriage Is to One Wife

Although Paul speaks only to the husband being bound to a wife,[2] by implication he definitely refers also to the sense of obligation that a married woman should have toward her husband. The singular usage of this noun, of course, indicates the constant, monogamous teaching of the New Testament. If Paul did not want to stress monogamy, he could have very easily just used the verb *dédesai*, "thou art bound." But he adds "unto a wife," indicating only one wife, not more than one.

Paul is speaking here to believers since he could not regulate the life of unbelievers. He wants to instruct believers what to do in the difficult situations of marriage which come about by virtue of changes in the circumstances of life. He has already given instructions to those who have never been married or who were married and have become widowed. They have the choice to marry or to stay unmarried. But to those who are already married, Paul teaches that they must remain married in fidelity to the principles of God and the pure life He desires for His children.

---

[1]The second person singular perfect indicative passive of *déō*.

[2]*Gunaikí*, the dative singular of *gunḗ*.

38

RATIONALIZING THE DISSOLUTION OF A MARRIAGE

... Seek not to be loosed ... —1 Corinthians 7:27

Here Paul gives a direct command: "Seek not to be loosed."[1] In this instance, as also in Matthew 2:13, 20 and Romans 11:3, we believe that the verb means to seek insidiously with a hostile or malicious design. The present indicative would lead us to believe that what Paul is trying to prevent here is an attitude in which a spouse constantly, maliciously, and by direct intention, is looking for an opportunity to dissolve the marriage. Such a temptation should never be allowed to take root, for marriage then becomes nothing more than an endeavor to give an evil motive to everything that one's partner does in order to achieve one's sinful design—the dissolution of the marriage.

Attitude is everything in marriage, and reactions to a spouse's actions are a demonstration of one's own attitude toward his or her spouse. What one spouse does can be considered either angelic or satanic depending on the attitude of the other. If one partner's heart is set on the destruction of the marriage, then nothing the other one does can be right. A far more harmonious atmosphere will develop if, instead of criticizing or attempting to change the other, that spouse works on changing his own attitude. With prayer and dependence upon God, it can be done.

The translation of one word, *lúsin*,[2] is expressed with four words in English: "not to be loosed." Actually the Greek text says, "Do not constantly seek dissolution," referring of course to marriage. It is the unbinding of the bond or chain of marriage. Here the verb *lúō*, "to dissolve or set loose or to untie," as generally in the New Testament, stands in direct antithesis to *déō*, "to bind, to tie." Do not seek to put asunder what God hath joined together. A Christian should not actively, personally seek the dissolution of marriage, but rather the strengthening and improving of it under all circumstances.

Guidelines if a Marriage Has Ended

Paul then proceeds to speak of the opposite eventuality. He says: "Art thou loosed from a wife? Seek not a wife." Again, he refers here only to the husband, but by implication the same truth applies to the wife. What is translated with "Art thou loosed" in Greek is *lélusai*,[3] "to dissolve or unbind." As before, Paul uses the singular and not the plural. He does not speak to both marriage partners because usually the dissolution begins in the heart of one of the two. Therefore this verb must be taken as inferring the personal responsibility as to the future state in which a divorced person will be found without reference to what led to the breakup of the marriage. It may have occurred by an unbelieving husband or wife who decided to forsake the newborn child of God rather than forsake his life of fornication.

The singular tense of this verb indicates that the person to whom Paul is speaking is no longer bound to the spouse. The other eventuality of a spouse being loosed from a marriage partner is when, on the authority of Christ's permission in Matthew 5:32, he or she leaves the marriage partner because the latter is unfaithful sexually.

On the above two reasons, the teaching of the New Testament has been, as we have already elaborated, that the innocent loosed partner is free if he or she so desires to remarry.

When Is a Christian Divorced Spouse Not Permitted to Remarry?

A third eventuality is if a Christian marriage partner, for no legitimate scriptural reason, leaves the spouse. In such a case, that partner is not permitted to remarry.

These details have already been dealt with, and what Paul says in this verse really does not affect those detailed situations that prescribe what a loosed marital partner can or cannot do. In this verse, the

Apostle Paul is giving his own personal advice as to what is better and more advisable for the Christian to do in view of his present situation of a dissolved marriage.

Learn From a Past Marriage Failure

Paul does not specify the reason for the dissolution of marriage. He simply says "Art thou loosed from a wife? Seek not a wife." If you are found in the state of a broken marriage, he is saying, let the past be a lesson for the future. Don't fall into the same trap or into the same propensity of desires. Examine the circumstances which may have contributed to the breakup of the marriage and don't enter into the same kind of circumstances.

In view of this, we must always remember what Paul said in verse twenty–six, that the unmarried person ought to view the present needs of life and accordingly decide whether marriage is the proper state to enter into or not. In the same way, if you find yourself loosed from a former marriage, have your eyes wide open and make your examination of the present situation absolutely complete and unbiased. Don't rush into another marriage that may result in the same fate as the first marriage.

Thus we see that Paul examines each state of the believer systematically. First, he examines those who have never been married, the virgins. Secondly, he examines those who have been married and are now single, perhaps because of death. And thirdly, he examines those who were married and are no more married because of the dissolution of their marriage, without referring to the cause of the dissolution.

As the virgins ought to consider the circumstances of life before they enter into marriage, so also those whose marriages have failed ought to consider even more carefully the circumstances which led to that failure in order not to repeat the same mistake. When Paul says, "Seek not a wife," it is not an expression of misogyny on his part. He doesn't express a hatred of women or a disapproval of marriage, because we find in the twenty–eighth verse that he presents the case of such marriage by both virgins and formerly married Christians. When he says, "Do not constantly seek a wife or a woman," he means don't rush into it, don't always have first and foremost in mind the desire to find another woman. Let your attitude rather be that of waiting upon the Lord.

The first consideration of the Christian should be a life of holiness and purity, a life of utmost glory to God who gives life itself. Since Paul actually does not limit his admonition only to formerly married men, the expression, "Seek not a wife," could be interpreted as following: Seek not a new marriage impetuously without due consideration of the past and present circumstances as relate to marriage and your total usefulness in God's service.

---

[1]In Greek the verb is *mē*, "not," *zétei*, second person singular present imperative active of *zētéō*, "to seek."

[2]The accusative singular of *lúsis*, "dissolution."

[3]Second person singular perfect indicative passive of *lúō*.

39

MARRIAGE IS A MATTER OF PERSONAL DECISION

But and if thou marry, thou hast not sinned;
and if a virgin marry, she hath not sinned. . . .
—1 Corinthians 7:28

When the Apostle Paul said in the previous verse, "Seek not a wife," he ran the risk of being greatly misunderstood. If we were to take this commandment or advice out of its context and follow it, many Christians would be unmarried because they would be afraid that marriage would add burdensome responsibilities in a world that is already full of difficulties and troubles.

A good example of this is the Shakers who espoused celibacy for their members. As a result, there was no propagation of their generations and the denomination has virtually disappeared. If all of Christendom were to follow this literally, Christianity itself would probably soon cease to exist.

"But and if thou marry, thou hast not sinned," continued Paul. The Greek expression *"eán dé kaí"* literally translated is "if and," or "but even."[1] This verse would be better rendered "Nevertheless, even if thou shalt marry, thou didst not sin." The suppositional sentence takes away from the previous one, "Seek not a wife," which has the strength of a command. It reduces it to simple, personal advice which is based not on a divine requirement or moral precept, but merely on expediency. It definitely allows for personal decision which should not be subject to criticism by other Christians.

What Paul said basically is that it is good to consider all the circumstances at the time that you are thinking of marriage to see whether those circumstances are the best possible climate and conditions for marriage, and how at the same time you can live a holy life and accomplish the purpose for which God has called you as an individual. That is all that can be read into that piece of advice Paul gave, "Seek not a wife."

To Marry Is an Individual's Decision

The fact that the verb "marry," *gémēs* or *gaméses* in Greek in this verse, is in the aorist indicates that this refers to the once–and–for–all entrance into the institutional bond of marriage. In modern Greek the word is *gámos*. While the noun gamos has maintained its ancient meaning of marriage, the verb *gaméō* has become corrupted in its meaning and refers to sexual intercourse, as if that were the only reason why one marries. In fact, there was recently an article in a Greek newspaper in which the writer was attacking the Scriptures as a book of vulgar expressions. He was referring to the use of the verb *gaméō*, taking it to mean what modern Greeks refer to as sexual intercourse instead of entering into contractual marriage. Unfortunately, in many instances marriage has become nothing more than a common bed instead of a oneness of life as God meant it to be.[2]

It is interesting indeed that the Apostle Paul speaks directly to the individual in this passage, not using the second person plural but the second person singular which is lost, of course, when one uses the personal pronoun "you" in the translation. In English this pronoun may refer to either one person or many persons, but it is actually in the singular, "thou." This is confirmation that the Apostle Paul wants the decision to marry to be an individual decision. It is a matter of personal, individual conviction, and not to be imposed upon anyone.

Not only is this word in the second person singular, but it is also in the active voice which indicates a personal, voluntary decision. This was the case with the Apostle Paul. The Lord never told him to stay single nor did any of the apostles. If, therefore, a believer is single because this state has been imposed upon him or her by a religious leader, by parents, or by any other person and not by one's own voluntary conviction, it is the wrong reason for being single. It must be a voluntary decision as the child of God carefully weighs his or her ability to

remain pure inasfar as sexual relations are concerned, and providing that sexual passion does not
cause defilement (v. 9), thus in any way detracting
from effective Christian living and service.

Must a Bishop or Deacon Be Married Only Once?

This verse together with the entire seventh chapter
of First Corinthians throws much light on the interpretation that must be given to the expression of
Paul as he writes to Timothy. In 1 Timothy 3:2, he
says that the bishop ought to be the husband of one
wife. This is also found in Titus 1:6 with the exception that, in the case of Titus, he refers to the elder
instead of to the bishop. For all practical purposes,
it is one and the same thing. This does not mean
that the bishop or the elder who ministers to a local
congregation, or who has any responsibility in the
church of Jesus Christ, has to be married. It means
that if he is married, he must be currently married
only to one wife, that is, that he be monogamous,
not having more than one wife at a time.

There is no justification in taking the expression
"the husband of one wife" to mean that a bishop,
deacon, or elder should not have been married previously because that would prevent a widower
from holding such an office. In Romans 7:1–3, we
are told explicitly that widows or widowers are free
to remarry. In this instance, an innocent party of a
divorce who remarries, even as a widower, is "the

husband of one wife." He is that now in spite of the fact that he had been married before.

The expression "the husband of one wife" in 1 Timothy 3:2, 12 and Titus 1:6 uses a genitive, *miás gunaikós*, which is called in Greek grammar the attributive genitive. This is used as an adjective qualifying the subject which is *anér*, "husband," in this instance. Paul says that the bishop and the deacon, in addition to being monogamous, should have the moral quality of full attachment to their wives. The whole context is descriptive of the moral qualifications of these church officers. Thus if a church officer is now married or if he will be married, he must be totally devoted to his wife.

The same is true with a similar expression in 1 Timothy 5:9 referring to a widow who is one husband's wife. That does not mean that if she had been widowed two or three times, she would not qualify. It rather means a widow who was morally faithful to her husband before becoming a widow. If she were an immoral woman who is now a widow, she would not qualify for church assistance. (See A.T. Robertson's *A Grammar of the Greek New Testament in the Light of Historical Research*, pp. 496, 502.)

Celibacy Is Not Inconsistent With the Office of a Bishop or a Deacon

If marriage were a requirement for a bishop or a ruling elder of a church, then Paul would not have qualified to be one, and he certainly was exercising the work of a bishop and a pastor in consequence of his calling and function as an apostle. Peter was married while Paul was not married, and both were perfectly acceptable to the Lord. When the Lord healed Peter's mother–in–law, He did not turn and say to Peter, "You would have been better off had you not married." Marriage was Peter's personal decision. Most probably he was married before he was called to become a disciple of Christ and to serve Him, and he continued to maintain his marital status. Paul was called to become a disciple and an apostle of Christ unmarried, and he maintained his single status. The first had no choice but to remain married according to the Scriptural teaching. The second could have married had he decided to do so. We must recognize that there are certain things in life that are voluntary and cannot be regimented by others.

Listen to the Apostle Paul writing to these very same Corinthians in 1 Corinthians 9:4, 5: "Have we not power to eat and to drink? Have we not power to lead about a sister, a wife, as well as other apostles, and as the brethren of the Lord, and Cephas (Peter)?"

By the expression "to lead about a sister, a wife," Paul did not mean to keep company with a woman while unmarried, but rather to be married and to have the company of a wife as even the other apostles had. This was within his authority even as to eat and to drink certain things that others may accept or reject.

Obviously, the matter of marriage is entirely something that pertains to the individual decision and prerogative, and not something that one has to abstain from or enter into because of the legislative or traditional powers assumed by any one individual or church.

It Is Not a Sin to Voluntarily Decide to Marry

"Nevertheless, even if thou shalt marry thou didst not sin." The word "sin" in Greek[3] as expressed here comes basically from an obsolete word, *hamartánō*[4] from which also it borrows most of its meanings: to miss a mark, to deviate from a way. In the New Testament it is used only in a figurative or spiritual sense, to sin in general, to deviate from the will or law of God (see Heb. 10:26, 2 Pet. 2:4, and 1 John 2:1; 3:8; 5:16) or of man as in Acts 25:8.

In 1 Corinthians 7:28, an older form of the word *hamartánō* is used. It is in the active voice which indicates that the sin that could have been committed is one for which the individual bears the responsibility, as indeed, one personally and ultimately must bear the responsibility of his choices. But one also must bear the responsibility of situations in which he is pressured by others and he chooses to accept. Choice always bears with it responsibility.

The second aorist in which this verb is found indicates that the sin was at a particular time in the past. When experiencing difficulties resulting from circumstances of life in a married state, one must not look back upon that moment of decision to marry and think of it as a sin committed at that particular time with the present sufferings the consequences of that decision.

Of course, this verse has nothing to do with an act of individual, willful disobedience as in the case of a Christian marrying a non–believer. It refers rather to the mere choice between staying single or getting married, and in the case of a Christian marrying a Christian. This basic requirement is already made very clear by the Apostle Paul in 2 Corinthians 6:14: "Be ye not unequally yoked together with unbelievers." The verb "unequally yoked" in Greek is *heterozúgountes*, which means to be yoked together with someone who is of a different quality and conviction. Also, the presupposed fact that a Christian ought to marry only a Christian is made very clear in 1 Corinthians 7:39: "She is at liberty to be married to whom she will; only in the Lord." This refers to a Christian widow whose husband has died. If she is to be married only in the Lord, so is every other Christian.

It Is Not a Sin For a Virgin, an Innocent Divorced or Widowed Person to Marry

But does this phrase, "Nevertheless, even if thou shalt marry, thou didst not sin," refer to only the virgins of whom he is speaking in verse twenty–five or to all the unmarried? It must refer to all those who are unmarried, including the divorcees and widowed referred to in the second clause of verse twenty–seven: "Art thou loosed from a wife? Seek not a wife." Immediately following that Paul says: "Nevertheless, even if thou shalt marry, thou didst not sin."

Of course, we cannot take what Paul says in the first part of verse twenty–eight as blanket permission and authority for a divorcee who is a Christian to be married again. From our in–depth examination earlier in this book, we have learned that it all depends on the conditions of the dissolution of that marriage. If he or she is the guilty party, then it has already been made very clear by the previous injunctions by Christ and the Apostle Paul that there cannot be remarriage. This applies to a Christian spouse who may have proven himself or herself unfaithful to the marriage partner, and the innocent marriage partner has divorced his or her spouse. Also, it refers to a Christian partner who has forsaken his or her spouse without the spouse being unfaithful. If, however, a divorced Christian has been the innocent party in the separation, then he or she can remarry and remarriage is not a sin.

A Virgin Maiden Does Not Have to Succumb to Her Parent's Desire for Her to Marry

The fact that the first clause of verse twenty–eight refers to all unmarried people, particularly to those who are in a state of singleness because of a justified divorce or widowhood, is proven by the fact that the second clause of the verse refers particularly to a virgin girl who has never been married before: "And if the virgin maiden shall marry, she did not sin."

It is again a suppositional clause, "And if," *kaí eán*.[5] It speaks of a personal decision arrived at as a matter of individual conviction to get married. By implication we could say that in view of the fact that the verb *gémē*, "marry," is in the active voice, he refers to the personal decision of a virgin maiden to marry,[6] although the custom at that time was that a father gave his daughter to marriage (*ekgamízō*).[7] This indicates that a Christian virgin maiden does not have to succumb to the desire of her father or her parents or others to marry somebody contrary to her own convictions. Many Christian girls today face this very difficult situation.

The fact that the Apostle Paul designates specifically the decision to marry by a girl and not by a virgin man in this verse is indicative of the above. He wanted to stress this in view of the custom that existed at that time in which many girls were forced into an unwanted marriage by their parents. Paul by implication here says: "Don't give in. When it comes to choosing whether to obey your parents or God, the latter takes precedence."

Obedience to God rather than man is taught throughout the Scriptures. What Peter and the other apostles said to those who would silence their testimony and Christian benevolence should characterize every Christian when the choice has to be made between obeying God and men, even if the "men" referred to consitute his parents. "Then Peter and the other apostles answered and said, We ought to obey God rather than men" (Acts 4:19). Paul himself would rather be persecuted and put in jail than disobey his heavenly vision. He said to King Agrippa in Acts 26:19: "Whereupon, O king Agrippa, I was not disobedient unto the heavenly vision." Therefore, a Christian girl should not allow her parents to force her unto an unscriptural marriage nor to marry one who, although a believer, according to her own personal conviction is not God's choice for her.

Paul says, "If a virgin maiden marries," not "is *given* to marriage," but marries of her own conviction and choice, "she did not sin." This is exactly the same verb as in the previous clause with the exception that it is in the third person singular referring to a maiden virgin's decision to marry. Such a woman should not at any time look back and consider her own decision to marry as a sinful act as long as that marriage was in accordance with God's prescribed will.

Such a thought of regret could destroy a marriage. It surely would in no way contribute to the peace and harmony that Christ desires in Christian marriages. Consider the day of your marriage as a day of your own personal decision by which you are bound for life and in fidelity to your spouse. A contrary attitude can be sinful in itself and wreak havoc on your marriage, yourself, and the entire family. As with any other sin, the consequences are not felt by the guilty party alone. Others suffer too. In the case of a broken marriage, children, parents, relatives and friends all must share in the grief.

---

[1]The same expression is used also in verse eleven. In verse twenty–one instead of using the particle *dé* which sometimes can be translated as "and" or the adversative "but," Paul uses the adversative *allá*.

[2]The Textus Receptus has this verb in Greek, *gémēs*, while the UBS text has it as *gamésēs*. The first is an older form of the aorist of the verb *gaméō*, "to marry." This verb, when used in the active, is properly spoken of the man as in Matthew 5:32; 19:9; 22:25, 30, etc. When in the passive, *gaméomai*, it means to be married and is spoken of the woman as in Mark 10:12 and 1 Corinthians 7:39. But *gaméō*, in the active, is also sometimes applied to the woman as in 1 Corinthians 7:28, 34 and 1 Timothy 5:11, 14. Another form of the verb *gamískō*, from *gámos*, "marriage," means to give in marriage as a father does his daughter. In the passive, *gamískomai* means to be given in marriage as a daughter by her father as in Mark 12:25. Yet another form of the verb is *ekgamízō* from *ek*, "out," and *gamízō*, "to give in marriage." It means to place out in marriage or to give in marriage, as a father gives his daughter in marriage as in Matthew 22:30; 24:38; Luke 17:27 and 1 Corinthians 7:38. Another form of this verb is *ekgamískō*, from *ek*, "out," and *gamískō*, "to give in marriage," as in Luke 20:34, 35.

[3]*Hémartes*, second person singular second aorist indicative of *hamartánō*, "to sin."

[4]In its original, *hamartéō* is derived from the negative "a," and *márptō*, "to hit the mark," or from *a*, negative, and *homartéō*, "to follow, accompany."

[5]This is followed by the subjunctive *gémē*, "marry," as in the previous clause with the exception that it is in the third person singular, also first aorist.

[6]Whereas in verse twenty–five Paul used the word *parthénos*, "a virgin maiden" in the plural, here he uses it in the singular feminine, *hē parthénos*. In Greek the word *parthénos* refers to both man and woman, but mostly to a woman. Here, however, the designation is a virgin maiden, *parthénos*, in the feminine.

[7]Matthew 22:30; 24:38; Luke 17:27; 1 Corinthians 7:38, and *ekgamískomai*, Luke 20:34, 35.

40

MARRIAGE IN VIEW OF THE TRANSIENCE OF OUR EARTHLY LIFE

But this I say, brethren, the time is short: it remaineth, that both they that have wives be as though they had none; And they that weep, as though they wept not; and they that rejoice, as though they rejoiced not; and they that buy, as though they possessed not; And they that use this world, as not abusing it: for the fashion of this world passeth away.—1 Corinthians 7:29–31

P aul instructs the Corinthians that attitude is the most important thing in all circumstances of life. He begins verse twenty–nine by saying, "This but I say," (and to put it in better English but change the order of the Greek words, "But this I say").[1] With the use of this verb, Paul is saying I bring to you a certain enlightenment in what I am saying. (And we find in the following verses that this enlightenment is in the form of illustrations about other situations in life.)

Paul, faithful to his custom even when he knows that there are people who disagree with what he is saying, calls them all *adelphoí*, "brethren."

The Opportunity to Glorify God in One's Life Is Short

Paul goes on to make one of the two statements on which his theory is based: "The time is short." At the end of verse thirty–one he says, "For the fashion of this world passeth away."

The word translated as "the time" in Greek is *ho*, "the," and *kairós*, better rendered as "opportunity." There are two words in Greek that are usually translated with one English word, "time." The one is *chrónos*, referring to time simply as a measurement or the length of a period of time. The word is used in English in the word "chronometer" which is a device to measure time but without any reference to the relation of time to the accomplishments that it permits. *Chrónos* denotes the length or space of time, but *kairós* signifies *eukairían*, "good or proper time, opportunity." With the definite article in 1 Corinthians 1:29, it means the opportunity to accomplish certain things and not simply time per se. Often when we say, "Time is short," we really do not refer to the measurement of time itself but to the accomplishment of a certain thing or project in that particular time. What Paul is stressing here as a basic consideration for life is that we merely have the opportunity of using a state of being to accomplish a desired goal. First, there must be the goal, and the goal as expressed throughout the Scriptures is the glory of God. The basic questions should be, "How can I best glorify God in my life? Is it through being married or being single?"

It is apparent from the teaching of Paul that honoring and serving God can be accomplished in either state of being, and the choice rests squarely with the individual. This time or opportunity to glorify God in one's life, Paul asserts, is short.[2] We don't have a great deal of time to accomplish all that opportunity presents to us in this life. The idea that the Apostle and other believers in Corinth considered the time short in view of the soon–coming of the Lord is not valid in my opinion. Life is essentially short, Paul is stressing, and we have so little time to fulfill God's individual plan for each one of us. Really, the time of the Lord's coming is immaterial, for it is each believer's duty to be redeeming what allotted time he has.[3]

Things as We Now Know Them Change

Before we examine the circumstances in life of which Paul speaks and what our attitude toward them should be, we must examine the other basic principle at the end of verse thirty–one: "For the fashion of this world passeth away."[4] It would have been better translated as "The form of this world vanishes." The image here is possibly drawn from the shifting scenes of a theater where the form or appearance of a scene is changed and presents an appearance which is entirely new. "Fashion" or *schēma*, is therefore the outer garment and not the essence. It is that which does not really belong to man as part and parcel of his being. It is a thing that he may lay aside to take on something which is different.

What is this world whose shape vanishes? The noun "world"[5] comes from the verb *kosméō* which means "to set in order, to adorn or to trim."

The noun as used by ancient Greek writers denotes order, regularity, ornament, but it also denotes the whole frame of the material heaven and earth so—called from its admirable regularity and beauty.[6]

In 1 Corinthians 7:31 which we are studying, this word refers to the things of this world, such as riches, honors, pleasures, etc., as also in Galatians 6:14 and 1 John 2:15, 16. Therefore "the shape of this world" means things as they are presently constituted in the world we now know. Institutions and things as we now know them are transient and temporary.

Two Basic Principles to Consider in View of One's Decision to Marry or to Stay Single

There are two basic principles that the Apostle Paul laid down for the Corinthians in the light of which they were to judge the decisions that they must make, primarily as to whether they should marry or remain unmarried.

One, the opportunity to serve our Lord is short-lived; and two, the scene or the shape of things as we now know them is changing. In the next chapter, we shall consider what effect these realizations should have on the believer.

---

[1]The verb translated "say" in Greek is *phēmí* and not the word *légō*. This word *phēmí*, "to say," is from the same root *pha* as *phaínō*, from which we have the idea of explaining, speaking, a development of the primary notion of enlightening, showing, and the elementary concept is manifestation. *Phēmí* in the *Odyssey*, Herodotus, and the Tragedians, signifies a divine revelation by words or signs (*phḗmē*, "a divine voice"). The verb is akin to *prophētikós*, "prophetic," that which belongs to the prophet or comes from him. In the New Testament it is found in Romans 16:26 and 2 Peter 1:19.

[2]The word "short" is expressed in Greek by the adjective *sunestalménos*, which is the nominative singular masculine participle perfect passive of *sustéllō*, from *sún*, "together," and *stéllō*, "to send or to contract." It is used only twice in the New Testament. The first time is in Acts 5:6 referring to swathing or winding up a dead body for burial. 1 Corinthians 7:29 is the only time that it is used in the passive form, *sustéllomai*, which means "to be contracted, to be short of time."

[3]The Textus Receptus has the expression *tó loipón*, from *leloípa*, the perfect middle of *leípō*, "to leave," meaning "henceforth," or "as to the remaining," between the words

sunestalménos, "contracted," and the verb *estín*, "is." The UBS has it after the verb *estín* and belonging to the next clause instead of to the previous one. The meaning is "as for the rest," or "henceforth," so that you may have the proper attitude in the following circumstances.

⁴This statement begins with the verb *parágei*, translated "passeth away." *Parágō* is derived from *pará*, denoting transition or nearness, and *ágō*, "to go, go away," consequently meaning to pass or vanish away." And what is it that vanishes away? "The fashion of this world." The word for "fashion" in Greek is *schéma*, from which the English word *schematic* is derived. The word *schéma* is from *eschémai*, the perfect passive of *échō*, "to have," or in its obsolete form, *schéō*, "to be." It means form or appearance.

⁵The phrase in Greek is *toú kósmou*, the genitive of *ho kósmos*.

⁶Plutarch says that Pythagoras was the first who called the system of the universe *kósmos*, from the order observable in it. It is used in this sense in Matthew 24:21; John 17:5; Acts 17:24 and Romans 1:20. It also means merely the earth as in Matthew 4:8; 13:38; Mark 14:9, and Luke 12:30. It also means the world, that is to say, the whole race of mankind, both believers and unbelievers, both good and bad as in John 3:16, 17; 6:33; 12:47; 14:31; Romans 3:19. It is spoken hyperbolically of a great number of men as in John 12:19; 18:20, and also of a number of persons from all the nations of the earth as in Romans 4:13. It also refers to the wicked part of the world which constitutes the larger number of mankind as in John 7:7; 15:18, 19; 16:20; 17:14; 1 Corinthians 11:32; 1 John 3:1, 13; 4:5.

41

HAVE THE PROPER ATTITUDE TOWARD THE PHYSICAL PRESSURES INCURRED BY MARRIAGE

. . . Nevertheless, such shall have trouble in the flesh: but I spare you.—1 Corinthians 7:28

Paul wants to be very honest in his opinion regarding those who decide to marry whether they be divorcees or virgins. This verse constitutes purely his own opinion and it cannot be of general application. In the cases of some believers, it may prove true, and in the cases of others it may not.

Tribulation in This Context Is Not Eschatological

It is our opinion that the word *thlípsis*,[1] "trouble or tribulation," has been misunderstood by some commentators as referring to the specific period which begins with the rapture of the Church. For believers it is known as the Day of Christ, and it is known as the Day of the Lord for unbelievers who will remain on this earth for a period of seven years at which time the Lord will return with His saints.

Christ identified this period when outlining the future of Israel to His disciples in Matthew 24:21: "For then shall be great tribulation, such as was not since the beginning of the world to this time, no, nor ever shall be." Similarly, the elder addresses John and says, "These are they which came out of great tribulation" (Rev. 7:14). The Greek text makes this period more definitive as it says "those which came out of *the* tribulation, *the* great one." This specific period of time of seven years is identified as the seventieth week of Daniel's prophecy in Daniel 9:24–27. The word *thlípsis* with this eschatological reference constitutes only a small portion of the use of this word in the New Testament as in Matthew 24:21 and Mark 13:19, echoing Daniel 12:1, 2 Thessalonians 1:6ff, and Revelation 7:14.

The general use of the word *thlípsis* has in it the idea of pressure, as of a heavy burden on the spirit which in the New Testament is translated with various English words such as "tribulation"(Acts 14:22); "anguish" (John 16:21); "affliction" (Acts 7:10, 11); "burdened" (2 Cor. 8:13); "persecution" (Acts 11:19); or "trouble" (1 Cor. 7:28).

It is doubtful that either the expression found in verse twenty–six, *enestósan*, "present," *anágkēn*, "necessity," or this expression in 1 Corinthians 7:28, *thlípsin*, refer to the eschatological use of the word. In other words, Paul was not advising that those who were considering marriage should not marry in view of the great tribulation that was to come upon this earth due to the Second Coming of Christ. This would have been tantamount to Paul saying, "Don't get married because the Lord is coming so soon, and His coming is going to be accompanied by great tribulation."

It is inconceivable that Paul, having on several occasions been the instrument of divine inspiration, would be so ill–inspired and ill–informed concerning the proximity of the Second Coming of Christ. Furthermore, it was the same apostle who wrote to the Thessalonians in the fourth chapter of his first epistle, verses fourteen through eighteen, that when that day comes the dead in Christ will rise first, and those who are in Christ but alive will be changed and will be caught up in the air. And in 1 Corinthians 15:51, 52 he tells us that this is going to take place with unimaginable rapidity.

If the general counsel of the Apostle Paul is followed that a Christian should marry a fellow believer, then the expectation of being caught up in the air or being raised from the dead is common to both. Therefore, suffering associated with the matter of marriage and the resurrection does not exist. If they have children, the great possibility is that these children will also be led to the Lord and will be enjoying the same privileges as the parents. That the Apostle Paul was advising people not to get married in view of the eschatological tribulation is really inconceivable.

The Burden of Marital Responsibilities

The meaning of the word *thlípsis*, therefore, must be the general pressure of circumstances and responsibilities that one feels toward the marriage partner and the family that may ensue. It is this added responsibility that Paul wants all Christians to consider carefully in view of the task that we have been endowed by God to perform and to which we are called. Marriage is to be contemplated and executed only in view of full recognition of the responsibilities in relation to the purpose and calling in the life of the individual.

The expression that Paul uses to identify the type of pressure, trouble, or tribulation coming is "trouble in the flesh." The dative *té sarkí*, "in the flesh," locates the area in which this trouble or pressure will be exercised. There are actually two words in Greek that are related and yet indicate a distinction in the kind of trouble that a person suffers. One is *thlípsis* for which the most common translation is "tribulation" from the Latin *tribulum*, "the threshing instrument," by means of which the Roman husbandman separated the corn from the husks. Though tribulation may crush and bruise us, it separates our chaff from the wheat so that we are prepared for the granary of heaven. This is generally the New Testament meaning of the word.

According to the ancient law of England, those who willfully refused to plead guilty to a crime had heavy weights placed on their chests. These poor unfortunates were sorely pressed and eventually crushed to death, that this was literally called *thlípsis*. On the other hand, if a person was placed in a cage, that was referred to as finding himself in a narrow *stenós*, "nonspacious," *chōrós*, "space." That is called *stenochōría* in Greek and occurs four times in the New Testament, in three instances associated with *thlípsis* (Rom. 2:9; 8:35, 2 Cor. 6:4) and by itself in 2 Corinthians 12:10. *Stenochōría* refers rather to the spirit as in Wisdom 5:3, and also by ancient writers such as Thucydides, 7:70. This word refers to the attitude of the spirit towards its circumstances. One may feel he is under pressure and in a strait and narrow place and yet abide in comfort. It is the attitude of the spirit versus the pressure of the actual circumstances.

The word *sárx*, "flesh," denotes the body in contrast to the spiritual part of man which is spirit as the element of his God–consciousness, and soul as the element of his environment–consciousness.

What Paul means therefore, with this unique expression, *thlípsin tē sarkí*, is the pressure that is put upon the body, not necessarily due to the fact of marriage, but due to the additional physical responsibilities that are incurred when a person is married. The pressure of responsibilities that is felt from the unavoidable circumstances of life is greater when a person is married and concerned about the spouse and their children than when a person is single. Recognize this added responsibility, is what Paul is actually saying when he says that the married ones, whether in remarriage or in the first marriage, are going to have trouble in the flesh. These are the inescapable pressures of life and those intrinsic to marriage.

Marriage Does Not Involve Constant Pressure

The punctiliar usage of this future verb translated "shall have"[2] indicates that such pressures will not be a constant companion of the one who decides to marry, but they will have pressures from time to time. Who marries and doesn't expect that? A person would be very naïve to enter marriage without realizing that there will be rough spots and sleepless nights. But Paul, not being married himself and unable to comprehend the advantages, does not at the same time emphasize the blessings of married life. Those who are happily married in the Lord know that they are many and varied, especially the blessings of the spirit in spite of the normal tensions of life.

Tribulation is not only resultant from marriage but from the Christian life itself. We should never forget the words of our Savior in John 16:33, "These things I have spoken to you, that in me ye might have peace. In the world ye shall have tribulation (*thlípsis*): but be of good cheer; I have overcome the world." In the same way there can be a family peace in the midst of physical pressures. That peace is what dispels our anguish, *stenochōría*, through the loving concern and comfort that comes from one member of the family for another.

The pronoun translated "such" in Greek is *hoi toioútoi*. It is prefixed by the definite article "the," indicating that it refers to a specific class of people. This class refers to all the married ones in contrast to the single, whether they were married before and became single by divorce or death, or those who were never married.

Paul's Tender Concern

Paul adds his paternal concern for the Corinthians whom he considered as his children in the faith. He closes this verse with the words "but I spare you."[3] The verb occasionally means "to treat with tenderness" or, in modern vernacular, "to avoid giving someone a rough time" (as in Acts 20:29, Rom. 8:32, here in 1 Cor. 7:28, and 2 Cor. 1:23). It sometimes implies forgiveness either with a genitive following as in Romans 11:21 and 2 Peter 2:4, 5, or absolutely as in 2 Corinthians 13:2. Sometimes it means "to forbear or abstain" as in 2 Corinthians 12:6. In 1 Corinthians 7:28, it means "I treat you with tenderness," and since it is in the present indicative, it is "I am treating you with tenderness." In other words, "Why should I make it any rougher for you, I, a single man, to tell you that you're having it so hard because you're married?"

Paul demonstrates the proper attitude of one class toward the other. The unmarried ones should look upon the married ones with tenderness as they may experience added difficulties of life, and the married ones should also exercise tenderness toward those who are unmarried and perhaps have no immediate family or loved ones to care for them. What a beautiful word, "tenderness," to be shown in our appreciation and evaluation of the troubles that others, whether single or married, are going through.

---

[1]This clause begins in Greek with the verb *thlípsin*, the accusative of *thlípsis*.

[2]*Échousin*, third person plural future indicative of *échō*.

[3]The verb in Greek is *pheídomai*, a deponent verb derived from *pheúgō*, "to avoid," *toú doúnai*, "giving."

42

OUR WHOLE LIVES SHOULD BE LIVED WITH ETERNITY IN VIEW

. . . both they that have wives be as though they had none; and they that weep, as though they wept not; and they that rejoice, as though they rejoiced not; and they that buy, as though they possessed not; and they that use this world, as not abusing it: for the fashion of this world passeth away.—1 Corinthians 7:29–31

What should be the attitude of the believer in view of the realization that our opportunities are short and things as we know them now will not always be?

This is given to us with the clauses introduced by the conjunction *hína*, "so that," or with simply "that" of verse twenty–nine. *Hína* is followed in Greek with the conjunction *kaí*, which should be translated as "even, so that even." Then follow five phrases describing situations in which a person may be found which should never be an end in themselves, but only a means to the goal of glorifying Christ and accomplishing one's calling.

Proposition One: Even if One Is Married, His Wife Should Not Come Before the Lord

First, Paul tells us, even they who have wives should be as those who don't have them.

Paul recommended the state of singleness as an advantage in accomplishing one's calling, and gave himself as an example. But he implies now that even if a man has a wife, she should not in any way reduce his dedication to the Lord and His calling. In other words, the Lord and His calling come first, but by implication we must understand also that there should be no neglect of one's marital partner.

This verse must be taken in conjunction with what Paul says in Ephesians 5:25: "Husbands, love your wives, even as Christ also loved the church, and gave himself for it." Love for one's wife has its place, but it should never be above the love that is due Jesus Christ. A spouse is human, but Jesus Christ is God and He should be treated as such and not as a mere human being even a husband or a wife.

Such should be the difference in the quality of love shown toward the Lord Jesus and toward any of our relatives, including our spouse, that our love for relatives in relation to the love for Jesus Christ seems like hatred. In this regard, we must recall the

320

words of our Savior in Luke 14:26: "If any man come to me, and hate not his father, and mother, and wife, and children, and brethren, and sisters, yea, and his own life (*psuché*, referring to the human instincts of man) also, he cannot be my disciple." This, however, must be taken in connection with Matthew 10:37 in which it is shown that hatred, as Christ refers to it, is a comparatively lower love for our relatives: "He that loveth father or mother more than me is not worthy of me: and he that loveth son or daughter more than me is not worthy of me." When it comes to the expression of a believer's fidelity to Jesus Christ, marriage should make no difference whatsoever.

Proposition Two: Sorrow Should Not Hinder Us From Glorifying God

The second proposition concerns sorrows in life. Paul says in verse thirty: "And they that weep, as though they wept not."

Paul recognizes that there are situations in life, both of the married and unmarried, when we cannot help but weep. The construction is exactly the same in all these clauses. It refers to certain people who are characterized by these circumstances, and not to everybody as if they all had the same experiences. Actually, it is not "they that weep," but "the weeping ones," *hoi klaíontes*, as in the previous clause, *hoi échontes*, "the ones having wives."

321

In other words, Paul is saying not to let tears, which represent sorrow in any way, diminish the full utilization of the short opportunity given to the believer on this earth to glorify Jesus Christ and to accomplish His calling. He does not infer in any way that it is wrong to weep. Even Jesus wept (John 11:35). Our Lord pronounced blessedness on those that mourn (Matt. 5:4) and on those that weep (Luke 6:21).

Proposition Three: Let Not the Joys of Life Hinder Us From Fulfilling God's Purpose in Our Life

The third situation in which a Christian may be found, whether married or unmarried, is that of experiencing joy. "And they that rejoice, as though they rejoiced not."

Again, the meaning is, let not the joys of life in any way detract the child of God from accomplishing for Jesus Christ what He has set before him. This in no way means that we should not rejoice in life. However, let us not consider the joys of this earth as the ultimate thing. This is too often the sin of otherwise virtuous Christians. They get caught up in the seemingly innocent pleasures of life. And when that one life given to them has come to a close, much to their regret they realize that most of the time and money God entrusted to them has been wasted in the pursuit of self–satisfaction and pleasure.

It is our heavenly reward that should produce our earthly joy more than anything else as our Lord said in Matthew 5:12, "Rejoice, and be exceeding glad: for great is your reward in heaven: for so persecuted they the prophets which were before you." There can be joy in the midst of suffering and persecution. As the same apostle says to the Philippians: "Rejoice in the Lord alway: and again I say rejoice" (Phil. 4:4). But again, Paul is concerned that our rejoicing on this earth may not in any way diminish our full utilization of the opportunity entrusted to us by the Lord for a short while until death overcomes us.

Proposition Four: Let Not Business Hinder Us From Accomplishing Our God–Given Goal in Life

Fourth, we should not allow our business transactions to stand in the way of the accomplishment of our divine calling. The last clause of verse thirty says: "And they that buy, as though they possessed not."

Buying things involves monetary prosperity and is basically amoral in itself. The same apostle in 1 Timothy 5:8 says: "But if any provide not for his own, and specially for those of his own house, he hath denied the faith, and is worse than an infidel." To provide for our own daily needs and those of our household is an imperative duty for each Christian. But involvement in business should never be at the detriment of the realization of our calling for Christ.

After all, business is only a means to an end and never should be the culmination of life itself.

The Greek verb translated "possessed"[1] in the phrase "as though they possessed not" means to hold or grasp as if it were going to be ours forever. Paul wants us to remember that that which we buy may be ours for a while and no more. We are not to become slaves to things that can be bought, sold, and lost.

Proposition Five: Proper Priorities Are Necessary for the Achievement of Our God–Given Goal

Finally, the Apostle Paul wants us to beware of abusing anything in this world that may be used by us. He says, "And they that use this world, as not abusing it."

The participial noun found in the phrase *hoi chrómenoi*, translated "they that use," is from the verb *chráomai* or *chrómai*; which with a dative means "to use, treat, behave towards." We can also translate it as "handling." We should use or handle this world or things as we know them now in their present form with care lest we abuse them. This can refer to any possession or thing that we have on this earth. The verb for "abuse"[2] means to use immoderately or to abuse as in 1 Corinthians 9:18. We should accept everything with thanksgiving in this life, but not use it immoderately or allow it to stand in the way between us and Jesus Christ.

There are two verses of Scripture that denote what Paul is trying to convey in this passage. The first is Luke 14:33 where our Lord says, "So likewise, whosoever he be of you that forsaketh not all that he hath, he cannot be my disciple." The Lord here refers to the possessions of life as well as the relatives spoken of in verse twenty–six. This whole passage in Luke 14:26–33 concerns discipleship. Also, in Matthew 10:37, our Lord says that we must not love any relative above Jesus Christ. We should place our relatives in their proper position and category. The same thing should be done with our belongings as with any material thing of this world. This is spoken of in verse thirty–three in which the verb "forsake"[3] gives the unfortunate connotation of reckless abandonment. Rather, the basic meaning is that we should place our relatives in their proper order under God and treat them as the Word of God specifies that we should treat them. The same applies to our belongings. We should place them in their particular category for the use that is meant for them and not make them part of ourselves since, in reality, only Christ indwells us. Therefore, to give undue importance and value to anything, including relatives or possessions, is to abuse these God–given gifts and will prevent us from accomplishing our particular calling.

It is interesting that in Luke 14:26, 27, 33 there are two parables that our Lord gave. The first concerns a tower that remains unfinished because the cost had not been counted, and the second describes a war that was not won because of lack of preparation. We cannot complete the task that God has called us to complete nor win the war that we are called upon to fight on this earth unless we conduct ourselves in the manner that He has prescribed.

Whatever this world of ours has to offer, let us use it, but never abuse it so that Christ and His Kingdom suffer in any way. The opportunity is short–lived. The shape of this world as we see it is a shifting one. We are here to work for that which is permanent and eternal.

---

[1]*Katéchontes*, the present participle active of *katécho*, from the intensive *katá*, and *écho*, "to have, hold."

[2]In its participial form it is *katachrómenoi* from *katachráomai*, or *katachrómai*, from *katá*, an intensive or denoting "ill," and *chráomai*, "to use."

[3]The Greek verb is *apotássetai* which is made up from the preposition *apó*, "from," and *tásso* or *tássomai* which means "to place in a specific category" (*táxis*).

43

THE CARES OF MARRIED AND UNMARRIED LIFE

But I would have you without carefulness . . .
—1 Corinthians 7:32

The goal of life must not be to be single or married; throughout this chapter, the Apostle Paul has endeavored to show us that the state of singleness or marriage is only a means to an end and should never be the end of life itself. The goal of life, must be to accomplish that which God's particular calling dictates for each individual. One must take into account his or her particular talents and endowments and determine to live his life to the best possible degree for the glory of God. If that glory can better be accomplished by being single, then there is nothing wrong with being single. And if it can also be accomplished by being married, then there is nothing wrong with being married.

Once a person has determined his calling and goal in life, then he should examine his God–given ability to be single or to be married. If an unmarried person is going to burn with sexual desire and expend a great part of his emotional life in suppressing that urge, then he would be unfit to accomplish the specific goal God has ordained to bring glory to His name. If, however, the sexual drive is well under control and one doesn't mind living alone, then the unmarried life is just fine for that person. After all, there are people who love to live alone and people who cannot live alone, and God can use all who are yielded to Him. We must be realistic in facing life.

In marriage, one should be careful lest he bring into that relationship a person who does not have the same inclination to press on and struggle in the accomplishment of his God–ordained goal for his life. Divergence of purpose between the individual marriage partners contributes a great deal to the breakup of many Christian marriages.

It is all this that the Apostle Paul has in mind in 1 Corinthians 7:32. He begins this verse with the verb *thélō*, as he does also verse seven: "For *I would* that all men were even as I myself. But every man hath his proper gift of God, one after this manner, and another after that." And also we see the same verb in verse thirty–two: "But *I would* have you without carefulness." What is translated as "I would" is the Greek verb *thélō*, which basically means to apply oneself to something or to will.[1] Therefore, Paul is trying to tell the Corinthians that all the advice that he has given is due to his desire that they be free of anxiety in life. He realizes that a person who does not have anxiety can accomplish the God–ordained goal and purpose of his life much more easily and effectively.

Consider the Anxieties That Accompany Married or Unmarried Life

Paul is not saying, "Don't get married so that you may not have anxiety in life." Rather, he is saying: "Don't allow yourself to be found in a situation where you have so many anxieties that you will be hindered from accomplishing your God–given call. Consider the anxieties that accompany the single or married life."

Before, Paul had said that if the anxiety of burning with sexual desire is unavoidable, then don't stay single. Also, he had said that if the circumstances of life are such that if you do marry you add to your anxieties, then don't get married. Paul's purpose in his advice about marriage was that each believer be found in the best possible situation for accomplishing God's divine call in life.

How did Paul want the Corinthians to whom he was writing, and all people in general, to be? When in 1 Corinthians 7:7 he said, "For I would that all men were even as I myself," or, "I would prefer all men to be like me," he was referring to being single since he was single and he speaks about marriage and singleness in this entire chapter.

And then in 1 Corinthians 7:32 he said, "But I would have you without carefulness," or, "I want you to be without anxiety."

The first thing that Paul implies is that he was
without anxiety, and it was because of his freedom
from anxiety due to his single state that his recommendation for all people was that they stay single.

To better understand Paul's comments, we must
examine the meaning of what is translated "without
carefulness" (amerímnous) in 1 Corinthians 7:32.[2] It
will help us a great deal every time that the word
merimnáō or mérimna (without the negative a meaning "to be without") occurs in the New Testament to
take it as meaning "being divided in ourselves and
putting persons and things in first place which really
are of second importance." At all times man's relationship with God should occupy first place.[3] The
meaning, therefore, of merimnáō is to allow something, a person, a thought—whatever it may be—to
crowd in and detract us from performing our main
duty or task. Generally in the New Testament, this
word is used with the sense of dividing and, as applied to the mind, of distraction.

Without a doubt, family responsibilities do entail a certain amount of concern and worry, and
Paul here referred to the anxiety which is created
for the maintenance of a happy marriage and the
care of family members. Marriage was regarded as
legitimate and honorable in the early church, but
Paul saw in the cares of married life a menace to
spiritual zeal and labor.

Paul recognized a lawful, temporal care in marriage. It was he who taught that the man who made
no provision (pronoeí) for those dependent upon

him, and especially for his own family, had denied the faith and was worse than an unbeliever (Rom. 12:10, 11; 2 Thess. 3:6–15; 1 Tim. 5:8). But how readily the cares of the world crushed out the love of God (2 Tim. 4:10; Heb. 13:5, etc.).

Marriage Should Not Relegate God's Kingdom to Second Place

The general tenor of the Apostle Paul's argument in First Corinthians chapter seven is that if one's calling and task has first place in life, there is nothing wrong with marriage, providing it is not allowed to relegate God's Kingdom to second place. Human care, including care for the marriage partner and the family, has its remedy in the spirit which puts first of all the kingdom of God and His righteousness in its proper category above the mundane things of life. The secret of Paul's indifference to personal loss (Phil. 3:7ff) and his contentment in whatever condition of life he happened to be (Phil. 4:11), lay in the fact that the ordinary human interests of life had become utterly subordinate to the interests of God (1 Cor. 7:21–31).

In addition, Paul taught that the strain of toil and the fret of care can be relieved by meditating on God's providence: "In nothing be anxious" (Phil. 4:6); "I will never leave thee, nor forsake thee" (Heb. 13:5); "Casting all your anxiety upon God, because He careth for you" (1 Pet. 5:7). Providence does not guarantee freedom from human pain, sorrow, and persecution (2 Cor. 4:8ff; 11:23ff, etc.), but embraces these and all things in a wide scheme of goodness (Rom. 8:28, 35–37; Matt. 10:28, 29). God cares for the sparrows that fall to the ground.

Worry is relieved for the Christian, not so much by the hope of change of human circumstances as by his changed attitude toward and estimate of human values. The word *amerímnos*, used only in 1 Corinthians 7:32 and Matthew 28:14, in the classics meant a man who cared for no one, or an unconcerned person. But in reality, the person who lives a blameless life cannot have an unconcerned direction in life.

In Matthew 28:14, we have the case of the chief priests and the elders who bribed the soldiers who were guarding the body of Jesus at the sepulcher. These leaders were afraid lest the governor would discover what they did and so they told the guards to lie about it. Don't be afraid if this is learned by the governor, they promised them; we'll persuade him and make you *amerímnous*, "secure." Now actually the word "secure" used in Matthew 28:14 is "without anxiety," exactly the word that we find in 1 Corinthians 7:32. In other words, "You don't have to worry about your involvement in the intrigue that we have planned in bribing you to lie that the body of Jesus was stolen."

The first thing, then, that Paul implies when he says, "I want you therefore to be without anxiety," is that there is an anxiety involved in marriage. This however refers to the commendable, careful concern that a married spouse should demonstrate for his or her family. It does not refer to the condemnable anxiety spoken of by the Lord Jesus in His explicit discussion in Matthew 6:25–34. In that passage the Lord condemns self–concern in respect to the future (v. 34), for the means of life (vv. 25–28), and for one's own life consisting of *psuché*, man's emotional life, and *sóma*, "body" (v. 25). According to our Lord, what makes a proper concern foolish is anxiety with the illusion, to which it gives rise in its blindness, that life can become secure through one's own concern and worry. Man can achieve ridiculously little by worrying, therefore worry is unnecessary. The Lordship of God should be the believer's first concern.

Are the Anxieties of Marriage Commendable and Unavoidable?

The second thing that Paul implies by this verse is that the anxieties pertaining to marriage are unavoidable as part and parcel of a believer's holy concern for others. Anxiety is condemned when it is for selfish interest or from lack of trust in God, but not necessarily so when it concerns others.

For instance, in 1 Corinthians 12:25, Paul speaks of the members of the body of Christ as having a moral obligation to be anxious for each other: "That there should be no schism in the body; but that the members should have the same care (*merimnósi*) one for another." In Second Corinthians chapter eleven

Paul enumerates his sufferings on behalf of Christ. He says: "Beside those things that are without, that which cometh upon me daily, the care (*mérimna*) of all the churches" (v. 28). He tells us here that every day he was anxious about the welfare of all the churches. That was not anything for which he was to be condemned, but rather commended. In writing to the Philippians 2:20, Paul expressed a deep concern that amounted to anxiety: "For I have no man like—minded, who will naturally care (*merimnései*) for your state." So we understand that Paul does not condemn the anxious care that a husband should have for his wife or a wife for her husband, and both parents for the children and children for the family.

Of course, if one did not marry he would not have these particular, anxious cares pertaining to the family. So Paul advises that if such family cares are going to detract a person from the accomplishment of his goal and call in Christ, then it may be better not to marry. He does not say that they definitely *will* detract the believer, but that *if* they are going to detract, then it is better to remain as he was, single. Thus 1 Corinthians 7:32 seems to be a further explanation of 1 Corinthians 7:7, "For I would that all men were even as I myself" (i.e., single).

With these thoughts in mind, it is easy to see how very necessary and important it is for the dedicated child of God to marry a person who will have the same goal in life, that is, the honor and glory of God. Those who love the Lord should beware of becoming yoked together with one who will be pulling in a different direction, thus causing division at the very roots of the family unity.

---

[1]There is another Greek verb *boúlomai*, which has more the meaning of a decree. From this verb is derived the word *boulé*, which in modern Greek has come to mean "parliament." Parliament decrees laws. It doesn't simply express desires and issues resolutions that have no binding effect. *Thélō*, however, means more "to resolve." Here the verb in the present indicative is used with the infinitive *eínai*, "to be," and it means "to like, love, delight, affect," as also in Mark 12:38 and Luke 20:46. It is equivalent to "purpose."

[2]In the Greek text the word is a compound one, *amerímnous*, the plural accusative of *amerímnos*, made up of the privative, *a*, and *mérimna*, "care or anxiety." The verb is *merimnáō*, which, along with the noun *mérimna*, is derived from *merís*, "a part," and the verb *merízō*, "to draw in different directions, distract." The verb *merimnáō* and *mérimna* have unfortunately been inadequately translated in many instances in the New Testament. Our translators render it by "being careful," Luke 10:41 and Philippians 4:6; by "caring," 1 Corinthians 7:32–34; and by "having care," 1 Corinthians 12:25 and Philippians 2:20. In other passages, however, they have translated it as "taking thought," Matthew 6:25, 31, 34 and Luke 12:22. At the time that the translations were made, the phrase, "to take thought," generally meant to take anxious thought or to be anxiously careful or worried. What actually they meant by "taking thought" was to be overcome or to draw aside from their principal task or purpose of life. Christ did not mean that man should take no reasonable and legitimate thought about his life, but that he should not be overtroubled or oversorrowful or overanxious to the detriment of his relationship with God.

---

[3]In this sense, the true meaning of the verb *merimnáō* is "to be distracted" and could be taken as a synonym of the word *thorubázō* or *turbázō*, which is coupled with *merimnáō* in the rebuke to Martha (Luke 10:41). The verb *turbázō*, translated "troubled," is derived from *túrbē*, "a tumult or multitude." The verb therefore means "to raise a tumult or disturbance, to disturb or bustle." It is the only place that it occurs in the New Testament.

44

WHO SHOULD COME FIRST IN THE CHRISTIAN'S LIFE?

. . . He that is unmarried careth for the things that belong to the Lord, how he may please the Lord.—1 Corinthians 7:32

In this verse, the word "unmarried" refers to either man or woman, although the adjectival noun is in the masculine. The verb "careth" in Greek is *mérimna*, the same basic word as in the previous clause. It is in the present indicative which refers to a constant, anxious care about the things of the Lord such as Paul exercised on behalf of others.

What Should Concern the Unmarried Believer?

And what are the things that the unmarried believer is concerned about? "The things of the Lord." This of course is not an absolute statement. Not all unmarried people give their full attention and concern to the things of the Lord. In fact, singleness sometimes deprives a person of the opportunity of living for others and being altruistic as the case

commonly is with a family person. One of the greatest advantages of living in a family is learning to be
responsible for others and to care and share with
them. The unmarried person lacks such a natural
opportunity and can more easily become self– cen-
tered. But the truth is that an unmarried person will
have more time for the things of the Lord, and he or
she will not be encumbered with family responsibilities. Paul here implies that anxiety for one's family
is a commendable must. However, there are those
who cannot handle both family and the fullest possible attention to the things of the Lord. If that is the
case, then one should consider marriage as detrimental to the best accomplishment of his call in
Christ.

One Who Loves the Lord First
Should Love His Family Best

The present indicative of the verb *mérimna*, "cares
with commendable anxiety," indicates constancy
and uninterruptedness, which in the case of a married person means that he ought to give due attention to his family. The one, however, is not exclusive
of the other because, as our Lord taught us, the concern and love that we show for our loved ones
should be of a type inferior to the concern and love
that we show for the Lord Jesus (Matt. 10:37; Luke
14:26–32). Our love for our Heavenly Father should
be a worshipful, venerable type of love, but this type
of love belongs only to the Godhead. On the other

hand, the person who has the opportunity of loving his family members appropriately can qualitatively love his Lord even in a very distinct manner above an unmarried person since he has a deeper comprehension of the familial relationships set forth in the Word of God; that is, the bride of Christ, the Father and the Son, etc. We should in no way ever think that a person who serves the Lord should not be a devoted family man or woman. Both Christ and Paul have chosen the bond of marriage to illustrate the relationship between Christ and the Church and, as such, it cannot in itself be a diminutive aspect of consecration to the Lord. It is entirely possible to please the Lord and at the same time please one's spouse. And in marriage, there can be a strengthening of one another in their service and prayers to God.

45

THE DECISION TO STAY SINGLE OR MARRY MAY BECOME A HINDRANCE IN THE ACCOMPLISHMENT OF ONE'S BEST FOR THE LORD

But he that is married careth for the things that are of the world, how he may please his wife.—1 Corinthians 7:33

Here in verse thirty–three the Apostle Paul does not speak of every married person, but of the possibility of some married people giving more attention to their spouse and to the things of the world than to the Lord. This is always a possibility, and what Paul is really saying is that if marriage will cause a person to do that, it is better to stay single. "But he that is married careth for the things that are of the world, how he may please his wife." All these verses must be taken as conditional, implying that either state, singleness or married life, may be a hindrance to the accomplishment of one's

341

goal, and if they are, then they are the wrong state to choose.

The Married Person Is Duty–Bound to Seek the Spouse's Satisfaction

Paul further explains how one eagerly cares for the things of the Lord by adding the last clause of verse thirty–two, "how he may please the Lord."[1] This verb *aréskō* originally meant "to please," but later on the meaning passed into "to be pleasing"; that is to say it passed from a relationship to behavior. It denotes intentional, deliberate, and continuous conduct and not a relationship. Accordingly, it means to satisfy, to make content, to give satisfaction to or to comply with. What Paul is saying here is that the unmarried person is not directly responsible to anyone else to whom he must make his conduct pleasing or to whom he must give satisfaction except the Lord.

And then in verse thirty–three Paul reverts to the married one: "But he that is married careth for the things that are of the world, how he may please his wife." What is translated here as "married"[2] refers to the moment that a person was married and not to the state of marriage. That decision to marry as a consequence has the constant, anxious care about the things of the world.

The verb translated "cares" is exactly as before, *mérimna*. The things of the world are called *tá toú kósmou*. The same word is used for "world" as in verse thirty–one, referring to the shape of the world.

It refers to earthly and mundane things which every married man must attend to. *Kósmos* here stands in contrast to the Lord. *Kósmos*, "world," refers to that order of things within which humanity moves, of which man is the center. Since the center of the world is man rather than God, then attention is directed chiefly to man.

Paul further explains what he means by anxious care of the things of the world by adding, "how he may please his wife." The verb is exactly the same, *arései*, which means "to be pleasing with one's conduct" and hence to make content. Paul does not imply that it is wrong in any way for a husband to make his wife content and to be pleasing to her. In fact Paul confirms this as a husband's duty. All that he says is that if the man were not married, then he would have only one to please, and that is the Lord.

---

[1]Similar expressions with the object being *tó theó*, "the God," instead of the Lord, occur in Romans 8:8 and 1 Thessalonians 2:15 and 4:1. The verb in Greek is *arései*, third person singular future indicative of *aréskō*.

[2]In Greek *gamḗsas*, a participial substantive, nominative singular masculine first aorist participle active of *gaméō*. In verse ten, the married ones are the *gegamēkósi* which is a substantive in the present perfect which refers to those who are in the state of marriage. Here in verse thirty–two it is *ho gamḗsas*, "he who was married," referring rather to the act of marriage.

46

IS IT WRONG TO WANT TO PLEASE ONE'S MARRIAGE PARTNER?

There is difference also between a wife and a virgin. The unmarried woman careth for the things of the Lord, that she may be holy both in body and in spirit: but she that is married careth for the things of the world, how she may please her husband.—1 Corinthians 7:34

As there is a difference between an unmarried man and a married man spoken of in verses thirty–two and thirty–three, there is also a difference between a married woman and a virgin woman which Paul now deals with in verse thirty–four. This verse begins with exactly the same verb used in 1 Corinthians 7:17 translated "distributed."[1] But here in 1 Corinthians 7:34, it means exactly what the King James Version says: "There is a difference between the married woman and the virgin."

Paul then proceeds to explain: "The unmarried woman careth for the things of the Lord, that she may be holy both in body and in spirit: but she that is married careth for the things of the world, how she may please her husband." Although previously he put the wife first in the clause "There is a difference also between a wife and a virgin," in the next clause he puts the unmarried woman first. He doesn't say the virgin maiden, *hē parthénos*, but *hē ágamos*, "the unmarried woman." He does so because he wants to also include the widow and the believing wife who has been discarded by her unbelieving husband. He refers to the state of singleness. This time, however, in addition to saying that the unmarried woman "careth (*mérimna*) for the things of the Lord," he adds, "that she may be holy both in body and in spirit."[2]

Why Doesn't Paul Also Speak About the Married Man Pleasing His Wife?

What does the Apostle Paul mean when he says that the unmarried woman cares for the things of the Lord "so that she may be holy, both in body and in spirit"?

Let us note first of all that what the Apostle Paul says about the unmarried woman, he did not say about the unmarried man. In the case of the unmarried man, he simply said that he cares for the things of the Lord how he may please the Lord. But in the case of the unmarried woman, he adds "that she may be holy, both in body and in spirit." Why is there this addition in the case of the unmarried woman? Because it is the woman who must spend the greatest part of her time in an effort to care for her husband and family through meal preparation, care of the home, personal adornment, etc. We should bear in mind that at the time Paul wrote this, unless a woman had a servant, she had no conveniences whatever as we know them today. Her work most likely would have been unending, leaving her little, if any, time to attend to the things of the Lord.

The meaning of being or becoming holy, *hágios*, must always be understood in the context in which it is given. As in 1 Corinthians 7:14, the word translated "sanctify" (*hagiázō*, derived from the same root as *hágios*) has the restricted sense of abstaining from fornication in the case of the unbelieving spouse as a condition for the believing partner to stay with the unbeliever. Here also, the meaning of the word *hágios*, in the case of the married woman, must be understood in a restricted sense as meaning that a married woman, in contrast to the unmarried woman, must spend much time in order to please her husband and family. The unmarried woman, however, is "set aside" or freed from many encumbrances of mundane responsibilities and the concern that she is found satisfactory to her husband.

This restricted meaning of the word *hágios* is strengthened also by the use of the phrase "both in body and spirit." This phrase is not found anywhere else in the Scriptures in this exact manner. It actually refers to the body as much as to the spirit. Paul in no way attacks a woman for trying to please her husband and family in any manner, even in personal adornment. But although Paul was not married, yet it was obvious that he could see that the women of those days considered personal adornment as very important. We must remember the worldly, carnal influence spread abroad by the immoral practices of the Corinthians and other godless cults at the time.

It seems that this carnal influence had permeated the Christian church to the extent that Paul found it necessary to write in 1 Timothy 2:9: "In like manner also, that women adorn themselves in modest apparel, with shamefacedness and sobriety; not with braided hair, or gold, or pearls, or costly array." And then in verse ten he continues: "But (which becometh women professing godliness) with good works."

Should the Christian Seek to Be Physically Attractive?

Using the term "adorn" metaphorically in Titus 2:10, Paul's advice for all Christians is "That they may adorn the doctrine of God our Savior in all things." It is interesting to note that the word in both instances translated "adorn" is the verb *kosméō* from the noun *kósmos*, "world," but which also means "adorning, ornament." This word is also found in 1 Peter 3:3,

348

"whose adorning (*kósmos*) let it not be that outward adorning (*kósmos*) of plaiting the hair, and of wearing of gold, or of putting on of apparel." And then in 1 Peter 3:5 we find the word "holy," referring to women, and used in connection with women adorning themselves (*hágiai gunaíkes . . . ekósmoun*): "For after this manner in the old time the holy (*hágiai*) women also, who trusted in God, adorned (*ekósmoun*) themselves, being in subjection unto their own husbands." In Revelation 21:2 we are told that John saw the holy city, New Jerusalem, coming down from God out of heaven, prepared as a bride adorned (*kekosmēménēn* from *kosméō*) for her husband. A truly Christian woman will not try to adorn herself so that her body appears differently than her spirit is. There will be a congruence between outward adorning and inward saintliness.

The unmarried woman who has determined that singleness is a way to accomplish her calling in the Lord will not be given to the craze for fashion and beauty as one who adorns her body and dresses in a way primarily to attract a man to marry her, or the one who is married and trying, by her appearance, to cause her husband to admire her. The Apostle Paul intimates here that there is a correlation between inward saintliness and outward modesty. The woman who seeks to adorn the doctrine of God will be modest, but also neat and comely, not bringing shame to the name of Christ.

The Lord Must Have First Place

The final clause of verse thirty–four is very similar to the final clause of verse thirty–two with the exception that here Paul refers to the woman who was married and wants to please her husband: "But she that is married careth for the things of the world, how she may please her husband."

What is translated by the clause "she that is married" in Greek is a participial noun *hē*, "the," *gamēsasa*, "woman who got married," in the aorist tense which indicates that reference is made to the time of marriage or the decision to get married. From the moment that a woman decided to marry, from that moment on she became engaged in anxious care about the things of the world. The danger is that a married woman will put the pleasing of her husband or family before the Lord. Indeed, there is nothing wrong with a married woman wanting to be pleasing to her husband or family, but she must remember that the Lord must have first place in her life.

The thesis of Paul throughout these three verses, 1 Corinthians 7:32–34, is that with the single state, there is less likelihood for an unmarried man or woman to put another person before the Lord. While it is possible for the married child of God to be equally as saintly as the unmarried, he or she should be on guard lest the duties of marriage become a distraction from the closest possible walk with the Lord.

---

[1]*Meméristai*; third person singular perfect indicative passive of *merízō*, from *merís*, "a part."

[2]The word "holy" in greek is *hagía* from the negative "a," and *gě*, "the earth"; that is to say, separated from earth. Or, it may be derived from *hágos*, "a thing sacred, purity," which in turn is from the verb *házō*, "to venerate." It is interesting, however, that Paul adds the two datives, *kaí*, "and," and *sōmati*, the dative of *sōma*, "body," and *pneúmati*, "spirit," the dative of *pneúma*.

47

BASIC CONSIDERATIONS IN THE DECISION WHETHER ONE SHOULD STAY SINGLE OR MARRY

And this I speak for your own proft; not that I may cast a snare upon you, but for that which is comely, and that ye may attend upon the Lord without distraction.—1 Corinthians 7:35

In all the advice that Paul has given in regard to whether an unmarried person should remain single or should marry, he might be misunderstood. Did he really have any grudge against those who decided to marry or, as we would call it today, a "sour–grapes attitude"? Would he accuse his fellow apostles who were married of having made a mistake and pat himself on the back that he accomplished more, simply because he remained single? Paul did not want anyone to think that his advice in regard to marriage was motivated by any pride over his own state and accomplishment. All that he said had as its basic motive the true benefit of those to whom he was writing and the desire to see the Lord served in an unhindered manner.

Thus Paul closes this section concerning the unmarried and widows, beginning with verse twenty–five and ending with verse thirty–five, with the phrase, "And this I speak for your own profit." That was Paul's basic motive. It was not to win more people to the state of singleness for which he had preference. It was not a matter of sinning or not sinning, being in the will or out of the will of the Lord, but it was a matter of judgment as to how the Lord could be served in the best possible way. Paul wanted every Christian, as he faced the decision of whether to marry or not to marry, to consider whether the single or married life would better profit his relationship to God.

When Deciding on Celibacy or Marriage, Should One Think Only of Self?

The word that is translated "profit" in Greek[1] has as its basic meaning "to bring together." When we speak of "profit" in English, generally we have only ourselves in mind and how it will benefit us. When Paul, however, speaks of *sumphéron*, "profit," he does not have someone's individual profit or advantage in mind. He is referring to that which brings the individual together with Christ, His purposes, or the benefit and advantage of the local Christian community or church. It is actually "to bring together" or "to cause common advantage." Therefore, when Paul said, "And this I speak for your own profit," he did not mean that the Corinthian Christians should consider whether to remain single or marry simply on the ground of personal benefit. They were encouraged to consider how that state of being would benefit others, the cause of Christ, the local community and Kingdom of God. It was to be anything but selfish consideration.

The profit at issue here is individual spiritual existence, the union of each Christian with the Lord and of the Lord with him. It is what he expressed in the previous verse, to be holy, both in body and in spirit. Therefore, *sumphéron*, "profit or experience," is that which edifies the community. If Paul had in mind that which benefits personally, he would have used another word, *óphelos* (1 Cor. 15:32; James 2:14, 16) or *ōphéleia* (Rom. 3:1; Jude 1:16), meaning personal advantage.

Does Paul Issue a Directive to Stay Single or to Marry?

We could therefore paraphrase the first statement of Paul in 1 Corinthians 7:35 as "I am not directing these remarks to you about singleness and marriage in order that you may find a state of personal and selfish satisfaction, but rather that which will benefit the glory of the Lord and the cause of His gospel on earth, and particularly the work of the local community."

The second statement that he makes indicates that he did not want his discussion and advice in regard to singleness and the married life to be considered in a legalistic manner. He said, "Not that I may cast a snare upon you."

The first thing that should arrest our attention is the verb that is translated "I may cast a snare upon you."[2] The verb transitively may mean, "to throw over" or "to lay on." It is used also in the hostile sense, "to break in." In the New Testament, the word depicts transitively the violent movement of "casting on or over" as in this case of 1 Corinthians 7:35. It also refers to "hostile seizure," as in Mark 14:46; Acts 4:3; 5:18. This word is also used in the fourth Gospel which shows that the Jews could not use force against Jesus until His hour had come (John 7:30, 44).

Here in 1 Corinthians 7:35, it is used transitively in a belligerent manner with the object being what Paul calls a snare. The aorist subjunctive tense refers to a once–and–for–all ensnaring of the Corinthians into a state of being to which they would find themselves enslaved. In other words, Paul is saying to these Corinthians: "Don't think I'm trying to bind you into something that you don't wish. The decision is yours personally to make and not a thing that I am to impose upon you."

When Paul speaks of a snare, he uses the Greek word *bróchos* meaning "a cord which one can tie or bind by transposition." It is what we call today a noose. In its figurative sense, as being a snare, it is used only here in the entire New Testament. What a gentleman Paul was! Even being an apostle, he did not want these Corinthians to consider the advice that he was giving them in regard to the single or married life as being a noose that he was throwing to entrap someone unawares.

The Decision to Stay Single or Marry Must Be Based on Inner Honesty, Not on Appearances

The first thing Paul had said was that his comments were for the purpose of the communal advantage of the church in Corinth and for the cause of Christ in general. Then he said that no one should consider it as an imposed snare. And now thirdly, he gives a positive statement which has as its verb that which he used in the first clause, "I speak." The purpose for which he is saying this is expressed in the preposition *prós*, "for or toward." "But (for the purpose) for that which is comely."

What is translated as "comely,"[3] when it is used of things as here and in 1 Corinthians 12:24, means "decent, becoming." However, the word used in this context would rather mean "honest conduct." Although the word originally referred to outward appearance, yet that meaning with the passing of time was changed to refer not only to the outward appearance but to the inner reality. It is used, for instance, in 1 Thessalonians 4:12: "That ye may walk honestly (*euschēmónōs*, the adverbial use) toward them that are without, and that ye may have lack of nothing." It is used also in Romans 13:13: "Let us walk honestly (*euschēmónōs*), as in the day; not in rioting and drunkenness, not in chambering and wantonness, not in strife and envying." It is used also in 1 Corinthians 14:40: "Let all things be done decently (*euschēmónōs*) and in order."

Thus what Paul explains in this third statement in this verse is that he has said all this so that the believer may be honest when considering marriage. Don't only look at the appearance but also at the reality of the matter. Is it going to be a help in living a better life to the glory of God? That is the answer that each individual must give personally and honestly.

The Basic Consideration Is Whether the Married or Single State Will Best Honor the Lord

There is yet another purpose for which Paul has written to the Corinthians which is expressed in the last clause of verse thirty–five: "and that ye may attend upon the Lord without distraction."

What is rendered as "that ye may attend" in Greek actually means "to sit well beside a task."[4] It refers to consecration and utter devotion to the Lord. This is actually what Paul means when previously he spoke of living in such a way as to please the Lord. It is sitting in the right place and doing the right things that honor the Lord Jesus Christ.

If *euschḗmōn* or *euschḗmon*, translated by "that which is comely," refers to the external aspect of the Christian life emerging from the reality of inner conviction, then *epáredron* refers to the relationship of the person spoken about to the source of goodness and honor in his conduct, and that is the *hédra*, "the seat."

This word *hédra*, meaning "a sitting place," does not occur in the New Testament, but it does in classical Greek. It used to refer, for instance, to a station for ships. When the Greeks spoke of something as being *ex hédras*, they meant that it was out of its right place. They referred to a bottom or foundation or base. Hence we find the adjective *hedraíos* in 1 Corinthians 7:37; 15:58 and Colossians 1:23, translated as "steadfast or settled." Accordingly, *epáredron* refers to conduct that emanates not only from the inner state of man, but from an inner state that is based upon the proper, good foundation which is the Lord Jesus Christ. It is not simply having good conduct that shows the reality of self, but self being conformed to the image of the Lord Jesus Christ and founded on Him. This is emphasized by the fact that *epáredron* is followed by *tó kuríō*, "upon the Lord."

Some manuscripts, instead of *epáredron*, have *euprósedron* or *prósedron*. The difference is that instead of the preposition *pará*, "by the side of," we have the preposition *prós*, which means "to," thus giving the Lord a very clear superiority as the Rock to which man's conduct should be attached and fastened. Essentially, however, both readings mean the same thing, referring to the Lord as the One who provides the basis for the conduct of the believer.

Consider Whether Marriage Will Help or Hinder God's Calling

Paul closes this section with the adverb *aperispá-stōs*,[5] "without distraction," which occurs only here in the entire New Testament. This adverb means to distract with different cares and responsibilities; one pulling, as it were, one way, and another in a different way. We find a good illustration of this in Luke 10:40 in the case of Martha. This word, *aperispástōs*, is one that is used commonly even in modern Greek today. Paul did not want the believer to be drawn in different directions. When one is married, he has the drawing of his family responsibilities and the drawing of his spiritual and moral responsibilities. Thus, the important question one must consider as he contemplates the matter of celibacy or marriage is whether this is a state which is going to distract from his main task in life, which is pleasing the Lord, or is it going to be a help. It all depends on the temperament of the believer himself given to him by the Lord, the task that he is called upon to perform, and the direct calling of God upon his life as to whether he can better accomplish his God–ordained task in life in celibacy or marriage.

Three Questions the Single Christian Should Consider

There are three basic questions that any single Christian ought to ask himself as he contemplates whether he should marry or not:

1. *Which State Will Provide the Most Honorable Conduct and Becoming Behavior (Schéma)?*

If I remain unmarried, am I going to be constantly flirting with the opposite sex and thus bring shame to the name of Christ while I maintain an attitude of the superiority of celibacy to indicate that I am "holier than thou" simply by being single? This is the height of hypocrisy.

In such a case, it is far better to get married. It is all too common today to find men who have determined within their hearts not to marry, who will yet court a lady, giving her hopes of marriage. Then when he perceives that the woman is becoming serious about their relationship, he backs out. This is no innocent pastime on the part of the man. He has been playing with the emotions of the woman, living a lie by allowing her to think that he is seriously interested in her, and then leaving her with shattered hopes and a broken heart. This is a devious sin that all too many single men fall into and for which they must some day give account to their Lord. The outside behavior of an unmarried person should conform to his inner conviction.

In which state, then, can I better demonstrate such outward behavior as the expression of inner conviction? If it is singleness, that's fine; if it is married life, that's fine too.

2. *Is My Conviction in Agreement With Christ's Teaching?*

My conviction and conduct must be *euparedron*, solidly anchored or moored to the immovable rock, Jesus Christ. I must not simply be satisfied that my ship is moored, but know on what it is moored. Is it on the Lord Jesus Christ? Would He be glorified not only through my outward conduct, but also by my conviction being in agreement with His teaching? In what state, that of singleness or of married life, can I be more firmly rooted in the Lord Jesus Christ?

3. *Which State Is Going to Distract Me Less, Celibacy or Marriage?*

I must decide which of the two states is going to provide for me a singleness of purpose in both outward behavior and proper conviction. It would be unwise to allow myself to get into a state which will cause me to be divided in my loyalty to a degree that I put the Lord second. If there is any fear that a man should love a woman or a woman love a man more than the Lord Jesus Christ, it is better to stay single. If, by becoming a parent, I am more likely to love my child or children more than the Lord Jesus Christ, then it is better to stay single. Will the one I am intent on marrying be a help to me in my endeavor to serve the Lord, or a hindrance?

Jesus Christ must be the head of the home. And when He has first place, then the family has the best possible environment for the fullest possible development and growth. If that cannot be the case, then Paul implies in his total teaching here that it is better to stay single.

---

[1]*Sumphéron*, a neuter participle used as a noun of the verb *sumphérō*, from *sún*, "together," and *phérō*, "to bring." Some manuscripts have the word as *tó súmphoron*, which for all practical purposes is the same as to *sumphéron*. Paul generally uses *sumphérei* as a verb meaning "it is expedient, it is profitable," or the substantive participle to *sumphéron*, referring to that which profits the spiritual life.

[2]In Greek it is *epibálō*, first person singular, second aorist subjunctive active of *epibállō*, from *epí*, "upon or unto," and *bállō*, "to cast, put."

[3]In Greek it is a participial substantive to *eúschēmon* from *euschémōn*, from *eú*, "well, good," and *schéma*, "form, fashion."

[4]It is just one substantive participle: *eupáredron*, made up of *eú*, "well," *pará*, "beside," and *hédra*, which in turn is derived from the verb *ézomai*, "I seat myself." *Hédra* is therefore "seat or sitting." Thus this term *eupáredron*, occurring only in 1 Corinthians 7:35, means "to sit well beside a task."

[5]This adverb is derived from the adjective *aperíspastos* which in turn comes from the privative *a*, and *perispáō*, "to distract." The verb *perispáō* is derived from *perí*, "about, around," and *spáō*, "to draw." This latter verb means to draw different ways at the same time.

48

THE DUTY OF PARENTS IN ENCOURAGING THEIR DAUGHTERS TO REMAIN SINGLE OR TO MARRY

But if any man think he behaveth himself un-comely toward his virgin, . . . —1 Corinthians 7:36

This passage is admittedly very difficult. The conclusion at which many commentators arrive, that this passage refers to giving away a virgin daughter in marriage by her father, is based upon the meaning of the verb *ekgamízō* (Textus Receptus) or *gamízō* (UBS), meaning "to give in marriage."[1]

Is It Wrong for a Father to Give Away His Daughter Unto Marriage?

Because of the use of this verb meaning "to give in marriage," we conclude that this passage does indeed refer to the parents, and particularly to the father, who may have retained his daughter at home.

In those days a father had much more authority over his daughter than is true in our western culture. He was without doubt the autocratic ruler of his family. One of the decisions of the father, and here Paul must have been speaking of a Christian father, was whether he should give his daughter in marriage or to retain her at home.

It seems to me that the interpretation of this passage ought to begin with verse thirty–eight. If the subject of the sentence, "So then he that giveth her in marriage doeth well" were the one marrying, it would have used the present participle active, *gamón*. This word is exactly the same as is used in Luke 16:18: "Whosoever putteth away his wife, and marrieth (*gamón*) another, committeth adultery; and whosoever marrieth (*gamón*) her that is put away from her husband committeth adultery." Therefore, the subject of the present participle *gamízōn* or *ekgamízōn* in 1 Corinthians 7:38, translated "giveth her in marriage," cannot be the one who gets married, but the one who gives his virgin daughter to marriage. If the subject of *gamízōn* or *ekgamízōn* were the would–be groom, then by virtue of the meaning of the verb, he would have to give away his own virgin. This is an impossibility. But if the subject is the father and the virgin spoken of as his own virgin daughter, then here we have the father of a single girl giving away his own virgin daughter to marriage. Paul says that if a father decides to do this, he does well. The decision is his, and naturally also his consenting daughter's.

How Can a Father Behave Wrongly Toward His Daughter?

Now we must go back to verse thirty–six to see what is it that has led such a father to give his daughter to marriage. Verse thirty–six says: "But if any man think that he behaveth himself uncomely toward his virgin." The principal verb in this sentence is *nomízei*, "think"—"if any man *think* that he behaveth himself uncomely."

In English, verse thirty–six says: "But if any man think that he behaveth himself uncomely toward his virgin, if she pass the flower of her age." In Greek, the construction of the sentence runs this way: "But if any man (anyone) acting (infinitive) uncomely toward his virgin, he thinks, if she is over age. . . ." This man spoken of is qualified as the one acting in an unseemly manner toward his virgin. What is the object of "he thinks"? It is the clause beginning with the infinitive *aschēmoneín*, "acting uncomely." "If anyone thinks that he is acting uncomely toward his virgin."

Now, why does he act thus uncomely? The answer comes after the verb *nomízei*, "he thinks." It is the clause "if she is overage," or as the translation has it, "if she pass the flower of her age. . . ." This would be better understood if we rendered to *ean*, "if," the meaning of "because"—because she is overage. The picture is that of a father looking at his virgin daughter who has passed the age of marriage and thinking that he acted in an improper manner, having kept her at home without the prospect of marriage.

Our next endeavor is to find out the meaning of the infinitive *aschēmoneín* from the verb *aschēmonéō*.[2] It means "to behave indecently, unseemly or unbecomingly." This word is used only one other time in the New Testament, where Paul says that love does not behave in an unseemly manner (1 Cor. 13:5). The use of the verb in this latter instance ought to throw some light on the meaning of the word as used in 1 Corinthians 7:36. The definition which the Apostle Paul gives in his hymn of love, *agápē*, is that it is the spiritual element in man which does not seek its own gratification but seeks to help another by discerning the need of that one.

Now, how can a father of a virgin daughter behave in an unseemly manner toward her? If he really loves her, he will never seek to determine the his daughter's future through selfish motives. There may have been a father who wanted to keep his daughter at home in order to serve him for the rest of her life and his, or he may have been refusing marriage for her in order to get the largest possible dowry from a prospective groom. This is not what a father who loves his daughter ought to do. He ought to put the future and the welfare of his daughter ahead of his own. There should be parental concern and love in the heart of a father, and his behavior toward his daughter ought to be the outward expression of that inner love which seeks always the benefit of his daughter.

The verb *aschēmonéō* in this context should not be taken as the father behaving in an immoral manner toward his daughter. If such were the case, the same word of condemnation would have come upon this father as the Apostle Paul had for the son who had married his stepmother in the fifth chapter of First Corinthians. Therefore, the proper meaning of the verb *aschēmonéō* is "has outwardly and unfairly treated his maiden daughter," or we could say, "If a father has been keeping his daughter at home for selfish purposes."

A Would–Be Groom Would Not Be Behaving Himself Uncomely *Toward* but *With* His Virgin

One more reason why we believe that this passage refers to the father rather than to the would–be groom is the use of the preposition *epí*, "toward" or "on," and not *metá*, "with." If the would–be groom had done something wrong *with* his virgin, then he wouldn't *think* so, but he would *know* so. The meaning of *epí* here is "over." The father of whom Paul is speaking has enforced a condition of singleness upon his maiden daughter for selfish purposes. This is what *aschēmoneín epí*, "to behave unseemly upon or over one's own virgin," means.

The necessary conclusion is that this Scripture refers to the father. If at any time he realizes that he is not treating his maiden daughter fairly in keeping her at home, he should act upon his conviction and should give her unto marriage.

---

[1]This verb is different from *gaméo* used repeatedly in the New Testament to indicate "to marry." In the active, it is properly spoken in reference to the male as in Matthew 5:32; 19:9; 22:25, 30, etc. In the passive, however, it means "to be married" and is used of the woman as in Mark 10:12 and 1 Corinthians 7:39. However, *gaméo* in the active is also sometimes applied to the woman as in 1 Corinthians 7:28, 34 and 1 Timothy 5:11, 14. The other verb that is used in 1 Corinthians 7:38 is *gamískō*, *gamízō*, *ekgamískō*, or *ek*, "out" (in the case of the last two), and *gamískō*, "to give in marriage." This latter form is used in Luke 20:34, 35, and the former form, *gamízō*, is used in Matthew 22:30; 24:38; Mark 12:25; and Luke 17:27; 20:35. All these instances are clear in the meaning of both verbs, *gaméo*, and *gamízō*, as referring to "marry" and "give to marriage."

[2]In verse thirty–five the Apostle Paul used the substantive participle *eúschēmon* referring to "good outwardly conduct that has its root in an inner conviction." The opposite of that conduct is *aschémoneō* made up of the negative or privative *a* and *schéma*, "behavior," usually outwardly resulting from an inner conviction.

49

MARRIAGE IN LATER LIFE

. . . if she pass the flower of her age, and need so require, let him do what he will, he sinneth not: let them marry.—1 Corinthians 7:36

The decision to give a daughter unto marriage whom a father has selfishly kept at home would be further accentuated if he finds another element that would influence his decision. This is given in the second suppositional phrase: "If she pass the flower of her age."[1] This word is used exclusively in 1 Corinthians 7:36, but its use in Classical Greek gives us a clue to its meaning as being beyond or past the bloom of youth.

A Father Who Has Unfairly Kept His Daughter From Marrying Can Still Do So Even if She Is Older

What is a father supposed to do who realizes that he has been unfair to his daughter in keeping her at home instead of giving her to marriage, and especially if he finds that she has already passed the prime of her age as far as marriage is concerned?

Paul says that such a father ought to give his daughter unto marriage even if she is older and perhaps beyond the child–bearing age. There is a subtle indication given to us here by Paul that the real purpose of marriage is not merely sex or procreation, but it is also companionship. Two people can be married and be happy without sexual relationships even if hindered by age or the physical incapacity of one or both.

That the father arrives at the conclusion that he must no longer keep his daughter at home unfairly is expressed by the next phrase in verse thirty–six: "and need so require."[2] The subject in this phrase ought also to be taken as the father and not the would–be groom. If it referred to the would–be groom having had relations with his virgin whom he wanted to marry, she wouldn't have been a virgin any more, and then the verb would not have been *gamízō* but *gaméō*. If this were the case, Paul would have brought about some condemnation upon such a would–be groom.

Therefore we conclude that the subject continues to be the father of the daughter. The principal verb continues to be *nomízei*; "thinks." If the father thinks that he has treated his daughter unfairly, even if she is beyond the normal age for marriage, and he believes that he should give her unto marriage, let him do so. If the subject were the would–be groom, Paul would not have said that he should do what he wants, since the would–be groom would have proven himself a sinner, a fornicator, by having sexual relations with a maiden to whom he was not married. The expression therefore "Let him do what he will," must refer to the father, and it must mean to let him give his daughter unto marriage, *ekgamízei* or *gamízei*.

This conclusion is confirmed by the next clause: "He sinneth not," *ouch hamartánei*. This could not have been said of a would–be groom who had sexual relations with his betrothed would–be wife. What the Apostle Paul is stressing here, that the decision of a father to give his daughter unto marriage, having considered all angles of the question, is not a sin on his part. Already Paul in 1 Corinthians 7:28 said of the virgins spoken of in verse twenty–five that if they decide to marry, they have not sinned. The same is true of the father who has finally decided to give his daughter unto marriage even though he had held the conviction for many years that it was better that she remain unmarried.

The Daughter of a Father Who Hindered Her From Marrying Can Decide to Marry

The verb appearing at the end of verse thirty–six expresses Paul's conclusion: "Let them marry."[3] The difficulty here is that in this verse we have the subject being the father and the object being the virgin daughter. Therefore, the marriage referred to here cannot be the father marrying the daughter. It could have referred to the would–be groom marrying the virgin, but this has already been excluded by virtue of what has already been stated by Paul. Therefore, the plural here can refer to the daughter and the man she wants to marry. Evidently the decision of the father to give his daughter unto marriage has been brought about by the appearance on the scene of a would–be husband for the daughter, and we now have a prospective bridegroom coming into the picture. The apostle says let them, the daughter and the prospective husband, get married. This is a directive to a father who selfishly withheld his daughter from marriage. After all, she herself ought to have a say in the matter of marriage. Hence, Paul says, "Let them, the virgin and the groom, get married."

The other possibile subject of *gameítōsan*, "let them marry," is the *parthenoi*, the virgin maidens referred to in this entire passage from verses twenty–five through forty. This portion of Scripture deals with the question of what should the virgins do, marry or not marry. It should be their own personal decision in spite of having been unfairly hindered from marrying by their own fathers.

---

[1]In Greek this phrase is *eán ḗ hupérakmos*: *eán*, "if;" *ḗ*, third person singular present subjunctive of *eimí*, "to be;" *hupérakmos* from *hupér*, "beyond," and *akmḗ*, "the acme or flower of age," particularly with respect to marriage as applied by Dionysius, Halicarn and Lucian.

[2]In Greek it is *kaí hoútōs opheílei gínesthai*: *kaí*, "and;" *hoútōs*, "thus;" *opheílei* "has an obligation;" meaning that one

is bound to make reparation to the party that has been injured as here and in Luke 11:4; *gínesthai*, the infinitive of *gínomai*, "to happen, to occur, to come to pass."

3This is the third person plural present imperative active of *gaméō*.

50

PARENTS MAY ACT WISELY IN NOT ALLOWING THEIR DAUGHTER TO MARRY UNDER CERTAIN CIRCUMSTANCES

. . . he that standeth steadfast in his heart, having no necessity, but hath power over his own will, and hath so decreed in his heart that he will keep his virgin, doeth well.—1 Corinthians 7:37

In this verse Paul gives the possibility of the opposite eventuality, that the father does not come to the conclusion that he is unfairly treating his virgin daughter by keeping her at home and unmarried. He says: "Nevertheless he that standeth steadfast in his heart." The verb *hestēken*, "standeth steadfast," is the third person singular perfect indicative of *hístēmi*, "to stand," that is, he who has been standing steadfast in his heart.

This verse speaks of the father who made the decision to keep his daughter at home and has never come under the conviction that what he did was wrong. He continues to believe that that is the proper thing to do in regard to his daughter. Observe that this standing is in his heart which refers to an inner conviction agreeing with his overt action. The adjective *hedraíos*, translated "steadfast," is to be related to the substantive participle *eupáredron*, "being well moored to the right foundation," which is, of course, the Lord. In other words, Paul refers to the father who continues to be under the conviction that his daughter will serve the Lord better in remaining single than in being married, and this is in accordance with the doctrine Paul has been promulgating. That is the first condition which makes a father not give away his daughter in marriage.

The Motive of a Father's Refusal to Give His Daughter in Marriage May Be Right

There is a second condition expressed in the phrase "having no necessity." The word translated "necessity" is *anággēn*. This is exactly the same word as we find in 1 Corinthians 7:26 which is translated "distress" in the phrase, "I suppose therefore that this is good for the present distress (*anággēn*)."

The word "necessity" in 1 Corinthians 7:37 must be understood as surerring back to the same meaning as in verse twenty–six which does not refer to the sexual needs of the would–be groom. So in verse thirty–seven, Paul speaks of the circumstances as discerned by the father lending themselves to the rightness of his conviction that it is better for his daughter to remain unmarried. Evidently, he sees no necessity for such a daughter to get married. She may not be oversexual, she may not be too anxious to marry, she may believe that she can accomplish more for the Lord in the unmarried state, or perhaps a man has not come along who would be worthy of this girl. In many cases, marriage can be detrimental to a woman instead of a blessing. It is quite possible that such a situation is one of a father who has a daughter so dedicated that she would prefer to serve the Lord on some mission field of the world alone rather than to be married and stay home with one who does not share her burden for the lost. When a woman is to decide between Christ or a husband, Christ must take the preeminence. Not, of course, that she cannot serve Christ being married, but if the choice must be made between Christ and a husband, it is better to fulfill the call that she has received from God and give up the idea of getting married.

A Father Has the Authority to Keep His Daughter From Marrying

The third reason for this steadfast decision of a father not to give his daughter unto marriage is expressed by the third phrase in verse thirty–seven: "But hath power over his own will." It is unfortunate that the particle *dé* has been translated as an adversative in this verse. It should be translated as a sequential conjunction *kaí*, "and." "And he has power concerning his own will."

379

The word translated "power" is *exousían*, the accusative of *exousía* derived from the verb *éxesti*, "it is possible," and would be better translated as "authority." It is having the right and the might to do something. The father in this instance has the right to keep his daughter at home and also the power to bring this about. The word translated as "will" is *thélēma* which denotes more the will as an expression of inclination or pleasure rather than a demand. The father here realizes that not giving his daughter into marriage is within his own jurisdiction, but in this instance it is a conclusion that he has come to after having considered all circumstances including the natural inclination of his daughter. The conclusion is his own will. He has the right to have it and also the right to execute it as well as the power. If he didn't have it, he couldn't exercise it.

When one considers the customs of that day, when because it was considered a great shame for a girl to remain unmarried many were forced into an unsatisfactory marriage, we can see the concern Paul is showing towards these women. He is saying that the father has the right to keep his daughter at home and protect her from an unsatisfactory marriage.

A Father Is Duty-bound to Protect His Daughter From What He Is Convinced Would Be a Bad Marriage

The fourth reason for the decision of this father to keep his virgin daughter at home is expressed in the next statement of our verse: "And hath so decreed in his heart." The word translated "decreed" implies a fixed resolution or determination[1]. Observe, this determination was made by the father in his own heart even as we have his own will spoken of in the previous clause.[2] This refers to his conviction about his daughter remaining single.

The verb *kékriken*, "he has decreed or made the proper judgment," has as its object "to keep his virgin." Actually it is "to keep his own virgin," *tēn heautoú parthénon*. "To keep" is the translation of the Greek infinitive *tēreín* of *tēréō*, "to keep, watch, guard."[3] It is actually the opposite of not allowing his daughter to go away but to keep her at home and give her protection. The verb *tēréō* occurs sixty times in the New Testament. Here, more specifically, it means "to protect" (see John 17:11, 12, 15). It refers to the fact that it is the duty of the father to protect his maiden daughter that she not be forced into an undesirable marriage or fall prey to circumstances which may cause her to make an imprudent decision to get married. In the spirit of Saint Paul's argument, this guarding or protecting must afford the maiden daughter the opportunity of greatest service to the Lord and of living in compliance with her Christian conscience.

A Father's Decision Not to Give His Daughter to Marriage May Prove a Good One

And finally, Paul closes verse thirty–seven by saying of the father, "he doeth well." Actually it would have been better to translate this "he will do well."[4] It refers to a definite act of the future. He will do well to guard his own daughter having had that conviction in his heart steadfastly for a long time and seeing that the circumstances of life are amenable to such a decision. This is stated in view of the fact that he has both the duty and the authority to cause his daughter to remain single, if she concurs with his decision.

In all this we must understand that there is a concurrence between the wishes of the daughter and those of the father, for the father must not force any daughter to remain unmarried if she wants to get married. Paul in this total discussion is delineating the duty of the father and, by implication of course. of the mother as well. For parents to keep their daughter at home and not to give her to marriage, if God's life long goals for the daughter, the circumstances, and the will of the daughter are taken into account, is not a bad decision after all. This is what Paul is saying.

---

[1]*Kékriken,* third person singular perfect indicative active of *krínō,* which means "to judge proper, to determine," as also in Acts 15:19; 16:4; 20:16; 21:25 and 25:25. In 1 Corinthians 5:3 it appears in exactly the same form, *kékrika.*

[2]*Toú idíou thelématos,* "of his own will," and *en té idía kardía,* "in his own heart."

[3]This is also used in Matthew 27:36, 54; 28:4; Acts 12:6; 16:23; 24:23; 25:4, 21.

[4]The verb is *poiései*, third person singular future indicative active of *poiéō*, "to do."

51

DID PAUL'S EXPERIENCE AS A SINGLE MAN INFLUENCE HIS VIEW AS TO WHICH STATE IS BETTER?

So then he that giveth her in marriage doeth well; but he that giveth her not in marriage doeth better.—1 Corinthians 7:38

In conclusion of the first instance where the father has decided to give his daughter in marriage, we have the first part of verse thirty–eight: "So then he that giveth her in marriage doeth well." The verb "doeth" is *poieí*, the present indicative of *poiéō*, which indicates that the father can do this at any time, no matter how old his daughter is. This statement should be connected with verse thirty–six.

The opposite eventuality is stated by the latter part of verse thirty–eight: "But he that giveth her not in marriage doeth better." The word "better" in Greek is *kreisson*, and it stands as the comparative of the adverb *kalós*, "well." It is not a matter of one decision, that is giving a daughter to marriage, being a sinful act and the other being a less sinful act. Both decisions may be right, given a full examination of the circumstances. In consideration, however, of all that the Apostle Paul said and in view of his experience and satisfaction being found in singleness, he expresses a personal opinion that the decision of a father to guard and protect his daughter in singleness is better than giving her unto marriage. It is his own opinion, of course. You and I have the right to disagree, and Paul expressed that right of disagreement on our part. He spoke as a man who had never experienced marriage, while many of us can speak as people who have already experienced marriage. Those who have found the fulfillment of life in marriage, and their opportunity to serve the Lord enhanced, may argue contrary to what Paul said and insist that he who gives his daughter in marriage will do better. Actually, the verb *poiései*, with which verse thirty–eight concludes, is exactly the same as that with which verse thirty–seven concludes and refers to a particular action in the future, being in the future tense.

52

AFTER THE DEATH
OF A SPOUSE

The wife is bound by the law as long as her husband liveth; but if her husband be dead, she is at liberty to be married to whom she will; only in the Lord. But she is happier if she so abide, after my judgment: and I think also that I have the Spirit of God.—1 Corinthians 7:39, 40

With these words Paul is completing the discussion of the subject of celibacy and marriage and the difficulties that each state may imply. While this word, however, is specifically for widows, it naturally includes widowers.

The first thing that Paul says is, "The wife is bound by the law as long as her husband liveth."[1] She is bound to her husband by virtue of the bond of marriage and not just because a law says so, but primarily because the law of Moses, conveying God's intent for marriage, says so. And for how long is a married woman bound to her husband? The answer is very clear: "as long as her husband liveth."

Paul discussed the other eventualities in verses eight through sixteen, wherein a marriage partner is no longer bound to a fornicator spouse or to an unbeliever spouse who leaves him or her. We must not see in 1 Corinthians 7:39 Paul delineating death as the only reason for breaking the bond (*desmós*, related to *déō*) of marriage.

If the husband dies, from that moment on the widow is free to marry whomever she wants. The Greek word translated "be dead" actually means "to sleep."[2] Death is usually designated as sleep, especially in the case of the believers. This verb, being in the aorist, indicates a particular moment when the husband dies. From that moment on a widow is free to be remarried. There is a definite distinction to the verb used for "be married" here and in the previous verse.[3] It is not to *be given* unto marriage but to *give herself* unto marriage. A widow is no more under the jurisdiction of her father at home as was the case with a virgin maiden spoken of in verses thirty–six through thirty–eight.

A Christian Widow May Remarry but Only in the Lord

Paul adds something extremely important at the end of verse thirty–nine. He says: "only in the Lord," presupposing that this widow is a believer, thus emphasizing that she should not marry an unbeliever. If this is true of a Christian widow, it must be true of all believers. They should not marry unbelievers.

The cases Paul discussed from verses eight through sixteen were those of a spouse becoming a believer, having been married originally as an unbeliever to an unbeliever. A believer, however, should at all times marry a fellow believer whether she be a virgin or a widow.

Of course the same thing would apply to a widower as Paul indicates throughout that what applies to a male spouse applies also to a female spouse and vice versa.

Blessedness

And then Paul adds a final conclusion: "But she is happier if she so abide, after my judgment: and I think also that I have the Spirit of God."

The translation of *makariōtéra* as "happier" is very unfortunate. "Happy" in English refers to a person's state of mind influenced by the circumstances of life. In contrast, *makariotḗs* is the state of the believer in whom God dwells because of Jesus Christ, and who, because of the presence of God within, experiences intrinsic satisfaction no matter what the outward circumstances are.

He who derives his satisfaction from outer circumstances or the good will of the demons (mythological gods of the Greeks) or luck (*túchē*) in Classical Greek, are known as *eudaímones* or *eutucheís*, two words which do not occur in the New Testament. It is therefore incorrect to translate *makárioi*, "blessed," as "happy." The blessed ones derive their satisfaction from God's presence within them because of Christ (Matt. 5:4–11 connected with "for my sake," Matt. 5:11).

Christianity never promises favorable circumstances of life, but does promise, as the outpouring of His grace, the indwelling of God within the heart of every believer. Consequently, that Godly indwelling results in the fullest possible satisfaction regardless of the circumstances of life. Whenever, then, the word "happy" is used in any translation, it is an improper rendering of the word *makários*, "blessed," *makárioi* in the plural, the peace within in spite of the circumstances without.[4]

Perhaps most Christians have heard of the beautiful illustration of peace. It is a painting depicting a bird standing on a rock on a dark night in the midst of a stormy sea. The bird is sound asleep with its head tucked under its wing and one foot raised as most birds sleep. That is peace.

So Paul tells us that a widow who does not marry after her husband dies is more blessed if she remains thus. Of course, that again was his own opinion, and he says so: "after my judgment."[5]

Paul's Subjective Opinion About the Remarriage of a Widow

Paul is giving an objective judgment or an objective opinion but he is giving a subjective opinion from his own experience. This is why he calls it very emphatically his own judgment.[6] It's all Paul knew experientially. Had he been married and been able to accomplish what he wanted to accomplish in and through a happy marriage, he might have had a different opinion. It is marvelous indeed to see the honesty of Paul in expressing an opinion that is subjective or giving a command that is objective.

Divergent Personal Opinions May Be Inspired by the Same Spirit of God

To qualify, of course, this subjective opinion he adds, "And I think also that I have the Spirit of God." What is translated as "I think" in Greek is *dokố* or *dokéō*, "to consider, to appear, to think." He says it appears to him "that even I (*kagố*) Spirit of God I have" (literal translation). It's interesting to know that Paul does not say *the* Spirit of God, but just Spirit of God. It is as if he were saying, please allow me my own personal opinion and don't reject it as opposed to God's Spirit energizing my own life.

The English translation of the last clause of verse forty does not convey the Greek grammatical construction. If this were to be translated literally, it would be thus: " I think and I also Spirit of God to have." It is not "I have Spirit of God" given in an assertive manner, but "I think to have Spirit of God."

To show his humility Paul does not use the verb "have" in the present indicative, *échō*, but he uses the infinitive *échein*, in avoidance of being thought of as bragging that because he was an apostle, therefore his decision to stay unmarried was the only proper one. Another believer may think otherwise regarding marriage and he or she may also claim to have God's Spirit.

This certainly ought to be the attitude of every believer when it comes to differences of opinion that concern individual decisions that in and of themselves could not be classified as either sinful or nonsinful. And indeed we ought to allow a brother or sister in Christ the privilege of making their own decision in such matters.

---

[1]This verse begins with the word guné, "woman," referring of course to a married woman or a wife. Then follows the verb dédetai, third person singular perfect indicative passive of déō, "to bind or oblige by a moral or religious obligation" as in Romans 7:2 and 1 Corinthians 7:27. The King James Version, having been translated from the Textus Receptus, has the addition nómō, the dative of nómos, "by the law." If we take this as the better reading, it should not be translated "by the law" but "by law." The definite article is missing. However, its absence really does not change the meaning of the statement.

[2]The verb koiméthé, third person singular first aorist subjunctive passive of koimáō, "to sleep."

[3]Here it is gaméthénai, first aorist infinitive passive of gaméō, and not gamízō or ekgamízō.

[4]For a detailed study of this subject, see the Author's book on the Beatitudes entitled *The Pursuit of Happiness.*

[5]The word translated "judgment" is not the Greek word krísis, "judgment," but the word gnómē, "opinion," which is derived

from the verb *ginōskō*, "to know, to think, to determine from experience."

[6]*Katá*, "according," *tén*, "the," *emén*, "my own," *gnómēn*, "opinion."

GUIDE TO TRANSLITERATION—FROM GREEK TO ENGLISH WITH MODERN GREEK PRONUNCIATION

Capital Letter	Small Letter	Greek Name	Trans–literation	Phonetic Sound	Example
A	α	alpha	a	a	as in father
B	β	beta	b	v	as in victory
Γ	γ	gamma	g	y	as in yell (soft gutteral)
Δ	δ	delta	d	th	as in there
E	ε	epsilon	e	e	as in met
Z	ζ	zeta	z	z	as in zebra
H	η	eta	e̅	ee	as in see
Θ	θ	theta	th	th	as in thin
I	ι	iota	i	i	as in machine
K	κ	kappa	k	k	as in kill (soft accent)
Λ	λ	lambda	l	l	as in land
M	μ	mu	m	m	as in mother
N	ν	nu	n	n	as in now
Ξ	ξ	xi	x	x	as in wax
O	o	omicron	o	o	as in obey
Π	π	pi	p	p	as in pet (soft accent)
P	ϱ	ro	r	r	as in courage
Σ	σ,ς*	sigma	s	s	as in sit
T	τ	tau	t	t	as in tell (soft accent)
Y	υ	upsilon	u	ee	as in see
Φ	φ	phi	ph	ph	as in graphic
X	χ	chi	ch	h	as in heel
Ψ	ψ	psi	ps	ps	as in ships
Ω	ω	omega	o̅	o	as in obey

*At end of words

GUIDE TO TRANSLITERATION—GREEK TO ENGLISH

COMBINATIONS OF CONSONANTS

Small Letter	Greek Names	Trans–literation	Phonetic Sound	Example
γγ	gamma + gamma	gg	g	as in go
γκ	gamma + kappa	gk	g	as in go
γχ	gamma + chi	gch	gh	as in ghost

DIPHTHONGS (DOUBLE VOWELS)

Small Letter	Greek Names	Trans–literation	Phonetic Sound	Example
αι	alpha + iōta	ai	ai	as in hair
αυ	alpha + upsilon	au	af, av	as in waft or lava
ει	epsilon + iōta	ei	ee	as in see
ευ	epsilon + upsilon	eu	ef, ev	as in effort or every
ηυ	eta + upsilon	eu	eef, eev	as in reef or sleeve
οι	omicron + iōta	oi	ee	as in see
ου	omicron + upsilon	ou	ou	as in group
υι	upsilon + iōta	ui	ee	as in see

BREATHINGS (Occur only with initial vowels)

(')   Smooth, not transliterated or pronounced.
When words begin with vowels, it may occur at the
beginning of words with every vowel or double vowel
(diphthong): ἔργον—*érgon*, work; εὐχή—*eúchē*, vow.

(')   Rough = h.
When words begin with vowels, it may occur at the
beginning of words with every vowel or double vowel
(diphthong). No distinction in pronunciation from the
smooth breathing. To indicate the rough breathing we
use "h" in the transliteration; ἕτερος—*heterōs*, another.

(ῥ)   Rho = r.
(ὐ)   Upsilon = u.
When this letter begins a word, it always has the
rough breathing. There they are transliterated rh, hu,
respectively, ῥέω—*rhéō*, flow; ὑπομονή—*hupomonē*,
patience.

Greek–English Index

Greek	English	Scripture	Page
adelphós	brother	1 Cor. 7:29	306
agápē	love	Eph. 5:25, 28, 33	36, 368
ágamos	unmarried	1 Cor. 7:8	105, 261
ágchō	to constrict		278
aggéllō	to tell		126
ágō	to go, go away		310
agorá	marketplace		242
agorázō	to buy	Matt. 13:44; 14:15; 1 Cor. 7:23	247
ákathanos	unclean	Acts 10:14, 28; 11:8; Rom. 14:14	176, 177
akmé	flower of age		374
akrasía	incontinency	Matt. 23:25; 1 Cor. 7:5	59
ákratos	incontinent		65
allá	but		302
allássō	to change, to alter		156
allélous	each other	1 Cor. 7:5	50
állos	another	1 Cor. 7:5	50
a	negative "alpha"		66, 168, 177
amerímnos	without carefulness	Matt. 28:14; 1 Cor. 7:32	330, 332, 335
aná	again, intensive		278
anággē	necessity	1 Cor. 7:26	278, 378
anér	husband	1 Cor. 7:2; 1 Tim. 3:2; Titus 1:6	295

déō	to bind		142, 283, 284, 286, 388, 592
desmós	bond		388
diá	through		27, 86, 111, 200
diabállō	to go in between		49
diábolos	devil		49
diallássomai or *dialláttomai*	reconcile	Matt. 5:24	155, 156
diá phthónon	for envy	Matt. 27:18	27
diá tás porneías	for the fornications	1 Cor. 7:2	25, 27
diatássō or *diatássomai*	to ordain, to set in order, to command, to arrange for one–self, get things arranged	1 Cor. 7:17; 9:1	84, 86, 155, 199, 200, 263
dídōmi	I give	1 Cor. 7:25	265
dís	twice		27
dokéō or *dokóto*	think		163, 391
doulóō	to reduce to the state of slavery, to be enslaved or be in bondage	1 Cor. 7:15	182, 186, 233
doúlos	a slave	Matt. 10:24; John 13:16	186
dúo	two		27
eán	if	1 Cor. 7:28	145, 367
eán dé kaí	but even, if and	1 Cor. 7:28	291, 374
echétō, see *échō*			

écho	to have	1 Cor. 7:2, 3	43, 310, 318, 391
egkrateúomai	to be continent	1 Cor. 7:9; 9:25	108, 112, 115
ei	if		194
eimí	to be		214, 277, 335, 374
eiségéomai	suggest		265
eisphérō	offer		265
ek	out of	1 Cor. 7:7	98, 99, 302
ekgamís- komai	to be given in marriage	Luke 20:34, 35	303
ekgamískō	to give in marriage	1 Cor. 7:38	302
ekgamízō	to give in marriage	1 Cor. 7:38	261, 300, 365, 366, 373
eklḗthē, see *kaléō*			
eklḗthēs, see *kaléō*			
ek sumphṓ- nou	with consent	1 Cor. 7:5	53, 54
eleēménos	one who has ex– perienced mercy	1 Cor. 7:25	268
eléō	to be merciful to		268
eleós	mercy		62, 266, 268
eleuthéros	free man	1 Cor. 7:22	239, 240
emḗn	my very own	1 Cor. 7:40	393
emérisen, see *merízō*			
en	in, upon, with		115, 167, 185, 187, 251, 256, 278

enístēmi	to be present or at hand		278, 312
en tē idía kardía	in his own heart	1 Cor. 7:37	382
entellomai	to command		212
entolé	commandment		85, 210–212, 214, 215, 269
entolón theou	of the command- ments of God		211
epeí	for otherwise, for then, for else		173
epí	upon, over		85, 86, 173, 205, 269, 363, 369
epibállō	to cast upon	1 Cor. 7:35	363
epispáō	to circumcize	1 Cor. 7:18	248
epispástho, see *epispáō*			
epitagé	commandment	1 Cor. 7:6	79, 85, 86 205, 263, 269
epitásso	to command		79, 85, 86, 269
epitáxis	seizure		86
estí, estín	is		177, 209, 214, 350
eú	well, good		39, 163, 363
eudokéō	to think well	1 Cor. 7:12, 13	163
eukairía	opportunity or proper time		54, 306
eúnoia	benevolence, or good will	1 Cor. 7:3	39, 43, 44
eupáredron or *prósedron*	well–motivated	1 Cor. 7:35	359, 362, 363, 378

GREEK–ENGLISH INDEX

hamartía(n)	sin		111, 297
háptomai	to touch with purpose	1 Cor. 7:1	10, 12
háptesthai, see *háptomai*			
háptō	to touch	1 Cor. 7:1	12
házō	to venerate		351
heautoú	of his own	1 Cor. 7:2	38
hḗ			253, 260, 261, 350
hē ágamos	the unmarried woman	1 Cor. 7:34	343
hédra	seat		359, 363
hedraíos	stedfast		378
hē parthénos	the virgin	1 Cor. 7:34	261, 343
hékastos	each one, every man	1 Cor. 7:2, 17	36, 83, 84, 92, 93, 194, 196, 217, 248
héo	for		38
heterozu-goúntes	unequally yoked	2 Cor. 6:14	298
híēmi	to send		136
hína	so that	1 Cor. 7:5	55, 59, 314
hístēmi	to stand, to be present, or at hand, or set in		278, 377
ho	he		306, 343
hó	who, which		256
ho adelphós	the brother		77
ho ápistos	the unbelieving one		186

ho gamḗsas	he who was married	1 Cor. 7:32	343
hoi chrṓmenoi	they that use	1 Cor. 7:31	324
hoi ḗchontes	they that have	1 Cor. 7:29	321
hoi klaíntes	they that weep	1 Cor. 7:30	321
ho kósmos	the world, people		310
ho Kúrios	the Lord	1 Cor. 7:17	197
hoi sōzoménoi	those who are being saved	Acts 2:47	190
hoi toioútoi	such people	1 Cor. 7:28	317
hōs	as		194
ho Theos	the God	1 Cor. 7:17	196
hos	he who		99
toioútois	such things, cir-cumstances, or cases	1 Cor. 7:15	187
hoú	of his own		38
hoútō peripateíto	so let him walk	1 Cor. 7:17	248
hoútōs	thus in this manner		99, 198, 199, 274, 374
huparchō	to continue to be	1 Cor. 7:26	274, 275, 277, 280
hupér	above		122, 374
hupérakmos	over–aged		374
hupér lian	overmuch	2 Cor. 12:11	122
hupó	under		99
idía	individually, severally	1 Cor. 12:11	94, 383
ídion	her own, his proper, one's own	1 Cor. 7:2	37, 93

kékleken	effective call		187, 200
kekosmé- méne	adorned	Rev. 21:2	349
kékriken	has decreed or made proper judgement		381–383
klésis	calling	1 Cor. 7:20	218, 253
koimáo	to sleep	1 Cor. 7:39	392
koinós	common	Acts 10:14, 28; 11:8; Rom. 14:14	176
kosméo	to adorn		308, 348, 349
kósmos	world		310, 342, 348, 349
krátos	strength, power, government		66, 115, 116
kreísson	better		116, 385
kríno	to judge	1 Cor. 7:37	382, 392
légo	to say	1 Cor. 7:6	102, 158, 309
leípo	to leave		309, 310
lían	very much	2 Cor. 12:11	122
leloípa, see *leipo*			
loipón	henceforth	1 Cor. 7:29	310
lúo	to free a prisoner		142, 286, 290
lúsis	loosing	1 Cor. 7:27	286
makários	blessed	Matt. 5:4–11	389
makariotés	blessedness		389
mállon	rather	1 Cor. 7:21	233
márpto	to hit the mark		302

mē	not		194, 205, 247, 290
mē aphiétō	let him not leave one		248
mē aposterésēs	defraud not	1 Cor. 7:5	47
mē apostereíte allélous	do not deprive each other	1 Cor. 7:5	47
mē chōristhénai	let not one depart		248
mē epispásthō	let him not become uncircumcised	1 Cor. 7:18	248
mē gínesthe	do not begin to be	1 Cor. 7:23	255
mē peritemnésthō	let him not be circumcised	1 Cor. 7:18	248
mē soi melétō	don't mind	1 Cor. 7:21	223
meínōsin, see *menō*			
melei	to mind	1 Cor. 7:21	222–224
melétō see *meleí*			
mélomai	to be concerned		223
mén	on the one hand		99
menétō ágamos	let one remain unmarried	1 Cor. 7:11	248
ménō	to abide, to remain		104, 105, 220, 248, 255
mérimna	anxiety	1 Cor. 7:32	333, 335, 337, 338, 342, 346
merimnáō	to be anxious	1 Cor. 7:32	330, 336, 343

ou kat epitagén	not of commandment	1 Cor. 7:6	81
pántas, see *pás*			
pará	near, by the side of		126, 254, 310, 359, 363
paraggéllō	to advise	1 Cor. 7:10	126
parágō	to pass away		310
paratheínai	to lay out		259
páresis	by–passing	Rom. 3:25	156
parthénos	virgin	1 Cor. 7:25	31, 259, 260, 277, 303, 374
parousía	presence		16
pás	every		92
patéō	to walk		200
peirázō	to tempt	1 Cor. 7:5	62
perí	about, around		200, 256, 363
peripatéō	to walk	1 Cor. 7:17	200
perispáō	to distract		363
phaínō	shine		309
phémē	a divine voice		309
pheídomai	to spare	1 Cor. 7:28	318
phēmí	to say	1 Cor. 7:29	309
phérō	to brine		363
pheúgō	to avoid		318
phōnéō	to speak		53
pistós	faithful, believer	1 Cor. 7:25	268
pistós eínai	ıs faithful	1 Cor. 7:25	268
pneúma	spirit	1 Cor. 7:34	351

poiéō	to do		383, 385, 386
porneía(s)	fornication	1 Cor. 7:2	22, 26, 27, 29, 35
pórnoi, see *pórnos*			
pórnos	whoremonger		24
pronoéō	make provision		330
prophētikós	prophetic		309
prós	to, for		55, 356, 359
prósedron, see *prósedros*			
prósedros	sitting near		359
proseuchḗ	prayer	1 Cor. 7:5	56
prós kairón	for a time	1 Cor. 7:5	54
prostássō	to order		214
protíthēmi	to suggest		265
psuchḗ	soul		108, 109, 321, 333
psuchikós	natural, soulish	1 Cor. 2:14	108, 112
púr	fire		116
puróō	to burn	1 Cor. 7:9	116
sárx	flesh	1 Cor. 7:28	315
schḗma	form, fashion, behavior		308, 310, 361, 363, 370
schéō	to be		310
scholázō	to give myself leisure	1 Cor. 7:5	55, 56
scholḗ	school, a place of leisure		55
soí	yours		223

sốma	body		333, 351
sốs or *sốos*	safe		192
sốzō	to save		192
spáō	to draw		205, 363
stéllō	to send or to contract		309
stenochōriá	distress, narrow place	Rom. 2:9; 8:35; 2 Cor. 6:4, 10, 12	315, 316
stenós	narrow, nonspacious		315
steréō	to deprive another of what belongs to him or her		47
suggnốmē	permission	1 Cor. 7:6	69, 86
sumphérei, see *sumphérō*			
súmphéron	mutual benefit	1 Cor. 7:35	354, 355
sumphérō	to be profitable	1 Cor. 7:35	23, 363
sumphốnon	agreement	1 Cor. 7:5	53, 54
sumphốnou, see *sumphốnon*			
sún	with, together		53, 69, 163 309, 363
sunérchēsthe, see *sunérchomai*			
sunérchomai	to pray	1 Cor. 7:5	66
sunestal- ménos	contracted	1 Cor. 7:29	309
suneudokéō	to be pleased together		163
sustéllō	to reduce in space		309
sustéllomai	to be short of time		309

tagḗ	order		85
taîs chḗrais	to the widows	1 Cor. 7:8	105
tássomai	to place in one's proper order or category		86, 200, 326
tássō	to categorize, to order		85, 86, 200, 269, 326
tá toú kósmou	of the world	1 Cor. 7:32	310, 342
táxis	category, order		85, 326
tḗn eautoú parthénon	his own virgin	1 Cor. 7:37	381
tḗ nēsteía kaí proseuchḗ	in fasting and prayer	1 Cor. 7:5	55
tḗ sarkí	in the flesh		314
tḗn opheilēn	that which is due		44
tḗn opheilo-menēn eúnoian	the favor that is due	1 Cor. 7:3	40, 44
tēréō or *tērō*	to keep, watch	1 Cor. 7:19	213, 381
tērḗsate, see *tēréō*			
tḗrēsis	the keeping, guarding		213, 215
téllomai or *téllō*	command, to charge		214
thélēma	will		380
thélō	I wish, I would		102, 328
Theoú	of God		335
thiggánō	to touch without influencing oneself or another		9

Scripture Index

Bibliography

Specialized Books

Gray, James Comper. *The Biblical Encyclopedia and Museum.* Cleveland, OH: F. M. Barton, 1900.

Staton, Julia. *What The Bible Says About Woman.* Joplin, MO: College Press Publishing Company, 1980.

Tock, Robert. *A Handbook of Biblical Difficulties.* London: Elliot Stock, 1886.

Wight, Fred H. *Manners and Customs of Bible Lands.* Chicago: Moody Press, 1953.

Articles on Marriage, Divorce and Remarriage

Abbott, Lyman. "Marriage and Divorce." *The Christian World Pulpit* 49 (January–June 1896): 204–07.

Horton, R. F. "Christ's View of Divorce." *The Christian World Pulpit* 99 (January–June 1921): 282–84.

Simpson, James Gilliland. "The Message of Malachi." *The Christian World Pulpit* 82 (July–December 1912): 353–55.

Dictionaries and Reference Works on the Greek Language

Arndt, William F., and F. Wilbur Gingrich. *A Translation of Walter Bauer's Griechisch–Deutsches Worterbuchzuden Schriften des Neuen Testaments und der Ubrigen Urchrislichen Literatur.* Chicago: The University of Chicago Press, 1957.

Brown, Colin. *New International Dictionary of New Testament Theology (Theologlsches Begriffslexikon Zum Neuen Testament).* 3 volumes. Grand Rapids: Zondervan Publishing House, 1975.

Bullinger, Ethelbert W. *A Critical Lexicon and Concordance to the English and Greek New Testament.* London: The Lamp Press, Ltd., 1957.

Buttrick, George Arthur. *The Interpreter's Dictionary of the Bible.* 4 volumes. New York: Abingdon Press, n.d.

Cremer, H. Edinburgh, Scotland: T & T Clark, 1954.

Douglas, J. D. *The New Bible Dictionary.* Grand Rapids: Wm. B. Eerdmans Publishing Company, 1970.

Friberg, Barbara, and Timothy Friberg. *Analytical Greek New Testament.* Grand Rapids: Baker Book House, 1981.

Grant, F. W. *The Numerical Bible.* New York: Loizeaux Brothers, 1899.

Gray, James Comper. *The Biblical Encyclopedia and Museum.* Cleveland, OH: F. M. Barton, 1900.

Hastings, James. *A Dictionary of the Bible.* 5 volumes. Edinburgh, Scotland: T & T Clark, 1901.

Hastings, James. *A Dictionary of Christ and the Gospels.* 2 volumes. Edinburgh, Scotland: T & T Clark, 1906.

Hastings, James. *Dictionary of the Apostolic Church.* 2 volumes. Edinburgh, Scotland: T & T Clark, 1951.

Kíttel, Gerhard. *Theological Dictionary of the New Testament.* 10 volumes. Translated by Geoffrey W. Bromiley. Grand Rapids: Wm. B. Eerdmans Publishing Company, 1968.

Lampe, G. W. H. *A Patristic Greek Lexicon.* 5 volumes. Oxford: Clarendon Press, 1968.

Liddell, Henry George and Robert Scott. *A Greek–English Lexicon.* Oxford: Clarendon Press, 1958.

McClintock, John, and James Strong. *Cyclopedia of Biblical, Theological and Ecclesiastical Literature.* 12 volumes. Grand Rapids: Baker Book House, 1968.

Meillet, A. *Apercu D'une Histoire de la Langue Grecque.* Paris: Librairie Hachette, 1935.

Moulton, J. H. and G. Milligan. *A Vocabulary of the Greek Testament.* Grand Rapids: William B. Eerdmans Publishing Company, 1957.

Nestle, Eberhard. *Novum Testamentum Graece cum Apparatu Critico Curabit.* Stuttgart: Wurttemburgische Bibelanstalt, 1952.

Parkhurst, John. *A Greek and English Lexicon to the New Testament.* London: G. G. and J. Robinson 1769.

Perschbacher, Wesley J., ed. *The New Analytical Greek Lexicon.* Peabody, MA: Hendrickson Publishers, 1990.

Rahlfs, Alfred. *Septuaginta.* Stuttgart: Deutsche Bibelgesellschaft Stuttgart, 1979.

Richardson, Alan. *A Theological Word Book of the Bible.* New York: The Macmillan Company, 1959.

Robertson, Nicoll W., Janet Stoddart, and James Moffat, eds. *The Expositor's Dictionary of Texts.* Grand Rapids: William B. Eermans Publishing Company, 1953.

Robinson, Edward. *A Greek and English Lexicon of the New Testament.* Edinburgh, Scotland: T & T Clark, 1829.

Smith, William. *Dictionary of Greek and Roman Antiquities.* London: Taylor, Walton, and Maberly, 1848.

Strong, James. *Exhaustive Concordance of the Bible.* New York: Abingdon Cokesbury, 1943.

Thayer, Joseph Henry. *A Greek English Lexicon of the New Testament.* Edinburgh, Scotland: T & T Clark, 1956.

Trench, Richard C. *Synonyms of the New Testament.* Grand Rapids: William B. Eerdmans Publishing Company, 1953.

Vine, W. E. *An Expository Dictionary of New Testament Words.* Westwood, NJ: Fleming H. Revell Company, 1966.

Weigle, Luther A. *The New Testament Octapla.* New York: Thomas Nelson and Sons, 1946.

Commentaries on First Corinthians

Barclay, William. *The Letters to the Corinthians.* Edinburgh, Scotland: St. Andrew Press, 1954.

Barnes, Albert. *Explanatory and Practical Notes on I Corinthians.* Grand Rapids: Baker Book House, 1949.

Beet, Joseph Agar. *A Commentary on St. Paul's Epistles to the Corinthians.* London: Hodder and Stoughton, 1885.

Bengel, John A. *Gnomon of the New Testament, I Corinthians.* Edinburgh, Scotland: T & T Clark, 1863.

Biblical Treasury, *A Magazine of Scripture Exposi-tions and Illustrations.* London: Sunday School Union, n.d.

A Brief Commentary. Society for Promotion of Chris-tian Knowledge, London: 1852.

Brown, E. F. *The Indian Church Commentaries, I Corinthians.* London: Society for Promoting Chris-tian Knowledge, 1923.

Calvin, John. *Commentary on the Corinthians.* Grand Rapids: William B. Eerdmans Publishing Com-pany, 1948.

Carr, W. G. *Commentary on First Corinthians.* London: Hodder & Stoughton, 1895.

Century Bible, *A Modern Commentary.* London: Cax-ton Publishing Company.

Clarke, W. K. L. *Commentary on I Corinthians.*

Churton, M. A. *Commentary on I Corinthians.* London: John Murray, 1865.

Dalton, W. *An Explanatory and Practical Commentary on I Corinthians.* Dublin: William Curry, Jun, and Co., 1840.

Darby, J. N. *Synopsis of I Corinthians.*

Dods, Marcus. *The First Epistle to the Corinthians.* Lon-don: Hodder and Stoughton, 1900.

Dummelow, J. R. *Commentary on I Corinthians.*

Edwards, T. C. *A Commentary on I Corinthians.* Lon-don: Hamilton, Adams & Company, 1885.

Exell, Joseph S. *The Biblical Illustrator.* London: Wilkes & Company.

Foster, H. J. *A Homiletic Commentary*. New York: Funk & Wagnalls Company.

Godet, F. *Commentary on the First Epistle of St. Paul to the Corinthians*. Grand Rapids: Zondervan Publishing House, 1957.

Goudge, H. L. *Commentary With Introduction and Notes*. London: Methuen & Co. Ltd., 1911.

Greek New Testament. *Epistle of I Corinthians with English Notes*.

Hodge, Charles. *An Exposition of the First Epistle to the Corinthians*. Grand Rapids: William B. Eerdmans Publishing Company, 1950.

Ironside, H. A. *Addresses on I Corinthians*. Neptune, NJ: Loizeaux Brothers, 1938.

Lange, J. P. *Commentary on I Corinthians*. New York: Charles Scribner & Co., 1868.

Lenski, R. C. H. *The Interpretation of I & II Corinthians*. Minneapolis: Augsburg Publishing House, 1961.

Lias, J. J. *Commentary With Notes and Introduction*.

Meyer, Heinrich A. W. *Critical Exegetical Handbook, I Corinthians*. 2 volumes. Edinburgh, Scotland: T & T Clark, 1872.

Moffatt, James. *The First Epistle of Paul to the Corinthians*. London: Hodder & Stoughton Ltd., 1938.

Morgan, G. C. *An Exposition of I Corinthians*. New York: Fleming H. Revell, 1946.

New Testament Annotations. *Annotations on the First Letter to the Corinthians*.

Olshausen, Hermann. *Biblical Commentary on I Corinthians*. Edinburgh, Scotland: T & T Clark, 1855.

Peake, A. S. *Commentary on I Corinthians*.

Poole, Matthew. "I Corinthians." *A Commentary on the Holy Bible*. London: Banner of Truth Trust, 1969.

Robertson, Archibald and Alfred Plummer. *The International Critical Commentary, I Corinthians*. Edinburgh, Scotland: T & T Clark, 1958.

Robertson, F. W. *Expository Lectures on I Corinthians*. London: Smith, Elder & Co.,1866.

Sadler, M. F. *Commentary With Notes Critical and Practical*. London: George Bell & Sons, 1898.

Schmidt, Paul W. *A Short Protestant Commentary*. London: Williams & Norgate, 1883.

Spence, H. D. M. and Joseph S. Exell, eds. *The Pulpit Commentary*. Vol. 44, *I Corinthians*. New York: Funk & Wagnalls Co.

Stanley, A. P. *I Corinthians With Critical Notes and Dissertations*. London: John Murray, 1858.

Sumner, John B. *A Practical Exposition of I Corinthians*. London: J. Hatchard & Son, 1843.

Turnbull, Ralph G. *Compact Commentary on the New Testament*. I Corinthians. Grand Rapids: Baker Book House, 1964.

Vine, W. E. *Commentary on I Corinthians*. London: Oliphants Ltd., 1951.

Weiss, Bernhard. *Commentary on the New Testament*. New York: Funk & Wagnalls, 1906.

Wenham, Alfred E. *Ruminations on the First Epistle of Paul to the Corinthians*. London: Alabaster, Passmore & Sons, 1912.

Wesley, John. *New Testament Commentary*. Grand Rapids: Baker Book House, 1957.

Books on Marriage, Divorce and Remarriage

Adams, Jay E. *Marriage, Divorce & Remarriage in the Bible*. Phillipsburg, NJ: Presbyterian and Reformed Publishing Company, 1980.

Bontrager, G. Edwin. *Divorce and the Faithful Church*. Kitchener, Ontario, Canada: Herald Press, 1978.

Bustanoby, Andre. *But I Didn't Want a Divorce, Putting Your Life Back Together*. Grand Rapids: Zondervan Publishing House, 1979.

Duty, Guy. *Divorce and Remarriage*. Minneapolis, MN: Bethany Fellowship, Inc., 1967.

Ellisen, Stanley A. *Divorce and Remarriage in the Church*. Grand Rapids: Zondervan Publishing House, 1980.

Emerson, James G. Jr. *Divorce, the Church, and Remarriage*. Philadelphia: The Westminster Press, 1961.

Epp, Theodore H. *Marriage and Divorce*. Lincoln, NE: Back to the Bible Broadcast, 1968.

Hosier, Helen Kooiman. *The Other Side of Divorce, A Christian's Plea for Understanding and Compassion*. Nashville: Abingdon, 1975.

Kilgore, James E. *Try Marriage Before Divorce*. Waco, TX: Word Books, 1978.

Kysar, Myrna and Robert. *The Asundered. Biblical Teachings on Divorce and Remarriage.* Atlanta: John Knox Press, 1978.

Lee, Mark. *Creative Christian Marriage.* Glendale, CA: Regal Books, 1977.

Leman, Kevin. *Sex Begins in the Kitchen, Renewing Emotional and Physical Intimacy in Marriage.* Ventura, CA: Regal Books, 1981.

Lovett, C. S. *Divorce Problem.* Baldwin Park, CA: Personal Christianity, 1964.

Meier, Paul D. *You Can Avoid Divorce.* Grand Rapids: Baker Book House, 1978.

Murray, John. *Divorce.* Philadelphia: The Orthodox Presbyterian Church, 1953.

Nordie, Donald L. *Divorce and the Bible.* New York: Loizeaux Brothers, 1958.

Plekker, J. Robert. *Divorce and the Christian: What the Bible Teaches.* Wheaton, IL: Tyndale House Publishers, Inc., 1980.

Rice, John R. *Divorce, The Wreck of Marriage.* Murfreesboro, TN: Sword of the Lord Publishers, 1946.

Richards, Larry. *Remarriage, A Healing Gift from God.* Waco, TX: Word Books 1981.

Snowman, Preston W. *New Light on Divorce and Remarriage.* Salisbury Center, NY: Select Publications, 1978.

Stott, John R. W. *Divorce.* Downers Grove, IL: InterVarsity Press, 1973.

Thomas, J. D. *Divorce and Remarriage.* Abilene, TX: Biblical Research Press, 1977.

Williams, John. *For Every Cause? The Question of Divorce*. Neptune, NJ: Loizeaux Brothers, 1981.

Williams, H. Page. *Do Yourself a Favor: Love Your Wife*. Plainfield, NJ: Logos International, 1973.

Reference Works Written in Greek

Archaioi Hellēnes Sungrapheis (Ancient Greek Writers). 150 volumes. Athens: Zacharopoulos, 1954.

Bibliothēkē Hellēnōn Paterōn Kai Ekklēsiastikōn Suggrapheōn (Library of Greek Fathers and Ecclesiastical Writers). 15 volumes. Athens: Apostoliki Diakonia, 1955.

Demetrakou, D. *Mega Lexikon Tēs Hellēnikes Glossēs* (Great Dictionary of the Greek Language). 9 volumes. Athens: Demetrakos, 1949.

Eleftheroudakis. *Enclyclopedic Lexicon*. 12 volumes. Athens: Eleftheroudakis, 1927.

Helios. *Neoteron Egkuklopaidikon Lexikon* (Newer Enclyclopedic Lexicon). 18 volumes. Athens: N.p., n.d.

Kalaraki, Michael and Nikolas Galanos. *Ioannou tou Chrisostomou ta Hapanta* (Complete Works of John Chrysostom), 1899.

Martinos, Ath. *Encyclopedia of Religion and Ethics*. 12 volumes. Athens: A. Martinos, 1962.

Papaoikonomou, George L. *Lexikon Anōmalōn Rhēmatōn* (Lexicon of Irregular Verbs). Athens: Kagiaphas, 1945.

Pursou. *Great Greek Encyclopedia*. 24 volumes. Athens: P. G. Makris, n.d.

Roosse, John, Th. *Grammar of the Ancient Greek Language and Especially in Attic Dialect*. Athens: N.p., n.d.

Triantaphullou, I. Delee. *Grammatical Skills, The Content and the Methodical Teaching of the Ancient Greek Grammar*. Athens: N.p., 1972.

Grammars of the Greek Language

Blass, F. and A. Debrunner. *A Greek Grammar of the New Testament and Early Christian Literature*. Translated from the German by Robert W. Funk. Chicago: The University of Chicago Press, 1961.

Burton, Ernest De Witt. *Syntax of the Moods and Tenses in New Testament Greek*. Edinburgh, Scotland: T & T Clark, 1966.

Buttmann, Alexander. *A Grammar of the New Testament Greek*. Andover: Warren F. Draper, 1891.

Cartledge, Samuel A. *A Basic Grammar of the Greek New Testament*. Grand Rapids· Zondervan Publishing House, 1959.

Chamberlain, William Douglas. *An Exegetical Grammar of the Greek New Testament*. Grand Rapids: Baker Book House, 1941.

Curtius, George. *A Grammar of the Greek Language*. London: John Murray, 1882.

Green, Thomas Sheldon. *A Treatise on the Grammar of the New Testament Dialect*. London: Samuel Bagster and Sons, 1842.

Harper, William Rainey. *An Introductory New Testament Greek Method*. New York: Charles Scribner's Sons, 1911.

Jay, Eric G. *New Testament Greek, An Introductory Grammar.* London: S.P.C.K., 1958.

Jelf, William Edward. *A Grammar of the Greek Language.* 2 volumes. Oxford: John Henry and James Parker, 1859.

Marshall, Alfred. *New Testament Greek Primer.* Grand Rapids: Zondervan Publishing House, 1982.

Metzger, Bruce M. *Lexical Aids for Students of New Testament Greek.* Princeton, NJ, 1981.

Moulton, James Hope. *A Grammar of New Testament Greek.* 2 volumes. Edinburgh, Scotland: T & T Clark, 1957.

Moulton, James Hope. *An Introduction to the Study of New Testament Greek.* London: The Epworth Press, 1955.

Robertson, A. T. *A Grammar of the Greek New Testament in the Light of Historical Research.* New York: George H. Doran Company, 1923.

———. *Pictures in the New Testament.* Nashville: Broadman Press, 1933.

———. *Practical and Social Aspects of Christianity.* New York: George H. Doran Company, 1916.

Seager, John. *Hoogeveen's Greek Participles.* London: A. J. Balpy, 1829.

Smyth, Herbert Weir. *Greek Grammar.* Cambridge: Harvard University Press, 1959.

Sonnenschein, E. A. *A Greek Grammar, Accidents.* London: Swan Sonnenschein and Company, Ltd., 1909.

Summers, Ray. *Essentials of New Testament Greek.* Nashville: Broadman Press, 1950.

Thomson, George. *The Greek Language.* Cambridge: W. Heffer and Sons, Ltd., 1960.

Vine, W. E. *New Testament Greek Grammar.* Grand Rapids: Zondervan Publishing House, 1965.

Wenham, J. W. *The Elements of New Testament Greek.* Cambridge: Cambridge University Press, 1981.

Winer, G. B. *A Treatise on the Grammar of the New Testament Greek.* Edinburgh, Scotland: T & T Clark, 1882.

Commentaries on the Bible

Abbott, Edwin A. *A Guide Through Greek to Hebrew Scripture.* London: Adam and Charles Black, 1900.

Alford, Henry. *The Greek Testament.* 4 volumes. London: Rivingtons, 1880.

Barnes, Albert. *Notes on the New Testament, Explanatory and Practical.* Grand Rapids: Baker Book House, 1949.

Bengel, John Albert. *Gnomon of the New Testament.* Edinburgh, Scotland: T & T Clark, 1863.

Bloomfield, S. T. *The Greek Testament Notes, Critical Philological and Explanatory.* 2 volumes. London: Longman, Brown, Green, and Longmans, 1845.

Churton, Edward and William Basil Jones. *The New Testament Illustrated.* 2 volumes. London: John Murray, 1865.

Commentary Wholly Biblical. London: Samuel Bagster and Sons, n.d.

Criswell, W. A. *The Criswell Study Bible.* Nashville: Thomas Nelson Publishers, 1979.

Dalton, W. *An Explanatory and Practical Commentary of the New Testament.* Dublin: William Curry, Jun. and Company, 1840.

Driver, Samuel Rolles, Alfred Plummer, and Charles Augustus Briggs. *The International Critical Commentary of the Holy Scriptures of the Old and New Testaments.* Edinburgh, Scotland: T & T Clark, 1907.

Ellicott, Charles John, ed. *A Bible Commentary for English Readers.* London: Cassell and Company, Ltd., n.d.

Jacobus, Melancthon. *Notes on the Gospels, Critical and Explanatory.* New York: Robert Carter and Brothers, 1866.

Jamieson, Robert, A. R. Fausset, and David Brown. *A Commentary Critical, Experimental, and Practical on the Old and New Testaments.* Glasgow: William Collins Sons and Company, 1870.

Lange, John Peter. *A Commentary on the Holy Scriptures, Critical, Doctrinal, and Homiletical.* New York: Charles Scribner's Sons, 1884.

Lapide, Cornelius A. *The Great Commentary.* Translated by Thomas W. Mossman Edinburgh, Scotland: John Grant, 1908.

Luckock, Herbert Mortimer. *Footprints of the Son of Man.* London: Rivingtons, 1889.

Meyer, Heinrich August Wilhalm. *Critical and Exegetical Handbook of the Gospels of Mark and Luke.* Edinburgh, Scotland: T & T Clark, 1880.

Morgan, G. Campbell. *The Gospel According to Matthew, Mark, and Luke.* New York: Fleming H. Revell Company, 1929.

The New Testament with English Notes, etc., (Greek). London: A. J. Balpy, 1831.

Nicoll, W. Robertson. *The Expositor's Greek Testament.* Grand Rapids: William B. Eerdmans Publishing Company, 1956.

Nicoll W. Robertson, ed. *The Expositor's Bible.* Grand Rapids: William B. Eerdmans Publishing Company, 1956.

Olshausen, Hermann. *Biblical Commentary on the Gospels.* Edinburgh, Scotland: T & T Clark, 1855.

Owen, John J. *A Commentary, Critical, Expository, and Practical on the Gospels of Matthew and Mark.* 1861.

Patrick, Lowth, Arnald, Whitby, and Lowman. *A Critical Commentary and Paraphrase on the Old and New Testament, and the Apocrypha.* London: William Tegg and Company, 1853.

Peloubet, F. M. *The Teacher's Commentary on the Gospel According to St. Matthew.* London: Oxford University Press, 1901.

Rebuilders' Guide. Institute in Basic Youth Conflicts, 1982.

Schaff, Philip. *A Popular Commentary on the New Testament.* Edinburgh, Scotland: T & T Clark. 1879.

Tuck, Robert. *The Preacher's Homiletic Commentary on the New Testament.* New York: Funk and Wagnalls, n.d. Reprint. Grand Rapids: Baker Book House, 1980.

Webster, William, and William Francis Wilkinson. *The Greek Testament with Notes Grammatical and Exegetical.* London: John W. Parker, 1855.

Weiss, Bernhard. *A Commentary on the New Testament.* Translated by G. Schodde and E. Wilson, with an introduction by James S. Riggs. New York: Funk and Wagnalls Company, 1906.

Whitby, Daniel. *A Paraphrase and Commentary on the New Testament.* London: Awnsham and John Churchill, 1710.

Wordsworth, Chr. *The New Testament.* 3rd ed. London: Rivingtons, 1864.

Young, Robert. *Literal Translation of the Holy Bible.* Grand Rapids: Baker Book House, 1956.